Sixty Odd Years

An Alaskan's Selected Reminiscences

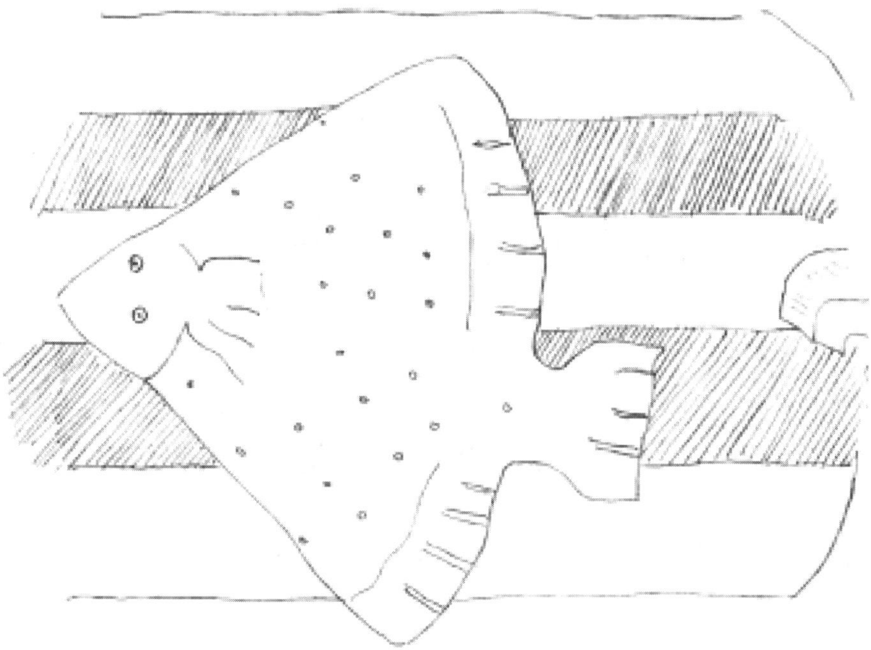

Dagmar J. Nye

Publication Consultants
PO Box 221974 Anchorage, Alaska 99522-1974

ISBN 1-888125-41-1

Library of Congress Catalog Card Number: 99-60555

— First Edition —

Front cover graphic and illustrations by Mike Nye

Manufactured in the United States of America.

To Jean
May all your endings
be happy!
Dagmar J. Nye

For Gladys

When evening waves her softly gentle plumes a hand creeps tenderly to me from one whose presence lies like mist upon the dunes and stealing inward over a starlit sea lights fires where never before a flame could be.

My father wrote that for my mother about the time I was born.

Acknowledgments

Heartfelt thanks to Becky Jensen, Bud and Mary Laws, Helen Jones and Gladys Stoffel who welcomed us to Anchorage. Boundless gratitude to the teachers at Anchorage Community College who helped us grow. To Suzanne Marie Nye 12, 000 thank yous for every word you typed into the computer, spell-checked and printed. To everyone else who made this epic possible a full measure of gratitude is hereby extended. May God bless you all.

To those faithful teachers who taught me the rudiments of American English and gave me invaluable lessons in syntax and proper grammar, in the tax-supported public schools of California and a private college in Pennsylvania, I am most grateful.

Table of Contents

One Loved Alaska — One Did Not

Chapter 1

You can't talk about Cal without talking about Alaska because he chose Alaska. He did not choose Wisconsin, where he was born, nor South Dakota where he lived after his father died. He joined the army at Fort Sill, Oklahoma when he was a broad-shouldered, husky twelve year old. In France, he learned too much about the trenches of World War I. The army sent him to the Philippines to help suppress an insurrection. He tried for a degree in mining engineering at Stanford. He washed out for hitting someone on the head with a chair in a fight. This was after he helped build a house for a fellow student who later became the California Fish and Game Commissioner. My uncle showed me the house and introduced me to the former official.

He worked on a fox farm in Washington state and sold a novelette to H. L. Mencken. Then he came to Alaska. He tried logging near Juneau until he found himself on a raft headed to sea. He worked in the Juneau Douglas Gold Mine. One day, he stopped for grub at a diner and met a waitress fresh from San Francisco. She was a Swedish girl with blonde hair and green eyes from Granholmen whose sister stayed in Carmel. Cal's brother stayed in Palo Alto and each became a community pillar and neither came to Alaska. The friend who talked Mama into coming to Juneau left before the snow fell. So these two were pretty much on their own.

The Justice of the Peace who pronounced them man and wife became a District Court Judge in the Territory and a friend. They took a steamer to San Francisco in time for me to be born at the University of California hospital. Cal tried living in Carmel when Mama took him to show her sister the new baby. He trapped moles on the Pebble Beach Golf Course but he could not fit in. He hated California so he brought us back to Juneau. There were pictures of me in lots of snow. When Cal lost his job at the mine, he went on assaying trips to Barrow and Nome. There weren't many nonnatives. Mama made clothes for the indigenous children. She had a sewing machine, lots of time and lots of clothes. Mama loved clothes and sewed very well.

Evidently, she ran out of her own clothes and whatever my aunt could send in the early days of the Depression. The native children lost their seamstress in the long winter. Fearing for her sanity, she took me on the first boat out in the spring. Cal came back from Barrow but he never followed her to San Francisco.

The Depression affected a lot of people. I could say we lost track of each other because I was three years old. I could say I forgot all about him but neither would be true. I remember standing on a bench in an anteroom of the court where Mama got her divorce. This made me tall enough to be able to show her my drawings. These were made with the pencil and paper with which I was supposed to amuse myself. "Look at all the people I made for Daddy," I beamed. Mama seized them and snapped, "You'll never see that man again." I made two decisions there and then: 1. If my Dad couldn't see my pictures I would never draw again; and 2. I was going to find my father if it took forever. So I was stubborn even then. I remembered he loved me. I remembered being happy when he was there. My stick figures wore triangle skirts or two lean rectangular pant legs, straight or curly hair or hats. They marched across a page crumpled on the floor. Mama almost dragged me from an anteroom of a Domestic Relations Court sometime in 1933.

The Boeing 747 circled Anchorage International Airport for three hours while Honey got sicker and sicker. "There was an obstruction on the runway" announced our pilot. When we finally did land an observant steward made sure Honey found a bathroom. He sent someone to stay with her till she felt better. Juggling our coats and carryon luggage I searched the crowd for David. Then someone came forward and a tall, lean and very dirty young man metamorphosed into my son. He and his friend got our foot locker and suitcases from the conveyor belts in the basement. Four of us squeezed into the cab of his friend's truck for the ride to Hope. I said afterward, "I fell in love with Alaska the minute I stepped off the plane." My son always clarified, "You couldn't see anything when you got off the plane. It was the middle of the night."

Cal believed his cabin was too small for bath or shower. In his letters he explained it was a one man cabin built after the '64 earthquake. Then he lost his home and got his picture in the Seattle paper. Someone sent the clipping to Mama who sent it to me. I sent my son to live with his grandfather when there wasn't enough room for him in his father's house. Then, I did temporary work for a year to earn enough money for two round trip tickets.

When the truck carrying Honey and me rolled along beside Turnagain Arm Beluga whales were playing in the moonlight.

Our heavy old luggage and my Navy footlocker were off-loaded beside the smallest cabin one could imagine sometime that early morning. When Honey and I finally crawled into our sleeping bags on the two cots we just lay there. For a minute we held each other's hand across the aisle. The room was so small and we were so weary. Our hands were much warmer inside the sleeping bags.

In the morning Honey was still asleep when I sneaked onto the front step and looked out at other mini-cabins. On a barbed wire fence a swallow, shiny green and not at all afraid, sang in the shower. It rained intermittently all day. We were alone in a small town crowded with mountains. We walked up and down the highway trying to find Cal or David or the truck we came in. After awhile my son found us and took us to Cal's cabin.

He was standing in the middle of the biggest mess I ever saw. Ancient *Life* magazines lay tumbled over towers of *Popular Mechanics*, becoming layered with dust and cobwebs. So did mounds of *Time* magazines and *Seattle Post Intelligencers*. In the background a bookshelf held grimy camera equipment and tools. A kettle and a blackened skillet were on the ancient stove. The wood for heating and cooking was on the porch by the chopping block and axe. Dirty clothes were in piles and I couldn't see any food at first.

He was standing there and my knees were jelly and I wanted to sit down. The two cots which lined the rear wall were so dirty. Both chairs supported quantities of ancient magazines. Logically, I should have thrown my arms around each in turn but I could not do so. He said, "I guess you didn't get my letter telling you not to come to Alaska because there aren't any jobs. And you sure can't stay here."

I said, "I guess you didn't get my letter which said I just wanted to see you guys."

So I made Honey and David carry old magazines to the dump. About ten per cent of them were rescued for the local museum. For three days we cleaned Cal's cabin, and there still was no clear place to sit. When David's friend had an errand in Anchorage we rode there in the windswept back of the truck. Quivering with cold, we bought a newspaper and found a mini-apartment "in town." One day later we three moved to Anchorage. Cal left us alone for five months just to prove he was right. I brought along his letter warning I would not be able to get a job for a year. It was in my purse when I went to work for a local tycoon. It was still there when I found Cal walking on a downtown street. He was clean, freshly shaved, with a recent haircut. In a shirt I got him for Christmas, he looked tall and strong and proud. When he saw me his face lit up like a Christmas tree. I was glad I kept my word. It did not take forever to find my father—just forty five years.

Long Ago/Far Away

Chapter 2

Long ago and far away, I was a child who ran along the city sidewalks beside my mother. I was always clinging to her coat pocket, always running, always trying to catch up. I remember standing once holding onto her pocket, reaching way up, watching an airplane. Lots of adults were also looking up, on the streets of San Francisco, watching an early airplane dip and soar. I remember Mama cried a lot and sometimes she sang "Marquita." In a Catholic school at night, a nun required me to kneel before a white marble statue. She insisted I must pray to have my sins forgiven. I wasn't there long. I was in bed much longer in a tiny one room apartment. Once a man brought me a painted Mickey Mouse on a board, manipulated with a string. He told me we were going to live on a ranch and I was going to have my own pony. I remember striving not to fall off a very high stool while he and Mama were in a nearby room making strange noises. Then Mama and I were on a train and I was being left with my aunt and my cousins. I remember baby carrots and oatmeal cookies and a clean bed and uninterrupted sleep and so much love.

I forgot how to knit. Mama taught me on the train to Ellen's home. But she was so impatient I hated the yarn, the needles, and especially my clumsy fingers. Now I smelled the heliotrope in Ellen's garden and the laundry soap in her basement. Now I swiped my cousin's tricycle and tore around the limestone patio until my cousin caught me. The patio was built with stones my aunt and uncle dragged from the beach. My older cousin, Keith, sometimes saved the frosting on his cake, insisting he didn't like it. George and I licked our lips and longed for the chocolate or vanilla or whatever icing Ellen used. Just before we left the table Keith scooped up the icing -savoring every molecule. Then, Mama came to get me and I found myself on a farm. We spent a rainy, muddy winter in a big, bare, cold farmhouse surrounded by cows and cow pies. The man who brought me Mickey Mouse in San Francisco became "Papa." He insisted I could not go near the barn. Mama didn't want me under foot in the house. One rainy morning Papa drove me to school in Stockton where I met my first teacher.

Miss Berglund was the angel from heaven who taught me how to read. She also taught other children, of course. "Run, Dick, Run. See Baby come," I pronounced carefully. I fell in love with Tommy, who came to school in a chauffeur-driven limousine. I can still see the comforting red bricks, the innumerable stairs and the long windows. I learned to sing too, and revisited jump rope and hide and seek. All of a sudden Mama was getting awfully fat and crying when she saw me, which made me extremely uncomfortable.

One day, after I came home from school, Mama and Papa had one of their arguments. I remembered the first home we shared. Mama was a cook and Papa was a foreman on a prosperous dairy farm. She bought him a brand new LaSalle sedan. "And what did you buy for me in those good old days?" she wondered aloud. I remembered Mama and I used to go for walks on a lane without cow pies. She took a picture of me in a beret, thin cotton dress, and sandals "skinny as a rail." She made such a fuss about hearing a meadowlark. Once I ran out to the yard to see something Papa wanted to show us. My new fuzzy slippers were ruined in the mud because I knew better than to make Papa wait. Papa was not happy with me! Still arguing, Papa drove Mama to town in the LaSalle sedan.

Now, alone as it kept getting darker, I wondered what I should do about dinner. A thunder storm blew down a power line. The lights went out. Lightning flashed. I ran from the kitchen just as a giant oak tree beside the house crashed against the stove and table. I stood on the porch, in the lee of the winds, watching the torrential rains. Then I sat on the porch, admiring the storm, until I got cold and went inside to bed. Mama said, later, she had her nervous breakdown because she was so worried about me and the tree. I didn't think so.

I had other gods in those days, my wonderful Aunt Ellen and scary uncle, and everyone speaking and laughing in Swedish. Both cousins, and their friends who came to play with us, spoke English. A neighbor child slammed the car door in my face when I was chasing him and my cousin through the car one day. It didn't leave a scar but my uncle insisted he wouldn't be responsible for me. So my aunt and uncle and I went to San Diego where I was almost adopted. My new "aunt" was very much like Ellen but without her vivacity and boundless energy. I was in bed again but this time not just looking at the walls, as I did under Mama's care. This time there were coloring books and paper dolls and snacks. There was even a Norma Shearer coloring book I shared with the girl next door when, too soon, I recovered. The girl next door chose a favorite color, Hunter Green, so I decided my favorite color was Burgundy. Now I had something to say when we went to the New Year's feast where almost no one spoke English. Like most children I understood the language of my elders in my infancy. Now I was limited to English and lutefisk and laughter but I felt included. Swedish New Year's was fun.

This new "Aunt" took the family terrier for walks and, when her fisherman husband was at sea, I went with her. She towed her Chihuahua past towering eucalyptus trees on concrete sidewalks, a few short blocks. One night a stranger approached as we neared a populated area. He offered Aunt Joey a one dollar bill, extending it in one hand, the other hand in front of his unzipped pants. Aunt Joey heard, "Give you a dollar, lady." She snapped, "Not on your life," tightened the Chihuahua's leash and clutched my wrist as we almost ran home. She locked the doors and moved a huge chair in front of each exit. When Aunt Joey's brother came back from his fishing boat he sang to me "Pennies From Heaven." I loved the song and dance act. He dropped pennies, lightly, into the parasol he brought me from Mexico before we even met. Aunt Joey taught me how to sew cross-stitch tablecloths and towels for my "Hope Chest." Aunt Joey and her husband took me to a department store where I asked Santa Claus for a long list of things I saw in shop windows. I especially yearned for the complete set of Dionne Quintuplet dolls. What I actually got was a handmade cradle from my "uncles" and a big Shirley Temple doll which fit into it. Was I really grateful? No. Not then.

My real aunt, Ellen, came on the train to get me and I was so glad to see her. We took the doll and cradle and things for my Hope Chest and my clothes with us back to Carmel. It was kind of a long trip so Ellen tried to teach me to knit on our way. It was fun this time. My uncle was captain of the port then. I remember how he hated to have his Sunday afternoon interrupted by someone trying to drown in the kelp offshore in his jurisdiction. I gained weight and poise and confidence. Growing was fun, just being with my cousin and his gang. One day I saw a van parked just across our street with two workmen going back and forth to it. Aunt Joey's frequent warnings to "watch out for kidnappers" were still fresh in my memory. I thought these men were behaving suspiciously. I told my aunt. She called the police. They were, of course, house painters starting a new job. My uncle was not happy with me!

Ellen and Cap left their boys with a neighbor. They took me, and my new possessions, in their car to an acre near Stockton. I knew it was an acre because I could read a sign on a bare patch of ground behind a barbed wire fence, "Garden Acres." Our home was a one-room shack with a double bed for Papa and Mama and a cot for me. There was a tall table, no chairs and no extra space at all except a narrow aisle. The baby slept with her parents at night, on my bed by day. A cat and several kittens hung around outside. With Mama's carving knife I made windows in a packing box. Then I moved the kittens in and out the windows to the disgust of their mother and mine. I planted brussels sprouts from somewhere in neat rows hoping they might grow into cabbages, which I liked. Papa brought home an enormous dog which growled, menacingly and loudly, whenever I came near his chain. I pumped buckets of water from our own private pump and carried them many yards to the shack. One day I was bringing more water when I heard Mama scream, dropped the buckets, and ran to her. The kerosene stove was on fire. Mama was carrying it through the door, dropping it on the ground, safely, outside the shack.

When Papa drove up from work he took her to the hospital in Stockton. I was left to watch the baby. In an apple box, I put a layer of diapers, a spare set of baby clothes, the baby, and a blanket, in that order. I pushed the box and its contents from the shack to the street in front of Garden Acres to the highway leading to Stockton. I was going to take the baby to Alaska, to find my father who loved me. He would certainly love the helpless creature who was left in my charge. Well out of sight of the shack I stopped pushing the box, wiped the sweat from my eyes, stood up and looked around. There was nothing but highway in either direction. On both sides were fields, no people, not even any animals. I stood there for a moment, apologized to God for not knowing what to do and pushed the box back to the shack. When I got there the baby started howling. I was walking toward a neighbor's house, just having left the baby in the shack, when Papa appeared. So did the neighbor. The baby got a clean diaper and a bottle. I got a scolding, but no strapping. Papa frequently threatened to use his razor strap on me but he never did. The neighbor, whom I never met before my aborted trip to Alaska, invited me to help her make brownies. We made brownies together and listened to her radio. I even brought some brownies home but I was forbidden to go back. Then it was time to go to school.

At school there was a tall, scrawny kid named Sadie who could throw up whenever she wanted to. This terrified me. An older boy occasionally let me ride on the front bar of his bike on the way to school. Another child, who lived near us, stopped by one day. Mama and I and the baby, in Mama's arms, went to a slaughterhouse to get bones for the big dog. The neighbor boy trudged ahead, both ways, as a good guide on a mission. We only made one trip to get bones before Papa sold the dog.

And then I was sharing a big bed with Mama and Papa in a dark and gloomy apartment at night. Mama was shouting, "I want to go to the river. I just want to touch the water." I thought that wasn't unreasonable because I saw a bridge over a river on the way to the apartment. Then it was morning and I was being put on a bus with a note for the drivers on my way to Carmel. Oh, was I glad to see Ellen!

Mama and Papa and the baby were up in the mountains at a logging camp which was destroyed by a forest fire. They were not hurt but their belongings were damaged. Mama was a cook for the lumberjacks, including Papa, and the baby was thriving, as I learned later. Back in Carmel I went to the beach with Roxanne and my cousin and a Scout Master. With the same people, we went swimming in a pool up the valley. As part of a summer swimming program, George and I went up the valley twice. Then I was eliminated for getting car sick on the winding roads. I loved to swim and did not mind getting sick but I could understand how the drivers felt.

My older cousin, Keith, was making his own sailboat in Ellen's yard. One day I smelled, then saw, smoke coming from the woods behind our home. Keith filled a water bucket and was bringing it when I came to tell him exactly where the fire was. At his instructions, I called the Fire Department. When the Fire Chief came roaring up in his hook and ladder he stayed for a while to make sure the fire was really out. He reminded us pine needles tended to smolder and might rekindle. I wondered where George was. Before the chief left, George confessed. He and Roxanne built a fire to toast marshmallows in the pine needles. Chief Norton called Keith a "real fireman" and me a "real detective." He warned George and Roxanne.

A few days later George brought me a ring, a "real" ruby he found. I wore it for several minutes before he asked me to give it back. I watched him put it on Roxanne's finger. By now, I was a reader devouring the books on Ellen's shelves. I passed the stage of longing for the tiny porcelain knickknacks in her China cabinet. The Fourth of July the Scout Master and Ellen took the boys and me down to the beach. Cap sat in his big chair in front of the radio keeping up with the world. Keith lit and tossed a firecracker which the wind deflected into my left eye, singeing the eyelash but doing no real damage. Of course, everyone hurried home. On Sunday George and Keith and I were picked up by the lady with a very large car. She always took us to Sunday School. I remember being so sad because I was going back to Mama the next day. Once again, Cap would not be responsible for Ellen's "sister's child."

Papa was foreman, again, on a turkey farm which also raised peacocks and guinea hens. Mama welcomed me with a glass of "real" grape juice, from concentrate, with which I fell instantly in love. The boss's wife suffered from a boil which I was invited to look at when Mama and I visited her. Then, she went to a hospital and Papa became foreman on another farm. Once he let me ride behind him on a tractor while he disked the hard ground. Near our house a huge field of rotting tomatoes turned into an insect paradise. Mama and I, with the baby in a blanket-filled box, picked cling peaches for money Mama "kept for me." Once I brought home a sparrow with a broken wing. Mama found another apple box for it. I brought it a jar lid of water and some weed seeds from plants in the yard, and went to bed. In the morning, the bird was gone. Mama said a cat probably ate it. We didn't have a cat, for once, but I didn't argue. I found another worry. Looking for something to wear to school, in the closet, I found Mama's medicine, a white powder in little packets which didn't taste like sugar. I spat it out and left the packet I found, opened, on the floor exactly as I found it.

Mama evidently didn't notice her face powder was also on the floor, also not entirely in its box. I was attending a country school, really in the country, walking through the fields which were mechanically harvested. They were now being used as fodder for a herd of sheep. The Basque shepherd's cart and his donkey were nearby but I never saw him. He was probably making breakfast since smoke curled from the chimney of his covered cart. Each morning, at the same time, I used this shortcut to the one room, eight-grades school house. I walked home along the road with an Okie girl whose family took Mama and me with them when it was peach picking time. Since she was older than I she stayed in school later. I waited at my desk making a handprinted copy of James Barrie's _Peter Pan_ on scratch paper. It never occurred to me to ask Mama if I could have a book so I was making one. Mama found my scratch paper book when we moved and, of course, it never occurred to her not to throw it away.

Back in Carmel, this time with Mama on a visit, Ellen gave me some tiny metal and glass animal charms. Mama seized my hand and squeezed and made me drop them. She was in a great hurry "trying to find a place" for me. The last time I was at Ellen's, George's new group of friends played Mah Jong and, one rainy afternoon, recited poetry to each other. I was spellbound listening to *The Wreck of the Hesperus* and *The Rhyme of the Ancient Mariner.* When I could, I asked the boy's mother if I could talk to her. Now, Mama visited her, with me in tow, so when I found her alone, I asked, "Could I stay with you?" I hardly dared to breathe. I was barely able to ask. "No, of course not," she said. Obviously, Mama did not come to see this particular "old friend" to "find a place" for me. I excused myself, left Mama there and ran sobbing back to Ellen's, stifling my tears on the way. Mama must have shared a good laugh there before she reluctantly took me back to the San Joaquin Valley where we came from, temporarily.

Rider's Run

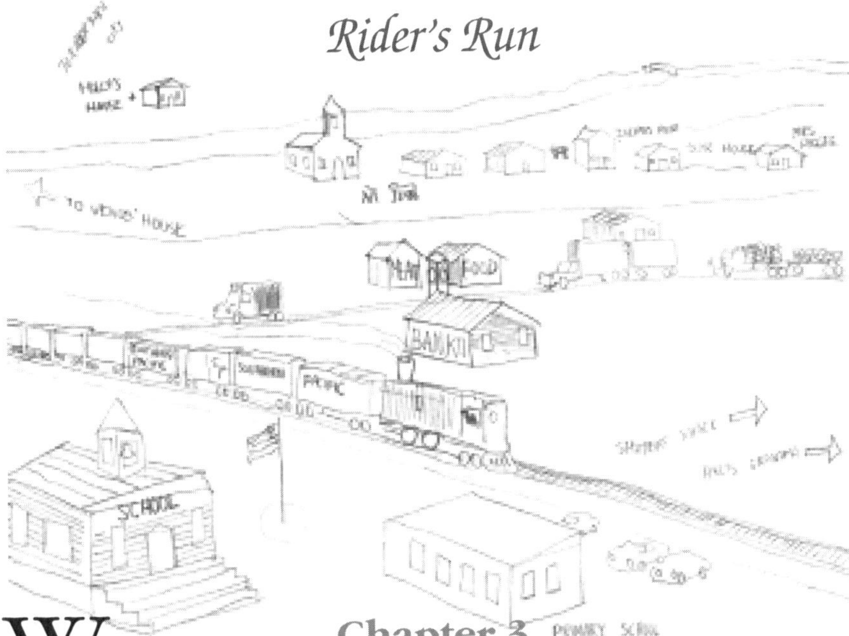

Chapter 3

We were here twice before—only without Mama. Once we were in a big house just two blocks from the home Mama and Papa bought on Church Street. Two blocks in the other direction rose the steeple of the New England church. Papa hired someone to care for the baby and me. I remember the very thin young lady's black hair. I only knew her for the few minutes she spent packing Mama's clothes and some household things. She didn't even say "Good-bye" or "Take care of the baby." She just charged through the door. Her arms were so full, she almost fell on the stairs. When Papa arrived, several hours later, he cried. Almost absentmindedly, he hugged me. He removed a miniature picture of my father from my locket, carefully inserting a picture of himself. Finally, he drove the baby and me to a German lady in Stockton.

Mrs. Percheron's husband owned a barber shop where Papa got his haircut. The barber and Papa originated in the same part of Germany. It was a case of instant hate between Mrs. Percheron and me. First she set me on the kitchen table. Then she seized a pair of scissors from a side table. Then she cut my hair extremely short. She made clothes two sizes too large for me to "grow into," six dresses from the same pattern. She made six hankies with crocheted edges which hurt my nose. For Pansy she crocheted caps, booties and blankets. She cooed and gurgled over Pansy while she bathed, dressed, and powdered her. Mrs. Percheron brought the usual cabbage, potatoes, and sausage directly from stove to table. She scooped from each onto individual plates and set the pots on the floor beside her chair. "Here, kitty, kitty," she called night after night. There were no pets. Her husband, son, and I dutifully laughed every evening.

After dinner, she hefted her bulk from the table, collected the pots and carried them to the sink. She sent me outside "to the fresh air" to sit on the steps alone with nothing to do. She talked to herself when she thought she was alone. She ignored her son as often as she ignored me. We were not allowed to play with each other.

One day we took the bus past a row of tall brick buildings with the usual high windows and a fence. "Your mother is in there. She's crazy," she informed me loudly. Everyone on the bus heard her and got a good look at me. Another time she took me into the biggest building behind the fence and right up to Mama. Mama sat in a clean print dress at a table with some hand sewing. Mama gave me a casual hug and chatted with Mrs. Percheron till the nurse who directed us to Mama came back. On our way out of the building, we walked past a long screened porch. Rows of old shriveled men and women sat looking through the windows. I noticed they had haircuts like mine and no teeth in their mouths. I was absolutely terrified. Not much later, Mrs. Percheron decided I was too much trouble. She notified Papa, who made a special trip to take me to my father's brother in Palo Alto.

My uncle's daughter, my age, was then attending a special school for very intelligent children. Eavesdropping on Mama and Ellen I learned my uncle's wife was a teacher who did not know how to cook. This was one of Mama's few understatements. We ate boiled peeled potatoes, boiled beef chunks and boiled peeled carrots for dinner. I was trying to understand what my uncle saw in this cadaverous female when a policeman appeared. Two minutes later I was in a police car being delivered to an orphanage. My uncle was at sea on a freighter. His wife would have nothing to do with me. I spent a few days alone behind a high fence. I sat on a metal swing, occasionally swinging at various speeds. The only other place to sit was bare ground. I spent a few nights in a metal cot watching young ladies. They changed diapers, bottle fed infants, and occasionally reassured me, "Someone will come for you soon. Now don't you worry." I was too old to cry and too numb to be helpful. I tried not to get in anyone's way.

Then Papa came and took me to another part of Rider's Run, up the hill from the town. Papa promised me a horse of my own before we left San Francisco. He almost kept the promise by letting me ride a work horse, twice, before we moved again. Two pleasant young ladies lived there. They made a card for Mama. One lady painted watercolor nasturtiums. Another did the lettering. It was a beautiful card. I made Xs and Os "for Mama in the hospital."

The third time we lived in Rider's Run was the charm. Papa drove up to the pink house on Church Street and began to unload our wagon load of household possessions. I only kept part of my attention on the crawling creature Pansy was now. The house was kind of attractive with peeling pink paint and a wide veranda. There were plenty of large, but not too large, windows. There were five rooms, an outhouse and bare ground in front with two olive trees. In the backyard was a barn, a rabbit shed, and our own garbage dump. The land slanted down to a wide valley beyond the barbed wire fence which marked the property line. It was a one story house with a two story house on each side. There were lilac bushes in the side yard, white and lavender. Papa cut down the olive trees but left the massive oak tree leaning against the veranda. When he was gone, which was often, I sat in the crotch of the oak. I thought long thoughts of school vacation.

Papa worked as a cow milker on a dairy farm on the other side of town. I first saw the Rider's farm when Papa took me there to shower. It was where the milkers washed up after work. The shower valve was too high for me to reach. I almost boiled my scrawny body. I was glad it only happened once. The shower was more exciting than my usual Saturday bath in the corrugated metal tub. Papa used the tub for scalding the pigs he slaughtered when he made sausage. When we used the tub for baths I was the last one. The water would be cloudy grey and cold. However, since this only happened once a week, how could I be anything but grateful?

Papa brought two goats, a cow, several rabbits, and a young pig to live in the outbuildings. He patched, roofed, and strengthened the buildings without disturbing much paint. On one side of us lived an Indian family with eleven children. Their pigeon coop was exactly on the property line three feet to the left of our house. I didn't mind the cooing pigeons or the yelling, rifle toting, and occasionally shooting, adolescents next door. Mama did. One day she and Papa left me in charge of the one acre homestead. While they were gone, two very clean early teenagers came up to our fence and called. They introduced themselves as real Indians. They were very nice to chat with. They told me about how far it was to school and gave me lots of useful information. The next time I looked over the fence they wouldn't talk to or even look at me. The day after that the whole family was gone, pigeons, pack of hunting dogs, chickens, and people. We had an additional two acres plus a two story house with big holes in its floors and walls. There was even a dugout where an animal shelter used to be. Papa acquired a garage where his car could be out of the rain when it was not at work. I missed the Indians.

Papa killed a pig. He borrowed a sausage machine from the Rider's Run butcher who owned his own shop. The butcher was glad to have a fellow German in this area. Here the Riders from old England had been multiplying for two hundred years. Papa and Mama converted most of the pig into sausage. I got to help with holding the various sizes of intestines Papa used to encase the various kinds of sausages. Mama canned some of the meat but it spoiled. Papa built a smokehouse where he smoked some of the meat and all the sausages. We ate well. Mama canned the gunny sacks of pears and peaches Papa brought home from nearby fruit farms. I got to help make catchup and wash all sizes and shapes of bottles and jars. Then I got to stir boiling fruit endlessly. Sweat ran from our bodies. Mama peeled fruit and boiled and sterilized jars. When the baby cried, I got to learn how to change and wash diapers. To rock Pansy to sleep, I moved my body up and down beside her on the big bed. Papa brought home apricots which Mama cut in half and dipped in salt water. Papa laid them on the racks he made. He set the racks under the almond trees where the Indians used to live.

I learned how to chop weeds with a solid iron bar attached to a hoe. I got blisters and muscles under the relentless sun. I also ate dried apricots every time I managed to pass the drying racks. I hulled walnuts and almonds from our trees and ate some of those, too, like a kind of commission. Sometimes, Papa sang German opera. Sometimes, Mama sang American Show tunes and Swedish Folk songs. They worked themselves into exhaustion. I stood on a chair at the kitchen sink to do the dishes. My dishwater came from a kettle on the stove. There was a single light bulb in the kitchen ceiling. Singing *Old Black Joe* and *Swanee*, I wiped those dishes with a greasy towel. Mama did not throw away the dish towels I cross-stitched for my Hope Chest. I brought them from San Diego only to wear them out in Rider's Run. I cut kindling, and heavier wood, for the big cast iron stove. I made the fire when it went out so I learned how to keep it going.

Papa brought home a doll with a sawdust body and a porcelain head. My San Diego doll cradle remained. Pansy and I shared a double bed exactly like the one shared by our parents. They shared a bedroom. Our bed and Mama's old steamer trunk furnished the front room. Except at mealtimes, a round table in the dining room held Mama's sewing. Here the Insurance lady came to talk to Mama and Papa and went away mad. Here the Union man came to talk to Papa and also went away mad. One day when we weren't all working too hard I wandered over to the Indian house and thoroughly inspected it. I had orders not to go anywhere near it, of course. At night I waited until Pansy was finally asleep. Then I walked cautiously through the normally unused front door. In the side yard I collected my doll and cradle and carried them up the creaking stairs at the old house. On each of several nights I brought more things to the upper room. I attached yarn to a loom I invented from an old sink drain board with nails on the ends. I got a candle and the candle holder Aunt Ellen sent me for Christmas at Garden Acres. At last, I could see well enough to work on the Indian rug I intended to make. The following night, Pansy suffered from indigestion. When she finally appeared to be sound asleep, I sneaked out of the house. Having a one-sided chat with my doll, Han San, I laid down the first threads for my rug. When I got really tired I blew out the candle. Then I waited till the wick felt cold to my fingers because I was terribly afraid of fire. At peace with the world, I returned to the sleeping Pansy.

The next morning, Mama was braiding my hair when Papa stormed into the kitchen. "You arsonist, are you trying to get us all killed?" he demanded. He was carrying my candle holder, the candle, and the box of matches from my "playroom." Mama yanked on my hair, "Speak up! What's going on?" I froze. She kept pulling my half finished braids. She demanded, "What did you think you were doing in that stinking hovel at night?" I realized Pansy was not sleeping while I worked on my rug. They ran out of things to call me before I found my voice. Papa spent the rest of the day building a four foot by four foot "playroom." There he installed Pansy and a blanket plus my doll with her cradle. Mama was "teaching me how" to pull the weeds in the flower garden, a job requiring more skill than hoeing. Contact with the principal garden weed, stinging nettles, reddened my arms. Later, we learned how to boil and eat those nettles. I never went back into the Indian house and I never used the "playroom." Neither did Pansy. Papa used the lumber for something else.

One of the Indian boys who lived beside us was about my age. He waited down the street, out of sight from our house, the first morning I attended Rider's Run Elementary School. He helped me get up on the front bar of his bike. With quiet dignity, he delivered me to a block from the school itself. There, by the railroad crossing signal, he explained his family was moving out of town. We would never see each other again. Then, with his hands on my shoulders, he pointed me toward the school. "Now get out of here, you little shrimp," he said. And that is how it happened I was not late on my first day of school in Rider's Run.

I was frequently late, thereafter, until I found a friend. She lived only three houses away and was even in my class. We would meet in front of her house and walk both ways together. From her I learned to carry a comb to keep what slipped from my swinging braids somewhat neat. She taught me a poem about glasses of beer. We sang "Ching a Chong a Chinaman sitting on a rail. Along came a Blackbird and nipped off his tail." Neither of us had any idea what it meant. When she moved away, I wrote a poem and gave it to her. It said, basically, "Thank You, Shirley, for sticks of gum, comebacks, and combs." I thanked her again for the book she gave me, *Whiter Than Snow*. Her desk at school was taken by a boy. He dipped my braids in his ink well until the teacher caught him.

I was late again afterward. Mama controlled the alarm clock. If she didn't wake up, I didn't wake up. If she did, she would stand inside the doorway while I stood on the veranda, aching to run. She would make me "straighten those socks" and "tuck in that shirt" and "stand up straight." When she, finally, let me go I ran as hard as I could. I reached the railroad tracks near the school streaming with sweat, fiery red of face. It was just in time to watch everyone else on the school steps have flag salute. When it rained Mama didn't have inspection on the veranda so I didn't have to be late. Since flag salute didn't happen outside on rainy days it didn't really matter. In that case, I would be sodden when I got to school. The rain would be squishing around in my shoes. My dress would cling to me. What I hated, really hated, was my handkerchief. Every morning, I started out with a clean handkerchief. After I blew my nose twice, it was no longer dry. All day I blew my nose in the same sodden hanky. Grimly, I threw it in the laundry pile every night. Mama used a washboard and clothes lines when we first came to Rider's Run. Then, a regular laundry man brought his truck once a week to our house. He took cloth bags full of dirty laundry and brought back cloth bags of clean laundry. He and Mama got along well together. I was still required to scrub Pansy's white leather baby shoes with an old tooth brush. I swabbed them with white liquid polish. I was able, and altogether willing, to forget how to use a washboard.

Golden Rule Days

Chapter 4

The first summer in Rider's Run, Mama created a birthday party for me. My birthday came toward the end of June. Mama made an Easter Bunny cake with marshmallow rabbits running around the top. My present was a set of hand tools for the garden which Mama used forever after. I invited Shirley and the Rider kids. Actually, I only invited Shirley. Papa brought the Rider kids to our house, and took them home afterward in his car. The Rider farm was, at least, fifty times bigger than our yard. Hide and Seek in their backyard would have been challenging. We played Hide and Seek among the outbuildings. Our game didn't last long. Papa was very entertaining. He showed us how to convert a hand rake into a back scratcher. As usual, he did most of the talking. Papa showed the guests the long zipper scar on his arm. With animation, he described the enemy plane coming toward him through the air over France. The other pilot also carried a revolver in his cockpit. The other pilot shot first. Papa even sang a little song in German.

April 1, Papa sent me to the German butcher with a message, in German, he made me memorize. In English, it meant, "hit me blue." Fortunately, my pronunciation was nowhere near exact. The butcher frowned a lot, tried to understand, and sent me home. The second pig grew up in our little barn, was smoked and/or made into sausage. Our goat provided milk and two kids which Papa sold. The rabbits died in the summer heat of their shed, except for those Mama canned. They spoiled before the winter. Another hard working summer followed a winter when Mama sewed for various people in the town. She also cleaned house for several local women. I hated her sewing for me. For hours I stood on a chair while Mama pinned and basted hemlines. Once in a while, Florence Rider walked part way home with me. She was taking piano lessons from her Grandmother. This distinguished looking lady lived alone in a big house I passed every day. One Sunday, Papa took Mama, Pansy, and me to the church at the head of our street. The Pastor said Mama's religion was a devil's invention. He probably never realized it was Mama's religion. Papa grabbed my hand and pushed Mama (who carried Pansy) right out of the church. I never got to see what Florence's Sunday school looked like.

One hot summer day, Papa let me ride on the left front fender of his car for two whole blocks. When I asked him how fast he went he lied, "Forty miles an hour." Florence Rider and I sat beside each other for a while in second grade. We shared a seat during singing periods. We played together at recess. Her aunt taught third grade. She made tassel topped green wool hats for three of us girls. The third girl often wore a scotch plaid skirt with a black velvet top. I thought she might be trying to wear them out before she outgrew them, like I did. In our school, most people started wearing their good dresses to school well before they replaced them. Although she lived much closer to school than most of us, she always came in a car. She owned a raincoat and an umbrella and a pair of galoshes! She was Florence's cousin, Holly. Her head was as covered with curls as mine was before I scissored them off. Mama frequently reminded me I cut my own hair while we visited her friend in San Francisco. Holly's mother was a former teacher. Every morning, when she delivered Holly, she arranged to chat with Holly's teacher the same afternoon. Once we three girls waved at Holly's father as he went by in the cab of a freight train. That's how close the school was to the railroad tracks and how close Holly was to her father. Our school population grew as Okies and Arkies fled from the Dust Bowl. One day, Florence and I were racing around the school building. One of these newcomers called me "A Redfaced Indian Squaw." He told Florence she looked like "George Washington."

In the fourth grade, a new teacher commuted from Stockton every day. One day, she mentioned she shared Mama's religion. I don't know how she knew because, to my knowledge, they never met. She created a library on a table in the back of the room. Later, she assigned book reports. As they accumulated, she asked me to help her correct them. I got into a yelling fight with Delphinia. This little Okie girl would not spell "once" like the dictionary did. She wrote it like she pronounced it, "one st." The teacher decided to correct her own book reports while I was at home sick. I was really sick a lot in those days. So was Holly. Once I went to visit her while she was ill. Her mother ushered me into her bedroom. There was Holly in a canopied twin bed with a radio on her nightstand. There was a lamp on her desk and another lamp beside a chair. I didn't even have my own room or my own bed. I didn't stay long. Holly said she wanted to listen to *Jack Armstrong, the all-American boy*. Each of us had measles. I had scarlet fever and scabies, a dreadful itching skin disaster. It taught me more than I ever wanted to learn about patience. I learned not to scratch. The itching continued, all over my body, for two or three eternities despite every ointment and salve the doctor prescribed.

Mama, and Pansy, visited a neighbor whenever the husbands were gone. Meanwhile, when nobody was around, I read books borrowed from the school library. It was California and winter and raining. One morning, one of the books fell from the end of my bed into a spot near the window. When I found it, the book was a sodden mess. Mama sent a note to my teacher, in a sealed envelope, with the book we tried to resuscitate. With these, I returned to school when my quarantine ended. Mama was as furious as she always was when I did something wrong. She forbade me ever to bring home another school book. This was too much for me to be able to do. I kept checking out library books. I hid them in the garage next door, read them there and checked them back in at school. I still did the dishes, straightened the house and made the beds after school. This wasn't an ordeal because no one was at home. When I finished I could run to the garage and read. I timed my return to Mama's kitchen for a few minutes before Mama scurried home from Mrs. Piggee's house. This was a few minutes before Papa drove home from the Rider's cow barn.

As it ages, redwood tends to splinter easily. Our floors were aging redwood planks. Every Saturday I scrubbed those floors. I started the process with a dishpan of water so hot it stung my hands. I grasped a bar of strong soap in one hand and a large hand scrub brush in the other. I kneeled on a gunny sack. Mama supervised from a nearby chair. Every Saturday Mama taught me how to clean the house Swedish style. So when I wasn't sick I was busy and when I was sick I was lonely. Florence invited me to her house to ride her pony. I went twice. We rode her Shetland "Champ" or a bigger horse retired from farm work. Sometimes we played Tarzan in their front yard, running around the trees, chasing or being chased by, her brother. I was always invited to stay for dinner which was always huge. We ate mashed potatoes, roast beef, corn on the cob, apple pie, and ice cream. We drank lots of fresh milk. The third time Florence invited me to her house, Mama supervised the Saturday morning floor scrubbing with unusual attention. I just couldn't seem to hold the brush right or slop enough water onto the bare

boards. I didn't use enough soap to make a lather. I was in such a hurry to go to see my friend. These visits were weeks apart. It kept getting later. Finally, I said, "Mama, you said I could go to Florence's house today." "Well, you can't go. You didn't get those floors clean. You can't go to Florence's house now or ever," Mama proclaimed. I ran from the house to the side yard, grabbed the hoe and tackled the five foot high stinging nettles. These tended to accumulate where the Indian pigeon coop used to be. Mama and I never discussed this matter because something else went wrong.

It was Fall. I was looking forward to going back to school. Mama's inspections weren't happening this year. She was as fat as she was before Pansy appeared. One Saturday, Mama made a picnic lunch and all of us dressed up. Papa drove half a day past the manzanita bushes of the Sierra Nevada to a sign which said, "RENO population xxxx." He parked in front of a church. As usual, I was left in the car with the sleeping Pansy. I was glad when we stopped. Something else made me happy too. This was the first time I ever travelled so far in a car without getting violently carsick.

At last, Mama and Papa emerged from the church. Mama said, "You're sure you put a stop to their announcement in the paper?" Papa said, "I'm sure. Don't worry. We are anonymous." Mama slid into the front seat and Papa drove us to a gas station. While he was taking care of the car, Mama cried, not very softly, in the front seat. She said, "I swore I was never going to get married again. After I divorced your father, I swore I was never, ever, going to get married again. I even had to use the ring your father bought me in Juneau. I remember when he told me he got it on the installment plan. I almost threw it at him. Now, here it is on my finger again." Papa slipped into the driver's seat and drove home. We picnicked beside the road and I got car sick.

As usual, one of Mrs. Piggee's sons delivered Papa's newspaper on Sunday. I saw the headline, "Hitler Invades Poland." It was September 3, 1939. The Reno newspaper relayed a local wedding announcement on the same day. I was just beginning to learn geography. I asked Papa where Poland was. He erupted, "The Fool. The Damned Fool. This war should never happen." He repeated himself several times. It was like the time I asked for help in arithmetic. Mama asked him to help me. He read the problem in my book. Mama added, "That is if your mathematics is better than your spelling. I saw 'P o t a t o e' farm on your old correspondence course papers." Papa made me scribble the numbers from the problem on a piece of butcher paper. From the closet, he extracted his night stick. This was an ornate cane left over from his chauffeur days. I knew I was in trouble but I had no idea why. "Put the hat on the five last," he insisted. He never actually hit me with the cane. However, my habit of making the number five like my schoolteacher did was cured immediately. Still upset, he stormed out of the house and drove away. I didn't solve the arithmetic problem and I didn't bring any homework to the dinner table ever again. If I couldn't do it at school, I didn't do it. Papa was gone again. Mama went to tell Mrs. Piggee all about her wedding while I put Pansy to bed.

The next morning, I walked to school eagerly-intent on not being too late for flag salute. I glided into a spot at the end of a row while the bell was still ringing. I smiled triumphantly at Florence. She glared at me. So did every other child on the steps in front of the school. I looked at my shoes, my newly remodelled dress, my clean fingernails. Why was everybody mad at me? What was wrong? After flag salute, as we headed for our classroom, Florence hissed,

"You German Pig." Holly muttered, "You little spy. At recess the kids edged away from me. We played baseball after one period. I hit the ball. I actually hit the ball. This did not usually happen. I ran to first base, to second, to third. I made the first home run in my entire life and no one cheered. We always cheered when anybody made a home run. The bell rang as I stepped off home plate. No one said anything. I ran to class with the others. Melvin leaned a mirror on his shoe for looking under a girl's dress When he saw me observe this pastime, he made a most unusually angry face. Without the usual chorus of good byes, except markedly to each other, the students headed home. I still had no idea what happened to my world.

Then, as I walked through the school gate, I saw the small crowd. Kids of all ages, most of them recent arrivals from Oklahoma and Arkansas, waited by the tracks. One of them threw a stone at me. All of them were suddenly yelling, "German spy, Nazi Pig, Dirty old hag." I ran for one mile without stopping. I ran and ran all the way home while the crowd grew smaller and smaller. There were still three or four kids left who found stones from my front yard to throw at me. I streaked into the back yard. I had my cry before I went inside to do my chores. As usual, no one was home.

At night Papa brought home a dog, a German Shepherd, named Rex. He said, "Take care of him. He's yours." I found a pie tin for water, another old pie tin for scraps. I petted him for a long time. He didn't mind even when I cried on his beautiful coat. And I did a lot of crying.

"You cannot choose your battlefield. The gods do that for you but you can plant a standard where a standard never flew." This was one of the sayings I culled from my books. The next morning Rex and I walked to school. As we neared The Soda Shoppe a tall, skinny, Okie boy came out into the street. He began a singsong "Here comes the little German girl. Here comes the little German girl." I was praying silently, "Please God, don't let any of those rocks hurt me." Suddenly, I started running straight at the person who was half again as big as I was. I flew at him, fists flying, pounding into his stomach. He just stood there. I was crying so hard I couldn't see. Finally, he grabbed both my hands and held them. "O.K. O.K. I got the message," he said. Other kids emerged from the shop. He added, "If I ever catch anyone even trying to make you feel bad I will personally take care of him. Just let me know who it is, little lady, and I will take care of him." In a dead silence I said, "Thank You." Then Rex and I walked to school. Rex was waiting for me afterward. After that, Holly and Florence indulged in subdued hisses and name calling every day for a couple of years. This practice continued until long after it became almost automatic. However, no more stones were thrown at me—even after my defender moved away.

Someone from the newly created Rider's Run Health Department typed a notice which the town Constable delivered to Papa. Papa promptly removed all traces of our animals, except Rex. He dismantled our barn, shed, smoke house, and drying racks. He sold the cow. Then, the Riders told Papa they didn't need him because there wasn't enough work. The work hadn't changed. They had. So Papa drove away at first for a day, then a week, then two weeks at a time. Pansy and I went to stay with Mrs. Percheron in Stockton. Mama's new baby was born in the county hospital. Mrs. Percheron joked with Papa. She missed no opportunity to remind me, "Your mother is crazy-a real crazy woman." I didn't know who to hate. How could I hate Florence for telling me, "All my relatives, even my uncles, hate your whole family?" Rider's Run overflowed with Florence's uncles. "I'll never stop hating you, you Nazi spy," she added. How could I hate Mrs. Percheron who so closely resembled the sow we formerly owned? I certainly couldn't hate the sow. It never occurred to me to hate Mama or Papa or Pansy or the new baby boy. Rex was still alive, and at home, when we went back to Rider's Run.

Ways and Means

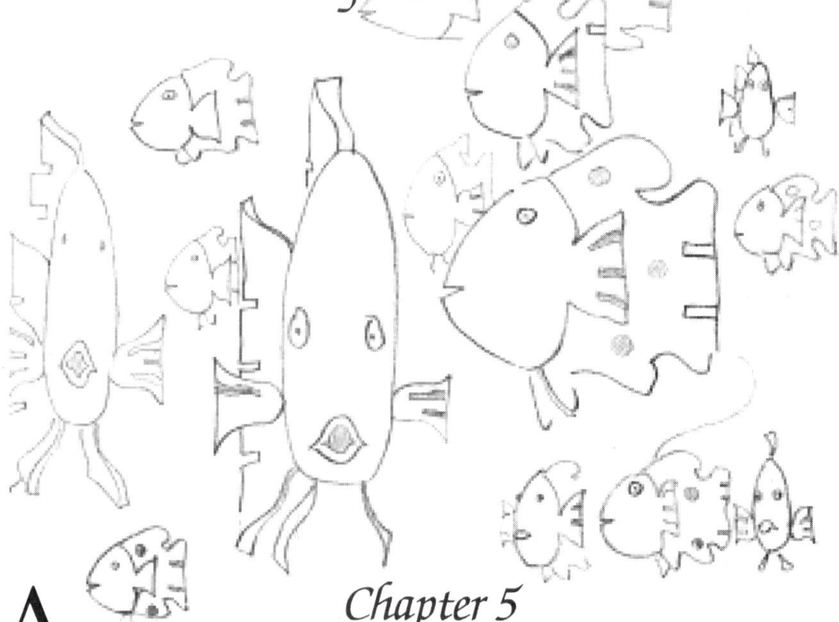

Chapter 5

A girl from my class moved in next door to us. I woke up very early one Sunday morning to find Mama making a real breakfast. The new girl, her mother and sister were in our dining room in their bathrobes. Her father came home drunk and brandished a straight razor exactly like Papa's. He threatened to kill everyone in the house. I was glad to see the girl until Monday morning in school. She suggested the other team captain find a stick so they could spit on it. This would decide which team was stuck with me. Three weeks later, the family moved away. Teams were even again.

Mama didn't cook unless Papa came home and he did so infrequently. I learned how to shop after school on credit, cream, mash or bake potatoes. Soon I learned how to fry or roast meats and to prepare vegetables. The first year of World War II there was a good garden from which Mama selected various zucchini, carrots, and squashes. She copied a Chinese apparatus-two identical bamboo baskets on a pole. I carried heavy loads of vegetables to the other side of town. The money I brought back was supposed to be spent for a bicycle for me. Religiously, I deposited the nickels and quarters and rare dollar bills in my own savings account at the bank. Mama made clothes from her old dresses for the next family who moved in next door. When there were no more donatable clothes for their children, these neighbors stopped speaking to us.

Mama found a reason to make real dinners for us. A Spanish American War veteran arranged to dine at our house in return for a portion of his pension. We enjoyed delicious dinners for almost a month. They were entertaining meals, too, because the bent old man recited poetry from his abundant memory. Longfellow's *Paul Revere* and Tennyson's *Ring Out Wild Bells* and *The Boy Stood On The Burning Deck* came alive. His right arm was a stump wrapped in black oil cloth and he limped slowly between his house and ours. One day at school Holly said, "I hear you Nazis are feeding that old tramp. He's an outlaw." I didn't reply, ever.

Papa came home and there was a long noisy battle in the kitchen. As usual, I herded the kids to another room and sneaked back. This time Papa slapped Mama-a really hard blow. I sprang into action, seized a log from the wood box and swung it against his knees. "Don't you ever, ever, hit my mother," I screamed. Then I ran from the house, two blocks, in sheer terror. I stopped, realizing Mama could still be in trouble. Then I thought, if he was going to kill me it better be now. I wouldn't be able to endure waiting. As I came near the house, I saw Papa was already in his car driving away. The veteran was forbidden to come back. I saw him now and then and we waved at each other. I missed him a lot.

Certain things I was not supposed to make, like desserts, not that I was much interested in extra cooking. It interfered with my reading. One day, while Mama was visiting I did make cupcakes, almost. I heard her coming toward the kitchen and threw the batter in the garbage. Mama advertised in the *Stockton Record* for someone to live in the front room. My room of my own, next to the kitchen, was formerly a storeroom. Mama and Pansy and the new baby slept in the big bed Papa formerly shared. This left the front room with its big bed, small table and newly acquired chair available. A family with two children came from a nearby town to chat with Mama. She looked really nice in a clean ironed dress, stockings, and shoes. Her clean hair was curled with the curling iron. Mama chatted happily and gave the visiting family fresh cookies. The very next week they brought the children's grandmother and her suitcase to the front room.

I think the grandmother's stay at our house was shorter than that of the veteran. She refused to eat, the excellent meals Mama provided, at our table with us. Instead, she insisted on standing at the sink, looking out over the valley, while she ate. Then, she insisted on sparse boiled meals. I remembered my Aunt in Palo Alto who refused to learn how to cook. Then, she insisted the children were too much for her. Then, her family came and took her away. She left a bottle of mineral oil she used to wash her face. I slipped it into the garbage, grateful to have the kitchen back again. Mama and the kids went visiting. I seized the chance to read when nobody was around. While she was there, she listened to the radio Papa brought home. After she was gone, Mama let us listen to the radio on Saturdays. We regularly heard *Armstrong's Theater of the Air*, my favorite, the *Kentucky Derby,* and the Opera.

Mama discovered the lending library in back of the Soda Shoppe. When there was no one to visit, she borrowed books. For a while we read a little bit each evening and a lot on Sunday. Mama read *Next to Valor* in a clear, loud voice and I loved every minute of it. In the back of the closet between her room and mine, I found *Anthony Adverse*. I read it from cover to cover. When my fourth grade teacher mentioned the Madonna in a history lesson, I said, "Oh, you mean like the statue in Anthony Adverse? The teacher's jaw dropped. I didn't usually interrupt anyone. Later, she told me I was too young to read such a book. Too late! Holly read something about a girl who dyed her hair green, which I thought was absurd. I was starting to read *The Bitter Tea of General Yen*. A green haired girl was so improbable, I missed a question about her on the Standard Test next year.

Once, when Papa came back, he took us shopping in Stockton. In the San Joaquin Valley we passed beautiful Nisei farms amid delightfully arranged trees. There were acres of carefully tended vegetables beside neat small houses. People bent over the rows, working together, pulling weeds by hand just like I did. I enjoyed this part of the long ride to Stockton for the first years we lived in Rider's Run. We made the trip to Stockton for staples and an occasional movie like *The Emperor's Candlesticks*. This time, some of those houses and outbuildings were gutted by fire. Some were flattened, some boarded up, some totally removed. All trace of the second generation farmers was almost gone. Weeds clogged their gardens. Papa explained the owners were in prison. "They were people who were born here just like you were," he added.

We filled the car with food. He visited the Percherons while the rest of us window shopped. Mama pointed out a burgundy princess style bathrobe in the window of a boutique. She murmured, "How would you like it for Christmas?. I actually tried on a fuzzy, white coat called mouton at a furriers. Neither the robe nor the coat accompanied us home. Papa didn't actually forget us. When Pansy was old enough to go to school, he brought her a real leather briefcase. It was too big for even me to carry comfortably. Now and then, he brought me a treasure like a dried Devil's Claw from the desert. He brought me a dried flying fish when he worked as a stevedore. He brought me a clear, green rock containing white polka dots like very miniature marshmallows when he was a lumberjack. I kept these gifts with the coffee cans full of rocks I collected for years. Secure under the part of the house which wasn't basement, they were eventually forgotten. Gradually, the jars of fruit and vegetables, canned in the good days before the war, were all consumed. Gradually, Papa's times at home became fewer.

When the last payment for the property became due, I was suddenly very important. In the bank in my account were $35. I earned them carrying baskets full of vegetables to sell in the hot summer afternoons. They turned out to be just exactly enough for Mama to get the title to "our three acres." Mama said, "It'll be your house, darling," She put the money I dutifully removed from my, now empty, account, into her purse. I didn't even mention a bicycle. It was probably the only time she called me "darling." It had a hollow sound.

Mama also forgot I ever wanted a bicycle when we went, with some neighbors, to the vineyards to pick grapes. As usual, she "kept the money" for me. I counted the boxes I picked. They were heavy lugs of purple, dripping, oozing, grapes. With sticky, black, grimy, hands I groped among the spiders and insects under leaves gray with spray and dust. I didn't hate to pick grapes. It was hot and horrible but it was a together thing, a group activity. Mama seemed to enjoy chatting and gossiping and keeping an eye on her kids playing in the dirt nearby. Other pickers, even other kids like me, were all helping the war effort as agricultural workers.

The first highlight of the summer was camp in the high Sierras. Somehow, I was included in a two week program for underprivileged youngsters. I always suspected it was my fourth grade teacher who sponsored me. She claimed the same religion as Mama. She was the one whose library book melted down in the rain. Individual campers were picked up by bus at our homes, I supposed. I know I was, carrying a lot of recently acquired "suitable clothes." For two weeks, I collected wildflowers from hiking trails. I pressed them in a book made of colored paper with cardboard covers. I ate a lot of great food, sang as loud as I could at each evening's campfire, ran, and played. I hiked and swam, even rode in a canoe. I even danced, on the last evening, with a boy in heavy hiking boots. I loved every minute of it. We sang, *We'll All Come Back To You* the last evening, with feeling.

The second highlight of the summer was my first crush. It was perfectly natural and totally innocent. When I came back from camp, Mama put me on the Calaveras Stage which stopped in Rider's Run. She gave me the usual note for the bus drivers on my way to Carmel. Coming down the hill into the sleepy town I felt the usual glow of welcome. I felt like I was coming home. Ellen arranged for me to baby-sit with some "Army Brats" and live in their house. One of them was my age. I actually wiped as many dishes as they did and shared their chores. They sang and played their piano. We chased each other around their big yard. The ten year old son and I went fishing. With his mother's encouragement, we took the bus to Monterey. At the wharf we each threw one end of a baited and hooked string into the oily water. Then of necessity, having no more fishing gear, we took the bus home. The son never forgave me for not having the sense to hold onto the string. I forgave him for not telling me he wasn't going to hold onto his end.

The love of my life was my cousin, George, who was actually younger than I. Ellen's only source of heat was a fireplace. She and Cap created it, from stones they hauled from the beach, in the early days of their life together. When Ellen was gone one evening, George telephoned me at my new abode. He spent an hour or two, in front of the fire in Ellen's living room, teaching me how to dance. In those days the dancers were very close together-supporting each other as it were. We danced till the fire smoldered and then I ran back to my current abode. This happened twice. Ellen was baby-sitting. Keith was working in a San Francisco shipyard. Cap was out drinking somewhere. Keith's dream of going to college was shattered. Cap refused to allow him to accept a rich man's offer to finance his education. While he was still attending high school, Keith designed, and built, a sailboat for the rich man. The sailboat won an important race with Keith at the helm. A trophy from the event remained on Ellen's mantelpiece.

I wandered over to Ellen's whenever I could get permission. The next time I did was after the second dance when I thought George's lips brushed my ear. Keith was at home playing *Skylark* on his clarinet. He let me stay and listen. It was beautiful. He was very sad and very tired and I didn't stay long. I asked him to say "Hi" to George and ran back to play with my charges. I heard again about the oldest girl's boyfriend. She was almost my age and she claimed to have a "boyfriend!" This particular evening, George came by and we went for a walk on the beach. George was very sad. He said he "asked a grown up person who knew all about such things. Anyway, there is a California law making it illegal to marry a first cousin. You are my first cousin so I won't be teaching you how to dance anymore. Anyway, we could never get married unless we left the state and I like Carmel." We were standing on the top step leading to the beach from Twelfth Street when he gave me my first kiss. Then, he said he would watch me walk home but he would not walk with me. I didn't say anything at all. I didn't even cry—then.

Once, when she got two jobs, Ellen arranged for me to baby-sit. Each of us worked, one night, for another new arrival at Fort Ord who also commuted from Carmel. I put the baby to sleep, found *The Prince and the Pauper* on a bookshelf and started to read. My employers let me finish the last few pages before they took me home.

Ellen was never one to carry a grudge. Grudges were Mama's department. One day, she telephoned my "Boss" to arrange for me to help her go shopping in Monterey. Keith took us in his new Rolls Royce convertible. We rolled over the wonderful hill to a Purity Store where Ellen was greeted like a major stockholder. Then, Keith bought ice cream for us and made the day into a party. By telling jokes and anecdotes from the shipyard, he kept us laughing all the way home. Another day, I walked from where I lived across Carmel to the Pebble Beach Golf Course. I walked right past a group of camouflaged soldiers guarding a gun emplacement. This sandbag-lined pit and its long khaki gun were planted squarely on the famous green closest to the sea. From here, later TV cameras got shots of golf clubs careening into the Pacific. The soldiers smiled and laughed and waved while I walked by them trying not to be noticed. Cap was still Captain of the Port where he now spent almost all his time. George's job was connected with keeping the pool clean. When I reached the pool area, I didn't see George, or Cap. I did see Keith, a very different Keith with glazed eyes. He saw me and called me onto the dock and then into a cabin cruiser. He, and a group of lifelong friends, were drinking beer. Once I was aboard, he showed me around the boat and introduced me to his friends. Then, very quietly and gently, he suggested I go home now. He said he was going to take the boat off shore. I walked back by the same gun emplacement, still trying not to be noticed.

In the evening, Ellen telephoned inviting me to go with her to visit a friend. I hoped it would be the lady with only one active lung. She always gave us tumblers full of fresh orange juice. Instead, it was an even more interesting lady. As we walked, Ellen explained I was never to go back to the Del Monte Lodge. To do so might embarrass Cap or jeopardize George's job at the pool. I understood. Our hostess heard part of this and was especially kind. She was a professional nurse, very interested in people, even me. We discussed Mama's religion. I shared what I knew from the Sunday School George, Keith, and I attended early in our lives. As our conversation dragged into the night, Ellen stretched out on the couch and slept. It was three o'clock in the morning when Ellen woke up. She politely ended the discussion and took me home to her house. For several hours, I was talking, with an adult, as an adult. It was a heady experience.

Then, the family with whom I stayed was transferred. Mama and Ellen decided I should go home. I discovered what Cap said about Papa was true. He was in jail, part of a roundup of aliens. The roundup resulted in the permanent departure of the German butcher from Rider's Run. However, Papa was no longer in jail. Shortly thereafter, he and Mama brought the family all the way to Del Monte Lodge. There officers, from the nearby bases, were crowding out the nouveau rich. Mama and Papa interviewed for jobs as kitchen help in the Lodge. Nobody hired either of them. I got a short visit with Ellen and a quick hug after a good meal. These followed the usual hours of Mama's crying and fighting with Ellen in Swedish. After another hug from Ellen, for me, we were back in the Buick heading for Rider's Run. Rex was glad to see me. I had strict orders not to tell anyone at school, of course. When everyone else described their summers, I went into great detail about the making of a picnic lunch. Even the teacher frowned as I gratefully slid back into my chair. Show and tell time was the almost exclusive property of our master of ceremonies. His parents always took him to the movies on Saturdays and he always relayed the plot to us.

Soon after my return to Rider's Run, Mama and I went to a pawn shop in Stockton. I saw a saxophone, pointed it out, and was steered away by Mama. When we left the pawn shop, I carried a violin, with a bow, in a case. In a paper bag, was a *Beginning Violin* book. For a while, I even tried to practice. The screechy sounds of my bow, on the insufficiently loved violin, were excruciating. After school started, there were two short lessons before I gave up. It was too easy, much too easy, to quit. As for show and tell, how many times could Holly and Florence talk about camp? How often could Holly tell everyone she owned a horse?

Show and Tell

Chapter 6

Something absolutely incredible happened on the first day of school. Rex and I walked sedately to the railroad crossing. Then, I spent several minutes trying to get Rex to go home. After he turned homeward, I walked as sedately as I could going fast. All eight grades, and three teachers, stood on the steps of the main building for flag salute. As I slipped into the end space no one hissed. No one whispered, "Nazi spy." A new person actually smiled at me. Florence and Holly almost smiled. Then, Holly remembered who I was and muttered, "Dirty Nazi pig." Florence snapped, "Stop it. It's over. This is the eighth grade. We're in the eighth grade!" Each week for two years, while the teacher graded papers, we sat with our hands folded. These periods of listening to *The Standard Hour of Music* were my respite from being hated. Now, it was like all the orchestras, at once, playing the *Ode To Joy.* I managed not to cry while we saluted the flag and moved into our classrooms.

"Show and Tell" blossomed this year. There were Boy Scouts who went to camp and Campfire Girls who went to camp. They needed a person to be a Campfire Girl so they could have a group at our school. Guess what? I was the person. It was not Regina, the girl with the explosive breasts, which all the boys somehow managed to brush against. They did this at least once, whenever we played softball, volleyball, or anything else. Logically, I thought it should have been Regina. When our little cluster of girls finally assembled, Venus, the new person, and I were last to arrive. Meanwhile, our Show and Tell master of ceremonies and two other Scouts presented a skit from Scout camp. One played a patient lying on the floor, another a doctor bending over him. Pulling a soup can from his jacket, "It's a can, sir," he announced. "It's a two more!" proclaimed a third Scout, bringing more cans from his jacket. World War II was still going on—but not here. Not now. I was in a daze most of the day. The new girl sat near me. So did Holly. At recess they told me about the Campfire Girls. After school, I got Mama's approval to join.

We got the uniform, the book, all the required paraphernalia. It looked like a breeze. So many of the beads rewarded things I did for, literally, years. Keeping babies from harming themselves, peeling vegetables, cleaning floors, changing diapers, food shopping, and washing dishes were my regular chores. A new teacher commuted from Stockton to teach the primary grades. She agreed to supervise The Campfire Girls. Supplies were needed for a special dinner party to mark our formal entry into Campfire. I got Mama's written permission to accompany the group to the butcher shop. I shopped there, after school, at least twice each week. When I got meat it was, "a pound of hamburger, please," or "two salmon steaks, please," deftly wrapped and plunked on the counter. The new butcher was not German, of course, but he was friendly and knowledgeable. He retained his composure while Holly examined a half side of beef. While we watched, he helped her locate exactly where the best hamburger came from. We watched while the beef was cut and ground, twice, into the entree. Our next stop was the grocery store. In those years, the grocer's wife owned the beauty shop next door. I was their baby-sitter. I was very quiet, very much in the background, while Holly chose the most expensive spaghetti, canned tomato sauce, and peas. We did the actual cooking in the small kitchen at school. Here Mother's Club members made lunches for kids who lived too far away to run or bicycle home for lunch. The Campfire official drove out from Stockton to be our guest of honor. She pinned a new triangular pin on each of us. The ceremony followed a dinner which was too bland to taste good. This followed a series of chats with the teachers and Holly's mother. It was the only time we saw an official until the Grand Council Fire in the spring.

Being an eighth grader brought new responsibilities. Our teacher was new to the area and not destined to stay more than part of the year. He bought a house, next to the doctor, to which he brought his wife and baby daughter. He walked to work instead of commuting from Stockton like almost every other teacher. Florence's Aunt, who taught the middle grades, always lived in Rider's Run. The new teacher-principal assigned Holly and Florence and me to Traffic Patrol because we lived in town. None of the eighth grade boys did. I was so proud to stand in front of the bank and watch for semitrailer trucks. These moved faster on their way to, and slower on their way from, the cement plants in Calaveras County. I stood under the town clock on the bank building for ten minutes before I ran home. Lunch was whatever leftovers I could find in the screened cooler attached to the kitchen. For another ten minutes after lunch, I stood there, on a regular basis, two days at a time. Then Holly, then Florence would stand watch at the corner. Each of us kept the younger children from dashing into Main Street—which was also a major truck route. When two or three eager youngsters were there, we listened for semitrailer sounds from behind a nearby curve. When it was quiet, the traffic patrol marched the children across. We would run across to the other side after lunch, of course. It was fun. Once in a while I suffered a nightmare about a semitrailer being unable to stop when kids were crossing. I was so grateful for the California law, "the pedestrian has the right of way." How else could we ever have dared to cross that street?

Florence lost Champ and the big white draft horse, Egypt, in a barn fire this year. Florence described the devastation of the fire. We were walking from school to the spotter's shack in another part of town. This area was mainly pasture. It was chosen for its distance from all buildings. Florence, Holly and another new girl, served watches as aircraft spotters to help the armed forces. Florence used the telephone in the shack to report all aircraft which came within sight of her binoculars. She let me listen to one call and look at the low flying, slow flying, small plane through binoculars. Then, she sent me home. I was impressed. I knew, of course, I couldn't be an aircraft spotter. I so recently stopped being a "Dirty German Pig."

Holly's mother made an arrangement with Mama. I should receive "a good breakfast" in return for staying all night with Holly's grandmother. For a few weeks, I walked with Florence to the Spotter's Shack and continued alone to Holly's Grandma's house. I quickly learned Grandma was accustomed to living alone. A recently broken bone was not enough to curtail her independence. I wasn't supposed to show up until dark, she insisted. For a while, I walked almost to her house and then to my house to do my chores. Then, I walked back to her house. Mama was always visiting and Holly's mother was driving into Stockton for war work. I continued to sleep at the ancient lady's house. I slept in a pre-civil war room with a wicker bed and an anti-macasser on a wicker chair. There was an oil lamp on a wicker table which I never even thought of using. We would listen to the radio together in her living room while I looked at stereopticon pictures. We separated to go to bed.

Every morning, we each ate a bowl of dry cereal with milk for breakfast. One day, she told me she could not afford my breakfast any more. I said, "Thank you anyway" and left her house for school half an hour earlier. This was presumably to get breakfast at home, actually to sit on the school yard swings. I watched the other kids arrive. This lasted until Holly's mother discovered the deception.

I wrote a poem and recited it for Show and Tell. Entitled *Dreamland*, it featured "rolling hills" and "mountain rills." It was conceived on the swings not six feet from the parallel bars where Holly and I first clashed. I recalled the day in third grade when Holly came to school as a new student. She cut in front of me in the line waiting to swing across the bars. I loved this particular exercise. When Holly squeezed in front of me, I bit her very firmly on the nearest hand. She made a terrible outcry, and was coated with several kinds of first aid antiseptics. Of course, I couldn't use the bars for a while. Now I was too tall for the bars, so I wrote poetry for at least two months. Then, the new Polish girl wrote a poem, *Six Little Puddings on the Windowsill*. It was a smash hit. We got to hear how each member of her family acquired a particular bowl of chocolate pudding. Two months later, Holly's mother drove Holly, Florence, and me to the young lady's wedding shower. Holly's mother taught us to say, "Best Wishes" to the Bride-to-be even though we wanted to say, "Congratulations." The "Congratulations" were for the Husband-to-be, a brand new sailor her brother brought home from Boot Camp. We weren't invited to the wedding. The girl left our area and was never heard from again.

After the annual battery of tests at school, the new teacher-principal invited me to dinner with his wife and child. I thought the invitation was, probably, about baby-sitting. These people actually involved me in conversation, for about two hours, while we shared a good meal. When I left, it was with an armful of his wife's "favorite books from girlhood." I read every word of those books. I considered, "Let's Meet by the Banks Where the Wild Thyme Grows." This was a clue in a game played by the heroine. She was "standing with reluctant feet where the brook and river meet-womanhood and childhood fleet." When I returned the books, there was nothing from them in my "Thought for the day notebook." This was not important because Mama found the notebook in the garage. She read, "If Mama really hates Papa like she says she does, why does she have anything to do with him?" Instead of answering this question, Mama burned my notebook in the kitchen stove. She kept yelling at me while the pages crinkled and smoked.

In the middle of the year the teacher-principal got a better job and immediately moved. A teacher who commuted before returned as eighth grade teacher and principal. She taught me before and did nothing to distract my tormentors. She ignored name calling, pencil stealing, all the little daily tortures of the early war years. I was not really delighted to see her again. To my astonishment she, too, invited me to dinner with her family. This involved an overnight stay. I enjoyed a good look at her salt and pepper collection. She told me my test scores were good enough for a college scholarship. After we shared dinner with her husband, I went to sleep in their den. Driving back to Rider's Run, she invited me to live with her and go to college in Stockton. I relayed all this interesting news to Mama. Mama washed her own ceramic tomato salt and pepper shakers, and sent them to the principal. Within the week, the principal ordered Bill Montana out of the classroom for shooting a rubber band. I just happened to look up in time to see Holly shoot the rubber band. I started to protest. I was sent out of the room. After school, the Principal told me the scholarship was out of the question. My "attitude was all wrong" and I "had no respect for authority."

As it happened, Bill Montana saved my life two summers before. Mrs. Piggee's sons, the neighbors who wore Mama's hand-me-downs and I participated in a swimming program. We walked along the highway to a large cattle ranch. The trees shading our way along its entire roadside property line were English Walnut trees. Each year, the owner harvested the nuts, sold them, and used the proceeds to pay his property taxes. Papa said he bragged about cheating the government in this way. I thought it was an ingenious solution to a problem.

At the pool, one of the Piggee boys noticed me and dared me to dive into the deep end. He insisted he would be right behind me. Into the pool I went. Bill Montana jumped in and pulled me out, sputtering, without even enough time to swallow much water. The lifeguard arrived, gave something to Bill, warned me, and gave the Piggee boys an excuse for not jumping in. Mama heard about it from the neighbor girls so I couldn't go back. It was all right. One of the neighbor girls confided she never ate until nightfall. She, and I, believed constantly chewing gum kept her alive between dinners. What if she fainted from starvation at the pool? I didn't want to have to help carry her home. I roller skated on the street in front of our house day after day. Sometimes, she did too. Mama called me a "spider."

So I lost my "scholarship." While we were both banished from the classroom, Bill Montana invited me to a party at his house. I thought I didn't like his sister, Rita. She was younger than I. After she shaved her mustache, an unsightly stubble grew under her nose. She wore makeup, lots of makeup, and it smelled like she smoked. When I saw her, in her own home, managing a spin the bottle game, I was impressed. Eighth grade boys, who couldn't bike to traffic patrol, demonstrated their prowess at kissing. The buxom Regina and some sixth and seventh grade girls encouraged them. Rita Montana ran the party like a parent might have—bedrooms off limits, no couples going off alone. I found myself playing spin the bottle. The second kiss of my life came from a seventh grader whose brother idolized the new girl, Venus. When the Montana parents suddenly appeared, the party ended. I accepted a ride home on the bike's handlebar of the boy who kissed me. Such was our first, and last, encounter.

Meanwhile, I filled in binder pages of things I did at home worth beads in a Campfire book. One day, while the family was shopping in Stockton, Papa took me to the Campfire store. Binder in hand, I bought a number of beads to string on my leather thong. When the primary teacher, our counselor, learned I shopped before she saw my list, she was irate. Nowhere in the literature was approval listed as part of the procedure. She was still considering what to do when I got another childhood disease and had to miss school again. This time the doctor gave me an injection so I could breathe. He said, "Pleurisy", and "Keep her in bed," to Mama and left. Mama snapped, "Pleurisy! Nothing but Pleurisy! I thought you were going to die! When I was in San Francisco I had Pleurisy all the time." I went to sleep.

I knew the Great Council Fire was coming. I was still weak but, on the day of the long awaited event, I got out of bed. I couldn't find my uniform in the closet because Mama finally sent it to the laundry. I found my best blue taffeta dress and my Campfire cap. I washed my face and brushed my teeth and hung my beads around my neck. I walked the eighteen blocks to Holly's house. I reached there just as Florence and Holly and Holly's mother were getting into the car. They took me to the counselor's house in Stockton. The counselor said, "I couldn't trust you alone here or I would certainly leave you here." Then she led the way from the house. At the Great Council Fire, I was the only one out of uniform. I sat Indian style, trying to breathe, in a large crowd of giggling young ladies. I was too sick to care about anything.

I slept on the way home from Stockton. Holly's mother woke me up in our driveway. I thanked her and stumbled into the house, totally humiliated. Mama didn't even miss me. She was still visiting Mrs. Piggee. I put my blue taffeta dress in the laundry. I threw my beads in the far corner where my dresser could have been. My room never contained more than a cot. I pulled the covers around me and went back to sleep. I was still under the doctor's orders to Mama not to go back to school until I got stronger. The counselor got her orders to report to the WAVES. I returned to school in time to say, "Good-bye." She was happy to be leaving our little hick town. She shook my hand warmly. Our Campfire group was disbanded forthwith.

You Lose Some

Chapter 7

We were fresh out of a "club." To the kids, around my desk, I suggested we make our own club. The banker's son wanted to call ourselves "The Eagles." He devoted most of an evening to wood burning an eagle onto a plaque. Meanwhile, I asked Mama if she could think of a name. On the table was the fiberboard trivet I brought from art class, a circle of leafy Bing cherries. Mama said, "Uh, why not call yourselves the Bing Cherries?" Innocently, I brought her suggestion to the group. Ben brought out his wood burned eagle plaque. Neither name seemed appropriate to Holly. She had a "better idea." Within the week, someone came from Stockton to teach crafts for several hours after school. We made raffia mats and covered coffee cans with drawings made on butcher paper. For me, "crafts class" lasted two weeks. Then Venus and Violet invited me to the movies.

Venus was the favorite girl of every boy in our class. She weighed 118 pounds when I was still trying for 95. She was stacked and smart. She and her sister Violet rode their bicycles three miles every day to and from school. When she invited me to the movies, I walked the mile from home plus three miles from the school. She let me sit on the seat while she bicycled all the way back to my house after our visit. This happened twice before it was decided I should stay overnight at her house. Venus worked hard. Every day, she made a hot breakfast while her parents milked their dairy cows. She made lunch while she and Violet got ready for school and Violet did the dishes. Then, they biked to school, ate in the lunchroom, and biked home at the end of the school day. Several nonconsecutive weekends I accompanied the family, in their car, to Stockton to watch the latest movie. When we saw *State Fair*, I was amazed how closely Venus resembled the star. She did chores, too. When I was there we did things for fun like riding the cows when her parents weren't looking. This was supposed to reduce the cows' milk supply. We usually just looked for four leaf clovers and talked. Venus found several four leaf clovers. She gave me one which I almost instantly lost. Finding four leaf clovers is not easy. I never could find a four leaf clover no matter how earnestly I tried.

Mama was making a graduation dress, a white see-through creation. It came with a non-see-through petticoat for which I thanked the Lord. It never occurred to me to suggest alterations to Mama. I went to school looking like Mata Hari. I wore form fitting dresses before I had a form to fit them. There I was, standing on a chair, when Mrs. Piggee brought the news. She looked at me critically and announced, "She is striking." Mama agreed, "Yes, not beautiful but striking—definitely striking, like a model." Mrs. Piggee possessed a telephone so Ellen called her with the news. We heard it at the same time. I felt like I was going to faint so I got off the chair. Then, I sat on it. Mama was threading the needle for basting stitches. Mama said, "Well! At last Ellen has a chance to find out what sorrow is!" I heard this—superimposed on Mrs. Piggee's, "Keith is dead and you're supposed to come to the funeral." The dining-sewing room whirled but I did not faint. Mama helped me out of the dress and went to use Mrs. Piggee's phone. I ran outside to cry.

Mrs. Piggee took care of the kids while Mama and I took the stage to Carmel. For the funeral, I brought a black dinner dress which originated with Mrs. Piggee. Mama remodelled it for me to wear someday. Someday came too soon and too sorrowfully. Ellen's house was different. A patio table Keith made in high school, and decorated with rope, was moved into the living room. The matching chairs filled everything but the fireplace. Cap still listened to overseas bulletins on his big Hallicrafters radio whenever he was at home. George's Model T was about half reconstructed in the area where Keith built his sailboat, his Curlew. The Curlew was an extinct bird. I remembered this—which also made me cry.

After high school, Keith joined the Merchant Marine. He built a fleet of small sailboats for the officers on his freighter. He watched them burn when the freighter was bombed. He was taken to Australia where he bought a motorcycle which he rode home from Seattle. In a hard rain, he reached

Carmel. Cap sent him to the hospital in "the city." Someone put him in a room with a guy who shoved him out a window.

Ellen and Mama argued relentlessly when they were alone together—which wasn't often. Ellen had many friends who came singly, or in groups, to comfort her. Always it was she who wound up comforting them. The trophy from the Curlew's first race was still on the mantelpiece. George made himself scarce. I found books in Ellen's bookcase. While people were retelling the story of how Keith died, I fled to the patio and read and read. Sometimes, Ellen sent me out of the area. I rode George's bike all the way around the point and out to Carmel beach and back. George taped his handlebars and grips with electrician's tape. This blackened my hands so I peeled it off and threw it away. George didn't even notice.

In Cap's car we went to Monterey. We sat in deck chairs while a minister addressed the large group of people who loved Keith. His best friends were pall bearers. George sat beside me trying to be a stone and not succeeding. I didn't dare look at him because I couldn't cry anymore. An enormous anchor of flowers was on the coffin. Ellen whispered, "It came from the man who bought the Curlew." Ellen was in complete command of herself and the proceedings. She did not cry. She wore a determined smile. Cap tried to be a stone and succeeded. Mama didn't cry either. She looked like her favorite word, "annoyed."

At last the funeral was over and Cap drove us back to Carmel. As we rolled down the beautiful hill with the entire Pacific Ocean at its bottom, I felt the familiar glow. I always felt this glow when I came home here to that view. Then, it was over. We were eating Ellen's wonderful food again and Mama was yelling at Ellen in Swedish. George snapped, "Shut Up! Won't you ever just please be quiet. I'm trying to hear Keith." He ran from the room. I watched him pass the hanging pots of fuchsias on Ellen's back porch. He stopped on the patio beside the curved stone seat Cap carved with a schooner like his father's. Cap took command of the real schooner when he relieved his dying father at the wheel. Cap was thirteen then, my age. He brought the ship home to port. Later, he carved it in stone. Even later, he commanded a similar ship in a Jack London movie. George looked at it and I looked at George through the huge kitchen window. The Pacific Ocean sparkled in all its glory. Mama snarled something in Swedish. Ellen finally broke down. It was Cap who comforted her after he told Mama to "get out of my house." Mama and I gathered our belongings and walked to the bus station.

We left the kids with Mrs. Piggee but nothing was said, or done, about Rex. Somehow, Mama notified Papa so he was there when we returned. So was Rex but, as Papa explained, someone gave him ground glass. Papa knew who it was—an old man with nothing better to do. He was our friend when we first came. This man laid his work hardened hand on my nose, when it was covered with fever blisters. He wanted to prove something to Papa. I was impressed when the fever blisters disappeared, exactly on schedule, the next afternoon. Evidently Rex wandered into the old man's territory while we were gone. Now, he lay suffering on the ground. I petted him and sobbed over him and he died. Instead of turning into the sniveling creature I fully expected to become, I hugged Rex. Then I hurried into the house to wash dishes and tried to be a stone. Papa took Rex away in his car and it was weeks before Papa came back.

I regularly shopped for groceries and picked up the mail at the Post Office in the new General Store. Usually there wasn't any mail. I faithfully deposited our copy of the food bill in Mama's desk. Actually, it was supposed to be my desk. Someone gave it to Mama for me to do my school work on. Somehow, it never got out of the dining room. Mama filled it with bills which I hoped Papa paid. Just before graduation I got mail for me, three cards, one from Holly, one from Florence, one from Venus. Holly's card read, "Some folks may wish you fame today and some may wish success, but here's an all inclusive wish, may you have happiness." Everyone in our graduating class got the same message from Holly. I didn't send any cards. The only cards sent from our house were to Grandparents in Sweden or Germany. Each year until the war, Pansy and I received a handkerchief with crocheted edges from Germany. Mama collected them in the big chest in the front room.

There was a consolidated graduation. Several small schools pooled their resources to rent a building. It was the same Grange building where Papa and I went before the war. Papa and Rex became part of a line of hunters determined to exterminate rabbits with guns. I stayed at the Grange hall helping robust farm women peel things for the meal following the slaughter. Now I was here again, no Papa, no Rex, no rabbits. It was strange. I must have looked sad after Keith's funeral. One day, Holly goaded, "You remind me of the Chinaman in my book, "No Mama, no Papa, no chow-chow." I was improving at becoming a stone.

I thought about how good those rabbits tasted when Papa made a stew. I recalled the German cherry soup with dumplings he made. I remembered the honey and milk he gave me for my throat when I was sick. Now Mama sat with Mrs. Piggee, who brought us. Holly and the other members of the consolidated band played *Pomp and Circumstance.* I marched into the auditorium with people I never saw before. When the diplomas were distributed I received Holly's. Mine was nowhere to be found. I passed Holly her tiny white rolled certificate of graduation in its blue ribbon. I thought, "now, I'll bet Holly goes to Stanford and I go to Hades." Holly eventually did go to Stanford, just like my own father whom I wanted so much to be like. On the way home Mama asked, "Why didn't you play in the orchestra? Why didn't you bring your violin?" I didn't even try to explain.

If she were at home when I was, she might conceivably have noticed I never practiced—or she might not have. The diploma found its way to me at Rider's Run Elementary School.

On the last day of school there was always a big party. Actually, most years it happened on Holly's birthday, as it did this year. There was a picnic under the trees by the primary building. Holly's mother presided over the food line. The games included relay races. The years I ran to flag salute finally paid off. In the upper grades relay race Florence chose me as the last member of her team. Holly chose a tall gangling seventh grader who loved to run. Holly expected to win. I found myself still waiting for the rolled paper baton from my team. The seventh grader took off and headed toward the bathroom building we were required to circle. I got my "baton" and shot straight for the building. I passed the seventh grader about two yards from the end of the race and won. I won! Holly took a box of Hershey bars from her mother. She handed it to me. I promptly distributed them, one by one, to the members of Florence's team. It was great!

We all agreed to get together in the summer but I didn't believe we would. When Papa brought Pansy and her brother a large tricycle to share, he brought me a bicycle. It was red and just my size. I used it to get mail and groceries and to visit Venus and Violet. One day's mail included an invitation to bring a lunch and go on a bike ride to Ione. We met at the Post Office, Florence and Holly, Venus and Violet, and me. It was like the early, prewar, days. Holly's mother used to take Florence, Holly, and me to a museum or a concert in Stockton. I was glad to be included again. We biked easily at first. Then, as the miles seemed to get longer, Holly or I would make a dash ahead. For a while we alternated in the lead, without words, just moving a bit faster. We stopped at the railroad station in Ione. Holly introduced Venus and Violet to her father. We ate lunch beside a stream and bicycled back. This time, I took the lead most of the way. Holly's family included her own full-time father. Holly intended to get a degree from Stanford like Mama told me, and I told Holly, my real father did. Suddenly, there wasn't enough space between me and Holly. I rode my bike into Rider's Run, waved at the others, and fled home.

Once, the November before, Papa came home. He brought a turkey for Thanksgiving. We ate somewhat uncomfortably. He and Mama were arguing bitterly. Mama wasn't going to leave Rider's Run. She liked her home overlooking the valley. When Papa came home at Christmas, she said something in a low voice. He stormed from the house, snarling, "You choose this time to breed!" No one ever bothered to teach me about the human reproductive process. Biology was not on my Freshman schedule. In its place, I chose Girl's Chorus. However, I watched Mama gain weight and guessed the reason. Early in July, Mama asked me if I wanted to invite Venus to stay with me. Mama was going to the county hospital to have another baby. So I bicycled out to see Venus with a note from Mama. I came back with a note from Venus' mother which gave her permission to stay with me for a week.

Mama walked over to Mrs. Piggee's house one day and didn't come back. One of the Piggee boys came to tell me she was being taken to the hospital. I left the kids where they were, at Mrs. Piggee's house, until after Venus and I came back together. We enjoyed the week. Venus cooked differently than I did but we survived, all of us. The kids seemed cleaner and less fussy under our care. I wore my sunsuit top and shorts. I danced on the lawn behind the house when Venus' boyfriend came over. They chatted and held hands and, occasionally, kissed each other. I pretended not to notice. I kept dancing farther from the house toward our private dump—which fell away into the valley. Boyfriends were not something I worried about then.

When Mama brought the new baby home, she arranged for me to spend a weekend in Lodi. The lady with whom I stayed was quite advanced in years. She carefully taught me how to iron a handwashed handkerchief by sticking it on a clean window. I recited the German prayer Papa taught me. She urged me to forget it for my own good, so I did. I never saw her again. I never was able to recall the German version of the Lord's Prayer.

Mama tried again to settle me in Lodi, where I would be attending the consolidated high school. It was arranged. I would be a live in baby-sitter for a family with two little girls and a new baby boy. On the first day of school, I walked instead of riding the school bus transporting students from Rider's Run. The family owned a piano. I was given three piano lessons and a permanent wave for my hair. This made me look like a mop on top. My new boss brought me, "on approval," a dress for Rainbow. Rainbow was something Holly and Florence got me into this summer. They tried to get me into the Jr. Women's Club. I balked at the initiation when we were blindfolded and told to strip to our underwear. Teams of current members painted the inductees, with lipstick, all over our bodies. Very fortunately, I got all of it off before Mama knew about it—if she ever did. Mama did not take kindly to such doings and, to my surprise, neither did I.

Rainbow was different. I loved it. I wore dinner dresses inherited from the daughter of Mama's friend in Lodi and from Florence. These girls grew faster than I did. I blew the baby-sitting job in Lodi because I bought a present for Mama. I was given an allowance which I spent for things like hair ribbons and lipsticks. Then, I passed a topaz pin in a shop window. I went in and asked the jeweler how much it cost. He told me. I began to save my allowance. The topaz was Mama's birthstone. In a tiny metal jewel box on Mama's dresser, she kept a topaz pin. She said my father gave it to her. Her birthday was coming. The only presents I ever gave her were things we made in school for Mother's Day or other holidays. Somehow, she never managed to keep them. I was sent on an errand to buy a few groceries at a neighborhood store. I thought the grocer gave me too much change so I kept the surplus. It was just enough to buy the topaz pin for Mama. I thought of it as a gift from God to Mama I was lucky enough to help provide. It never occurred to me I was breaking one of the Ten Commandments-Thou Shalt Not Steal. It never occurred to me to doubt my arithmetic.

No one ever told me I did something wrong. I was simply informed the dress for Rainbow was being returned to the store from whence it came. I was going back, with my belongings, on the bus to Rider's Run. Then, I was on the bus. Then, I was home. Mama didn't say a word, not one word, until I brought her pin from my baggage. Awkwardly, I presented it to her.

She threw it across the room, box and wrapping and all. "You little thief! You little thief!," she shouted.

Gradually, I understood. My store-bought gift for Mama came, and went, so quickly. I kissed the baby a lot on the top of his head. It was good to be back. Riding the bus to high school was more fun than walking with an old friend of Venus. And I still belonged to Rainbow with Holly and Florence.

You Win Some

Chapter 8

Mama's friend in Lodi, who got me the job I so quickly lost, did not forget me. She found another job for me. As usual, no one consulted me. It was arranged. I was expected to walk several blocks, after school, to a small cottage. There a young lady did people's washing so she could care for her husband and their young son. At the beginning of a law career, her husband became blind. My job was to read the Bible aloud for him, for about half an hour, twice each week. Then I ran back to catch the bus in front of the high school. Florence was struggling with Latin in the library. Holly was working on a life saving certificate. I was not missed. On the bus, I could still go over and over Florence's, "Hic, Haec, Hoc, Huyus, Huyus, Huyus," which I memorized long before she did. I could still help Holly by being her "victim" in the pool after classes. For my own lifesaving practice, I could not lift the weighted bag from the bottom of the pool. I could bring it up part of the way. Then, needing air, I would invariably drop it. The reading job did not last long. The lawyer asked me how much I was being paid for my reading, with which he found no fault. I answered truthfully "Nothing." He told me he loved to hear my voice but he could not allow me to work for nothing. I missed him.

For the first couple of weeks I was one of the Freshmen without a regulation gym suit. Although my gym class was not shared by anyone from Rider's Run, Venus noticed I wasn't carrying the suit. She went with me after school to buy a gym suit. I chose a one piece monstrosity which looked like it would last forever. I forgot two things: one—I was growing and two—it wasn't like everyone else's. Venus, Holly, and Florence wore neat white shirts with navy blue shorts. I wore a solid, heavy, navy blue romper, to my deep chagrin. The consolation was—we never appeared together. In my class, I wasn't too noticeable. One day one of the girls asked if I wanted a pair of Levis. When I said, "Yes, I'd love it," she handed me, with a joyful grin, two towels. Made by the Levi Strauss company, they were to be put in the swimmer's laundry chute. Swimsuits designed in the 1890s were provided and laundered for us.

Holly and Florence and Venus all took Biology class together. I deviated, this once, from my College Preparatory Course, to take Girl's Chorus. I wanted to learn how to read notes. This was something I managed to miss learning in the nine elementary schools I attended. It was a large group, so large we met in the Band Room. I sang like I always sang, by ear, loudly and clearly, until the last week of the semester. No attempt was ever made to do anything but sing from the sheet music. From these sheets, I learned the words. Then, we faced individual tests. When my turn came, and I looked at a page of notes without words, I froze. The teacher looked at me like I crawled out from under the rug while she scribbled a D. Angrily, she suggested I not try to take her class again. Meanwhile, the other Rider's Run girls learned how to make lockets from quartz. They learned how to identify the rocks I collected for years and how to dissect frogs.

I met other girls in my classes. One of them was related to a world famous explorer. She was very sweet to everyone and better dressed than anyone from Rider's Run. Although we each wore a white blouse, navy blue skirt and blue cardigan, her cardigan was cashmere. There were so many ways to illustrate how rich one's parents were. There were variations in the cut of the skirt or blouse, the pins and watches. I even wore a skirt with an inch of green material at the bottom for a while. I loved it because it was different. Someone gave it to Mama. She remodelled it for me. There was another girl who liked to look different. She wore a headband or a scarf and knew a lot about books. One day she wasn't in class. I asked about her the next day. She died. I never knew more about her. It changed my life because suddenly a lively, happy, person just wasn't there. I wondered if there might be something I could do for fun before I, too, died.

Venus was invited to the Baptism of a friend of hers from school. Her parents wouldn't let her drive all the way to Lodi alone. She invited me to go along. It was still wartime, of course. Holly and Florence and Venus acquired legal driver's licenses. This was right after they reached the magic age of fourteen. It was, presumably, to help in an agricultural program. Of the three, only Holly didn't have any connection with farming. Her grandparents died and their farm was sold not long after her horse died. Two or three times Holly drove Florence and Venus and me to Stockton to ice skate. Holly did most of her driving with her parents, as did Florence. Venus even drove her family's tractor! So we went to Lodi. On the way, my first menstrual period brought me the fiercest pain I ever knew until then. I was so sick I stayed in the car while Venus went into the church. When I thought I was going to die, I left the car. I walked up to a nearby house. Grimly, I asked the lady who answered the door if I could come in. She threw the door open and made room for me on a couch. Then she brought me a glass of warm milk and honey and told me about the new invention-Tampax. She must have been someone's beloved mother. I fell asleep. The lady watched the car in front of her house. When Venus came out of the church, she ran to talk to her and then woke me up. Venus bought Kotex on our way home.

I did something on my own, besides Girl's Chorus. I signed up for the Prop Mistress job on the school play. Everything was fine until I missed the bus after a rehearsal. I walked to the nearby house of the lady who got me my two Lodi jobs. Her daughter performed a supporting role in the play. I thought she would not mind driving me the seven miles home. She could chat with my mother, I thought, and everyone would be blessed. Wrong again! She took me home after letting me see her beautiful house and her daughter in a designer bedroom. Far from fellow-feeling because we were both involved in the class play, the latter wanted nothing to do with me. The lady did have a long chat with Mama and I gradually dropped out of the play.

Somehow, I managed to do enough to be personally invited to the after-play party. I invited Venus to go with me after we attended the performance. My name was on the program. Like most of my classmates, I suffered a huge crush on the star. He totally ignored me of course. Venus told me I could probably have him as a boyfriend. We were driving home through the starlit night. I said, "He actually asked me what I was doing next Saturday night and I said, Nothing." Venus stopped the car and turned to face me. "You blew it! You should have said, 'I don't know.' This leaves room for him to ask you to go somewhere. Next time just say, 'I don't know.'" There was no next time. A few days later, I went to the bathroom a bit ahead of my class. There I found the overly made up daughter of Mama's friend from Lodi with another equally popular, equally wealthy, friend. They were trying to open a window to clear out the smoke from their cigarettes. They made me promise not to tell anyone. I didn't even tell Venus and I certainly didn't tell Mama. Later, Mama told me the girl smoked. The girl believed I told on her or, at least, she acted like she did. I thought the wrong girl died.

When I was looking for something one day, I opened a drawer in Mama's dresser. Of course, I was forbidden, years before, to touch things belonging to Mama. Now, I discovered groups of letters tied with ribbon. Gradually, over a period of a few days, I managed to read some of them. They were from my father. They said, among many other things, "I'm taking the skiff through Taku Harbor into Juneau." "I wish you would just let me write. Only, please let me write." "I love you and I miss you both." I wrote a note to Papa saying, "When I am eighteen please send me to my father in Juneau." Then, I promptly forgot the note and the letters. The note was in Papa's part of the dresser. The next time he came home he took us to Stockton. As we left Rider's Run, Papa inquired, "So you want to go to Alaska?" Mama said, "When did I give you permission to read my mail?" I broke into tears and huddled in the back seat. The next time I was home alone I looked in the dresser. His things were gone. Her underwear was where the letters were. I searched the house. All I found were moleskins rotting on frames my father used at Pebble Beach when I was a baby. Why Mama kept them I couldn't imagine.

In one of my classes was a really beautiful girl who walked with an exaggerated limp. She invited me to stay at her house one weekend. When I walked home from school with her, another girl came with us. This second girl was someone both boys, in their groups, and girls, in their groups, could be heard talking about. I heard about her on the bus while the Chemistry teacher delivered us to our various dropoff points. Now I found myself liking her. Gloria's parents were gone for the weekend. Gloria pointed out where the edibles were and then led the way into her bedroom. It was comfortingly messy with a full set of well used furniture. She sat on her bed and took off her leg. I was in shock. There was a black oil cloth cover near her hip above where the hinged knee attached. Her friend pulled a pack of cigarettes from her purse, offered one to me, then, to our hostess. Gloria tossed her wooden leg aside and eased back against the wall which abutted her bed. Of course, I took a cigarette and, of course, I smoked it all the way to its end. We deposited the ashes in an ashtray Gloria brought forth from under her bed. The other girls smoked before but they gave no indication they even suspected I did not. We enjoyed a lively discussion about the boys they knew and the girls they wished they didn't know. We considered the difficulties of being a Freshman in a consolidated high school with all those farmers. "Farmer" did not have a pleasant connotation. We parted at the school entrance on Monday. I was delighted to hear Gloria agree when her friend told me, "You definitely are not a farmer."

The following week there was a Rainbow meeting. The little wooden box on its tray with the small racks of black and white marbles stood on a table. The membership stood in line to vote. Two girls were candidates to join our select body. The first girl got only white marbles. The second girl was Gloria's friend. I put my white marble in the box, grateful at last here was someone I knew. The box was removed by the officers who promptly returned. Someone put a black marble in the box. Gloria's friend must have been really hated. We voted three times before there were nothing but white marbles in the election box. Whoever blackballed her did not give any sign whereby we could identify her. I felt a shiver of fear.

My Spanish teacher was a charming young lady from Mexico via the University of California, Berkeley. I loved her and the class. I made a habit of not missing any questions on her tests. I loved to speak Spanish in class. One day I missed a question. At the top of my paper the teacher wrote, "Lo siento mucho, chica." She actually regretted I missed one! I was in Freshman heaven all day.

Holly's English teacher was probably a draft reject although he certainly looked able-bodied. To me he seemed to be a trifle bullheaded. When flyers came out for an essay contest, I pushed mine into my English notebook and forgot about it. Two days later, Holly told everyone on the bus how much trouble she was having with her essay for the American Legion. She was, "going to quote Herbert Hoover and Calvin Coolidge and ...." I stopped listening. How could I possibly find someone important to quote? We didn't even have Bartlett's Familiar Quotations at home. We had no thesaurus, just one battered dictionary and Mama's useless books.

I did have paper in my notebook and a pen which worked and several hours before Mama would bring the kids home. I didn't bother to wash the dishes or make the beds. The dining table contained something Mama was sewing. So I sat on the kitchen floor and wrote my essay for the American Legion contest. I didn't quote anyone. I just wrote from my heart. Being an American was very important to me. I remembered the news reels of the Chinese baby sitting alone in the smoking rubble while bombers roared overhead. I remembered the dime, from our floor, I carried to my fourth grade teacher to buy a Defense Stamp. I counted the words, copied my essay on the right kind of paper and stored it carefully in my notebook. Then I did the dishes. I was making the beds when Mama came home.

Sometime later, the bullheaded English teacher, who did have a head resembling a bull, called me from class. In a nearby room, he showed me my essay. "Where did you get this?" he wanted to know. I just stared. "Where did you find the original? Who did you copy it from?"

"I didn't copy it. I wrote it," I said. He stared at me, decided to believe me, and sent me back to class. At the winter awards assembly he reluctantly handed me a check for $7, First Prize from the American Legion. My English teacher started the applause. We spent our English periods in her class writing about intellectual curiosity and Darwin's Theory. She knew I knew how to write English essays. She made sure I read some of the best original essays in the English language. With my $7, I bought material for a dress for Mama to make for me. Venus and I went shopping together after school. We just made it back in time to catch the bus. It turned out to be insufficient material. Mama made it into a sleeveless sheath which I wore once. It shrank in the laundry. I was very sorry because the fabric design was Egyptian. It looked good on me. I learned a valuable lesson about fabrics from this experience.

Mama's comment about the essay contest I won was short and pointed, "You aren't brilliant. Your father was brilliant. You are a plodder." I won another contest this year. Holly won essay contests, too. Fortunately, there were several contests. Holly's teacher always beamed when he presented her first prizes and almost held his nose when he gave me mine. Mama noticed I no longer gave her the money I won to "keep for me." She decided I was old enough "to learn how to iron." This was before ergonomic furniture. Mama's ironing board was the right size for her but too high for me. The iron was awesomely heavy. The laundry man still brought bags of clean clothes when he took away bags of dirty clothes. Ironing was torture for me. I ached all over after each of Mama's screaming, "You hold the collar with one hand and the shirt should be flat. Sprinkle some more. It isn't damp enough." The good thing about these housekeeping lessons was Mama's absolute need for adult companionship. I never qualified. The bad thing was Mama became so enraged at my clumsiness she erupted one evening. "Your father was shell-shocked in the first War. I don't see how you can even think of trying to find him. He was epileptic. He had fits. He was reading a book in the Philippines, lying on the ground, when a wild boar charged him in the head. He hit a man on the head with a chair at Stanford. He was so crazy I found him trying on one of my dresses."

"Stop!" I screamed and ran outside. Thereafter, Mama did all the ironing when everyone else was sleeping—even me.

Mama was proud of her ability to do electric wiring. With a screwdriver she repaired her own iron and sewing machine. I walked home from the front of the General Store where the school bus dropped off the Rider's Run students. One afternoon, I heard the fearsome clang of the Fire Bell. Then I glimpsed the volunteer firemen running beside, and behind, the Rider's

Run Fire Department hose cart. They ran around a block while I spotted billowing black smoke in the direction of our house. Then, I outran them heading the same way. Mama was standing in her bedroom throwing furniture through the window. A neighbor attempted to catch a dresser drawer and decided against it. It shattered on the hedge. Someone with a bucket was dousing something in the kitchen. There was a bucket brigade in action from a neighbor's house, behind and to the right of Mama, and lots of smoke. Mama saw me and yelled, "The house is on fire!" Volunteer firemen attached the big fire hose from the cart to the hydrant in front of our house. A few minutes later, everyone went home. The fire was out. We spent the night in the garage behind the Indian's house.

In all the excitement, Mama's eldest son decided to help. He pulled the axe from the chopping block and aimed it at a chunk of wood. He wanted to split the wood like Papa split it when he was at home. He watched me split firewood when I was at home and, if I could do it ... The axe dug into one of his legs. One of the Piggee boys, watching the fire, tried to prevent this. He reached the child too late and carried him to Mama. Mama sent a neighbor to get the doctor. I stopped trying to piece together parts of Mama's dresser. I ran to get some old sheets to stop the blood. The doctor sewed stitches in the leg and gave Mama lotion for the baby.

In the garage, when we finally moved my cot and Mama's bed there, everyone laid down but no one slept. The newest baby had a terrible rash which he continuously tried to scratch. His hands were sweating in the mittens supposed to prevent him from hurting himself. I tried to create an atmosphere of quiet. Mama yelled "Shut Up" now and then, almost out of habit, although it certainly did not work. I spoke softly to myself quoting the Lord's Prayer and the Twenty-Third Psalm and "In my father's house are many mansions. If it were not so, I would have told you. I go to prepare a place for you but I will come and receive you unto myself that where I am ye may be also." Half way through the Lord's Prayer again it became quiet in the airless, steaming garage.

When I paused for a breath, Mama said, "I didn't know you knew so much of the Bible." I didn't break the silence which followed.

The next morning I needed an excuse for being out of uniform. My uniform required washing before it could be worn again. The Dean of Girls was a little gray haired lady smaller than I was. In our talk, she asked me to check back with her when I became a Senior. She was "keeping an eye on me and my grades and wanted to be sure I would get a good scholarship." A friend told Venus I was in the top ten on our latest Standard Test. The consolidated high school student body was huge. The ranking, with the Dean's suggestion I could get a scholarship, sent my spirits soaring.

Mama restored our gloom in the evening. We tried to sort out the damaged household things from those which were still useful. Suddenly,

Holly was walking all around inside the blackened rooms. I felt so insulted. She didn't say anything except, "Hi" when she saw me. She made a tour, in so far as it was possible, and bicycled away. Papa came home and rebuilt the house. He even added a back porch with a toilet and a shower enclosure in part of "my room." Mama told me the Principal at Pansy's school gave

$50 to the Red Cross. The money was collected in the Elementary Grades to help Mama recover from the fire. Mama said, "the Red Cross got the money because your friend Holly told them there wasn't any serious damage." Mama added, as she always did when anyone mentioned the Red

Cross. "I was in San Francisco working for the NRA and you were sick. I went to the Red Cross and they called Ellen and sent a telegram to my family in Sweden. They gave me this handkerchief." She kept the handkerchief in "my desk" where it was easy to find. Papa burned the timbers from the kitchen, dining room and "my room." He replaced the roof, and repaired the veranda. He made a big bon fire of the rubble and the outhouse. He replaced some of the bare furnishings, got back in his car, and departed. We moved back out of the garage.

By this time, Mama acquired shutters for the windows Papa made for the garage. Mama put an ad in the *Stockton Record* and two black people came to live in the garage "apartment." There was a performance of the *Barber of Seville* at the high school. Mama sent me with a note to Holly's mother. She read the note, gasped, and led me into her dining room. She brought clothes from Holly's bedroom closet. I was completely dressed, head to toe. These things were wrapped and I carried the package homeward. Each item was carefully noted, verbally. "You have to bring back this brown jumper. It still has some wear in it. You can keep the shoes. Holly doesn't wear them anymore. You can keep the underwear. You have to bring back the blouse." I carried the package home to Mama.

Holly's mother came to pick me up on the day of the Opera. Florence and Holly were already in the car. We were still living in the garage. When I saw their car pull up before our burned home I ran over to meet them, fully dressed in Holly's clothes. The Opera was so much fun! I heard it before as one of the Sunday afternoon operas. We heard these gems on the radio Mama let us listen to when Papa wasn't home. The auditorium was full of parents and teachers and children. I waved to my Spanish teacher and she waved back. The costumes and lighting, the programs, were spectacular. Holly's mother probably should have sent a note home, along with the clothes, or waited for me to take them off. I could not remember which item belonged to me and which did not. I never wore any of them again but I was too humiliated to take them back.

When school was out for the summer, Mama borrowed a suitcase from the black couple. She arranged for me to live with a lady who owned a business and wanted a companion. I would be studying Marine Biology and Typing in Pacific Grove summer school. For once, I thought, Mama has done something right.

Between Classes

Chapter 9

I was invited to Holly's birthday party. As I left the house, Mama handed me a tissue paper-wrapped gift which I delivered to Holly. It was a lawn party with decorated cardboard candy baskets. They reminded me of the May Day baskets Holly and I made one Saturday before the war. It was much more subdued at her house than at school with fewer kinds of refreshments. Fewer guests came and there were no relay races in our good dresses. When Holly opened "my gift" we discovered a ceramic religious plaque. Holly turned red and mumbled, "Thank You." I said, "You're Welcome," with meaning. I wondered when and how Mama got the plaque. Did someone give it to her for my room? The only plaque I wanted was the one in Ellen's bedroom. Keith gave it to her when he was in the fourth grade. It began, "A wonderful being is a mother. Other folks may love you but only a mother understands." I wanted to be this kind of a mother some day!

In Pacific Grove, I went to live with a buxom business woman. Having inherited, and successfully managed her husband's bank, she was accustomed to authority. She met me at the bus station, took me to my room, told me what she expected and left. I was expected to get myself into the summer classes at Pacific Grove High School. The house we lived in looked very much like Holly's grandmother's home in Rider's Run. It even had a stereopticon by which I was expected to be entertained. The work was negligible, a few dishes, some dusting, being there at night so she would not be alone. Like Holly's grandmother, she didn't consider me a confidante.

Marine Biology was glorious. Our class went to tide pools at the foot of the street where I lived. Our teacher pulled up fragments of loose kelp to reveal the wondrous creatures living underneath. We used microscopes and petri dishes, examined nudibranches, memorized phyla and genera. We dissected flatworms and watched the halves become wholes again, cut kelp apart, learned scientific names. I could have spent my whole life in Marine Biology and never noticed the passage of time. The second day Roxanne appeared, George's friend who got "my Ruby ring." She came with a friend of hers from Monterey. They entertained the class while both of them did makeup work from a previous semester. After class, I went down to the beach to swim in the public pool. I got a good tan and met a copper colored lifeguard who invited me to go to the movies. Then he changed his mind and took Roxanne.

In typing class, I met another person who was making up credits. Unlike Roxanne, he was quiet and shy. He invited me to go to church with him and the lady banker approved. I found myself in a strange church whose doctrines of eternal damnation sent shivers up my spine. After church, my new friend took me to a park with a lawn. We sat on the crabgrass while he put his arm around me and we kissed. It was immeasurably boring. Fortunately, there were two active youngsters in the same class who offered me a lift home one day. The driver, who drove in spurts, spent a lot of time looking in the rear view mirror. In those days people maintained high hedges to prevent passersby from looking into their homes. One block, at least, faced hedges on every corner. Inevitably, we stopped at the stop sign while all three of us looked both ways. The driver stepped on the gas. So did the still unseen driver at a right angle from us. In the ensuing crash, no one was hurt but our driver was "grounded" for a while.

Due to circumstances beyond my control, otherwise known as Mama, I reached typing class two days after the summer session began. This meant the big poster of "The Home Keys," which hung above the blackboard, was covered with a sheet. I did a lot of groping on the keyboard before I memorized the home keys. The lady banker offered to let me use her personal typewriter. I declined. It would have been in the evening. This was her quiet time for the newspapers she pored over after our makeshift dinners. I thought she really needed an adult to cook real meals, care for the house, and chat with her. The semester was less than half over when she decided she could not afford to keep me any longer. I told Roxanne's friend, Jody from Monterey, who instantly invited me to spend the rest of the semester with her. I did. Jody used a couple of quotations I promptly adopted. "Quick, a glass of water. Here comes a pill" was whispered when someone she didn't like appeared. Another whisper was calculated to dismiss someone in the same category, "Fall fatally flat on your face five times."

Jody had several brothers, a mom and dad who were splitting up, and no pretensions at all. After the banker's house it was like fresh air, sometimes in gusts. It was also the only possible way I could have come to know Lawrence. He was a tall, thin, very pleasant young man who didn't have any money either. He liked to take walks and talk and stand on a bridge and watch stars reflected in moving water. He walked me home from our typing class and gave me a good night kiss. We decided we were too young to get married and there was too much to do first. Dreamily, we agreed to find each other when we were forty years old and educated. This would be soon enough to get married and have a family. Jody spent very little time at home, day or night, so no one minded when I came in late. Actually, the only difficulty was the radio which was never off and always blaring. Lawrence and I got Bs in Typing and I got an A in Marine Biology. Jody shook hands with me when I left to catch the bus for home.

I spent two weeks there, renewing my acquaintance with the kids, before Mama sent me back to Carmel. Mama was remodelling a dress for me when she remarked, "You have good teeth and legs." I wasn't too flattered because a few minutes earlier she caught me scratching a mosquito bite on my chest. It was below the neckline. Papa strolled by. Mama forcibly turned me around on the chair where she was adjusting my hem. She whispered, "Don't touch your breasts when he's around." I didn't have any breasts. I began to suspect Mama's motive for sending me away again.

So I was going to be a Sophomore in another school. Only this time the school was the new high school in Carmel. Before it was built, Keith and his compatriots rode a bus or drove a car to Monterey. I spent one day in Sunset School with George when we were much younger. Now, three months after George graduated from Sunset, he was a Freshman very much involved in Shop courses. We never met at school. I walked, at first from a house overlooking the Mission, almost on a level with the high school. The lady, whose companion Mama expected me to be, was very old. The first name of her tenant meant cup in Spanish. She was so sweet. We only knew each other for a few days before she found another room. I was left alone with the very old lady. Her concept of dinner normally began with one measured cup of cooked white rice and one peeled raw carrot. One thin slice of boiled fish or one small greasy meatball and a glass of skim milk completed the meal. I began to starve immediately. Breakfast was a cup of cornflakes thinly coated with milk and a small glass of canned orange juice. I could buy a hot dog at school for lunch.

The first thing I noticed was a change in my sight. Things would blur when I looked at the blackboard. I took the bus to Monterey at the old lady's suggestion. Her optometrist handed me a box of eye exercises very much like the stereopticon. His diagnosis was "lazy eyes." The optometrist sent the bill to the lady with whom I lived. She promptly notified me I no longer lived there. I went to an employment office where I found another lady who lived in the same area. She was younger and much more cheerful with a healthier appetite. I personally returned the box of eye exercises to the optometrist. My explanation, "since I was obviously cured there was no further need for them" brought a sigh. We felt sorry for each other. Aunt Ellen became involved because these ladies telephoned Mama. Ellen came with me to my new abode to meet my new "Aunt"—Miranda.

Miranda was of Mama's religious persuasion and a Canadian background. Her niece was presented to the Queen of England. Miranda's living room contained a portrait of her with three ostrich plumes to prive it. There was also a stack of Chinese tray tables, a silver tea set, a large, full China cabinet, thick rugs, etc.. She showed Ellen and me the house and pointed out my "room." After Ellen left she said, "I can't believe you are related to her. Can you imagine, she actually wanted to see my Bendix washing machine!" Since Ellen still used a hand wringer and galvanized tubs, her interest was real. My Aunt Ellen was probably the only person in the world I really loved. Miranda just lost whatever points her house made with me.

My room was incredible! The furniture matched. The bed was a double bed with curtains, white, fluffy, lace curtains like those crisscrossing the picture window facing her patio. A huge curtained dressing table, dresser, a large closet, night table, thick rug, lamps on the table and desk were there. It looked like something in the Sears catalog. Actually, the house was featured in *House Beautiful* magazine. I slept in the room exactly one night. In the morning, Miranda announced she was going to rent it. She needed enough money to give me an allowance and some appropriate clothing. It was a great relief not to have to sleep with so much furniture. I moved into the den. There was a day bed, desk, chair, and bookcase in a small area.

The blackboard was no longer blurred. A friend of Miranda's donated some of her daughter's clothes. Of course, there were no school uniforms in Carmel except for the white blouse and navy blue shorts universally required for gym. I could pay attention in class. I loved all my teachers especially my World History teacher, an austere man. He told us he originally intended to become a businessman like his father. When he read Liam O'Flaherty's *Famine,* he decided to change his profession. He used lots of maps In his class I met a girl from the Philippines whose father was a Japanese prisoner of war. It was necessary to replace everything they left behind when they came to Carmel. Her mother bought her beautiful new clothes. One day, after school, she showed me a portrait of her family. Nearby was a small picture of what her father looked like in the prison camp. I didn't envy her.

I invited a girl from my Geometry class to meet Aunt Miranda. They chatted over tea in the living room while I listened. Another girl I invited brought her mother who also chatted over tea. Miranda liked the first girl, a doctor's daughter, whom I only invited because Miranda wanted me to bring home a friend. I didn't have any friends except two younger girls who gave me rides to school each morning. I would go to Jane's house, an incomplete log cabin in the woods which was unbelievably crowded. From there we would walk to the house of another girl whose father dropped us at school on his way to work. We listened to, "Fred Waring and His Pennsylvanians" on their radio every morning. These girls would have been too busy to have tea with Aunt Miranda. Miranda told me she purchased a membership at the Del Monte Lodge just so I could take Jumping lessons. I took two Jumping lessons at Del Monte Lodge Country Club. I learned how to hold the horse's flanks with my knees and to stay on while he jumped a series of hurdles. I remembered from Florence's Champ how to hold the reins. It was fun. The doctor's daughter and her, even more colorless, friend and I constituted the Jumping class. They evidently considered me beneath them so the lessons ended abruptly.

Meanwhile, Aunt Miranda invited a California Senator and his wife, another couple, and a man of her own age to tea. She produced a lacy white cap and a frilly white apron and showed me how to hand someone a tea cup. She did the pouring, of course. On the appointed day, I tried to act like a maid—only there were no dress rehearsals. I didn't spill anything but I almost did. I felt like a knot of elbows and knees. The Senator came into the kitchen where I was washing the teacups. He warmly asked me, if I ever needed help in getting a good education, just to call him. He would help me get a scholarship to Berkeley. I thanked him and kept washing the dishes. I didn't want to go to Berkeley. I wanted to go to Stanford like my father. Such was the first and last time I played a maid.

A little Jewish boy invited me to The Sophomore Hop, a formal dance. His religion didn't matter to me. Papa insisted he, "could smell a Jew a mile away," but I never believed him. This boy's mother was a professional furrier. Aunt Miranda didn't know this when she draped her scratchy fur coat over my dinner dress. The dress was outgrown by the daughter of one of Miranda's friends. We enjoyed the dance. His mother took us there and came to take us home.

Then, Aunt Miranda was driving me, in her car, all the way to Stockton. Together we walked into the tall brick building behind the barbed wire fence. A nurse pointed out where Mama sat chatting with a group of toothless old ladies. Later, Miranda and I saw Mama on the witness stand in a sort of courtroom. She was fresh and clean in a print dress, telling the court Papa came home from a long absence. He drove her to the asylum swearing, verbally and on paper, she was incompetent and unfit to care for her children. After a while, Aunt Miranda took the stand as a character witness for Mama. Aunt Miranda was draped in a fox fur stole over a trim business suit. She wore high heels and a frothy blouse collar just visible at the neckline. This day was the first (and second) time she ever saw Mama. She left the stand and walked back to me. The Judge conferred with someone, and called Miranda, who conferred with him. Then, she drove Mama and me, with Mama's belongings, back to Rider's Run. We left Mama enroute to Mrs. Piggee's to pick up the kids and catch up on the gossip. We stopped in Stockton where Miranda bought a fuzzy white coat for me. At Pajaro Valley, we stopped on a peak to survey a valley much larger than the one behind Mama's house.

A few weeks later, Aunt Miranda accompanied a friend to Santa Barbara. She urged me to invite the doctor's daughter to stay overnight. This friend of mine didn't appear until 10 P.M. so there was never an opportunity to talk or eat together. She was evidently obliged by some social code to accept Miranda's hospitality, but not mine. She went to bed in Miranda's room as soon as she arrived and rushed away, breakfastless, in the morning. Feeling unclean, I took an extra bath before I went to the house of another of Miranda's friends. This lady treated me like a member of her own family. She taught me how to use my fingers on her harp and kept me fed and housed for a week. The next Saturday, the furrier's son had a date with me. He called Miranda before she left. With all the arrangements Miranda made, she forgot to mention the cancelled date to me. I sat in Miranda's living room and read *Frenchman's Creek* from cover to cover before I relocked the house. Sadly, I went back to her friend's home. Monday I told the furrier's son I waited most of a day for him. He explained Miranda knew he wouldn't be there. He still took me out afterward with everyone's apparent approval. The doctor's daughter belonged to a small but exclusive group. Among its members was a relative of John Steinbeck. She referred to him as "the black sheep of the family." I did not mind being on their "Black List" in such distinguished company.

Another friend of Miranda's was still chatting with her one Saturday night when I had to go to bed. She was using my den room because a couple from Fort Ord was renting my original room. Something was being done with paint in her own home. Obviously, she could not sleep in Miranda's bed so I slept on the couch. In the excitement, I forgot to wash my hair. During the evening, I heard the visitor say, "So how is it going in Sunday School?" I popped up with, "Oh, I love to go to Sunday School." Embarrassed, I popped back down into the couch. The next morning Miranda woke me up for Sunday School. I remembered my hair was still unwashed. I explained this. Knowing it would never dry if I washed it then and there, I requested I not go this once. As Miranda and her friend left for church, the friend chortled, "Oh, I love to go to Sunday School."

The extra credits from summer school resulted in an extra period. Instead of a study hall I was assigned the job of office runner. It was a prestige job.

We delivered dental appointment reminders and collected detention slips. On rare occasions, I managed to misfile a detention slip if a penitent athlete begged. The other office runner was a senior whom everyone loved. She gained my attention by announcing her impending death. Once, she casually remarked she was going to die before she reached thirty. One sunny April afternoon we were practicing archery on the playing field below the library. The senior came running down the hill from the office. This day was rare for Carmel, not a trace of fog on the mountains, just glorious spring. The runner called us together and told us the news. President Roosevelt was dead. I remember it was like statue tag. No one moved. We just stood there, silently, till someone sent us home.

One of the teachers at school was converted from Mama's religion to Catholicism. One morning I started to walk to Jane's house for my ride to school. This teacher pulled up beside me in her car. She invited me to go to the Mission with her so I accepted. It was sunrise and the old mission was radiant in the early light. We were the only ones there and the experience of watching her devotions was impressive. After school, I wrote one of the many poems constructed in Miranda's den. Some of these made it into the school paper by way of my English teacher's desk. This was, "Thank You for this lovely morning which no other dawn has ever brought, could ever bring." It was entitled *Mission San Carlos Borromeo.* A days later, when I came home from school, Miranda waved the poem at me. She demanded "What is this supposed to mean and why did you lie about loving Sunday school?" She wanted to know, "Why didn't you water the lawn the day you waited for your date?" "Where are my two missing silver spoons?" she shouted. I couldn't reply. She let me stay the rest of the week till school was out for the summer. Meanwhile, I discovered she made reservations for Santa Barbara two weeks earlier. I felt better when I learned this. No spoons were missing when I counted them.

Learning Experience

Chapter 10

As part of my usual College Prep Course, I learned more Spanish. Two languages doubled my vocabulary. Meanwhile, my English teacher conducted her annual High School Best Program. She selected one of my poems for publication in the *Carmel Pine Cone*. I was delighted to have my, "wings, strong, courageous. God, teach me flight. Make not my course an easy nor overwhelming one" ... appear in print. I thought there was something to share with Cap. His life was reviewed, with many pictures, in the *Pine Cone* sometime before. Mama's copy was somewhere in the muddle of her closet floor. Now, I brought home my copy with my poem. As usual, it went on the pile under the hanging clothes. The desk was for smaller things like bills.

In time, the Indian house tilted into its bare basement. Papa planted potatoes in the hillside behind it. The towering bamboo plant still flourished. Without asking, one of our neighbors regularly cut himself a fishing pole. The dump at the bottom of our yard slid partially down the hill overlooking the valley. I climbed over the fence, one day, to look for four leaf clovers. A very large bull found me. I heard a loud snort, looked up and into his eyes, then at his sharp horns. I stood up, turned and walked quietly away. I remembered not to run. Shaking, I returned to the potato plants. In my right hand was a shovel. My left hand firmly grasped one leafy plant. Shovelling loose the earth, I found more than enough "spuds" for dinner. The half acre of potatoes Papa planted lasted a long time. Rosemary Mama planted was well grown and decorative in front of the Indian house. I clipped some with garden scissors whenever I made spaghetti for dinner. Of course, I made my own sauce.

Our neighbor on the other side of the Indian house died. Her cow was sold. Her barn and outbuildings were levelled to make room for a new house. Now, only one cow remained between our place and the church. It was right behind the church and belonged to the lady who collected ceramic elephants. Mama brought her a ceramic elephant from a shopping trip in Stockton. I got to see her collection-tables and cabinets of sitting, standing, walking ceramic elephants. I noticed, behind the house, a barnyard with a Holstein cow. This was years after the Health Department forced Papa to get rid of our cow and the outbuildings. The lady was related to the Constable. On two different occasions, I ran to him for help. My intent was to stop Papa from manhandling Mama. Each time, Papa drove away before the Constable reached our house.

Mama taught me her "kid them along policy." This was useful to protect a child from doing something drastic. I used it to keep Pansy from throwing things. However, Mama did not just adopt the "kid them along policy." She used it regularly. Mama discovered it was possible for me to graduate without completing my senior year. Mama didn't tell me she intended to subtract the senior year of high school from my life. Instead, she took me into Lodi to sign up to work for Continental Can Company. I completed the application while Mama discovered the only opening for me was on the night shift. No one would be responsible for my transportation.

The next thing Mama tried was a bar in Lodi to which I could bicycle. Sweating in the sun, I rode my bike there one afternoon. For six hours, I carried full drinks on trays to tables and empty glasses on trays to the kitchen. There I found, "Regina the buxom's" equally buxom sister who looked old enough to be her grandmother. An efficient waitress, she worked hard and long. Hers was a remarkable supply of common sense. At quitting time, she loaded my bike into the back of her pickup. She drove me the eight miles home through the dark. On our way, she pointed out she already quit my job for me. She handed me the ten dollars I earned. She made me promise never to go to a bar again, at least not until I was "legal". At home, I parked my bike and slipped into my cot. Mama found the ten dollar bill and kept it.

Mama was really frightened when Papa incarcerated her in the insane asylum. After years of threatening to do so, she actually filed suit for divorce. She invited Mrs. Percheron to be a witness on her side, along with the kids and me. I thought this was strange. Never did I hear Papa's friend say anything good about Mama. Papa must have wanted the sour relationship to end. Mrs. Percheron described him as several kinds of bad guy. He was depicted as a true villain, who did not deserve a cultured lady like Mama and, even, "lazy". I thought that was too much. One thing Papa was not was lazy. My turn to testify finally arrived. I was dozing, in a sitting position, on a bench beside Mama's other three children. Sleepily, I repeated the accusations I heard. The Judge looked at me compassionately and, almost immediately, sent me back with the kids. He granted the divorce. As we left the court building, Mama pinched my arm. "You didn't sound like you meant it. You sounded like it was something I told you to say." Actually, it was.

I spent the summer reading books from the lending library and roller skating on the street in front of our house. There were two memorable games of touch football with neighbors across the street who didn't stay long. I did all of Mama's housework and cooking and lots of babysitting for a new couple across the street. There was another Red Cross Swimming program, and comparative peace at home. I finally got to catch the bus in front of the General Store and go back to Lodi High School.

Home Economics was required. I was paired with a girl I never met to make cupcakes which we forgot. They, therefore, burned. I chose a pinafore as my sewing project because it looked easy to make. While everyone else made straight skirts or basic sheaths or aprons, I struggled with belt pieces and shoulder straps. Of course, Mama was not available to help. The class was overcrowded. I cut out the pieces and basted half of them together. It never occurred to me to try to use Mama's ancient sewing machine. At semester end the project was half finished. I put it, with the pattern, in its original bag, in the bottom of Mama's closet. Mama asked me how it was possible to get a D in Home Economics. I briefly considered saying, "It wasn't exactly easy," but settled for, "I don't know." I decided next time I sewed I was going to take a sewing class and really learn how.

We were Juniors, Florence and Holly, Venus and I. We went to Rainbow. I wore Florence's old dinner dresses, and loved them, when there was a dance. I invited a boy, who sat next to me in English class, to escort me to a Rainbow dance. He drove all the way to Rider's Run with a corsage of rosebuds. They adorned the shoulder of a blue-gray gown with a sweetheart neckline. He shook my hand at my door when he brought me home. A couple of weeks later, he invited me to a Sea Scout Ball in Stockton. Again, he drove seven or eight miles to and from my house in Rider's Run to Lodi. There we boarded a chartered bus which took us the rest of the way to the Ball.

He was not happy because I wore a red and white flowered dinner dress. The color matched and, therefore, concealed the rosebud corsage he brought. It was fantastic. I was really impressed when the bus driver pulled into a fast food diner and parked. He waited while everyone went inside for hamburgers. This time my date kissed me good night and it was very sweet. On Monday, in English class, I found myself considered part of a foursome. His friend, who sat beside him, brought his girl to the same dance. They were all in the high school band it was impossible for me to join. This friend teased me a lot. One day he remarked, "I like you because you can take the teasing." Gradually, we stopped chatting in the halls. Another boy invited me to the Junior Prom and became upset when I failed to talk enough. He considered himself a conversationalist. I didn't. I preferred to be teased in a friendly, funny way. For a while I had a crush on a football player. Otherwise, I actually studied in Study Hall. Now and then I asked another girl to draw pictures for my notebook. She could dash off a movie queen, or a nude, in a few seconds.

While I was away, being a Sophomore in Carmel, Florence decided to follow her mother into nursing. Holly decided to go into Biology. Venus got practical art experience working on the yearbook. I scored high on the annual tests. Venus' boyfriend assured her I was still qualified to be called "bright." I belonged to the Spanish club wherein everyone spoke only Spanish. At one after-school meeting we practiced Spanish marriage proposals. I faced "the suitor" and mumbled, "me amo." Everyone broke into laughter. The teacher suggested I should say, "te amo", or, "le amo a usted." I said, "I love me."! Before he could answer, the bell rang and I took my red face to the bus, earning more friendly kidding.

This year, the Nisei children came back to schools in the San Joaquin Valley. The war was over. Two gentle, graceful, young ladies in the same uniforms we wore, only neater, came to my classes. Except for "Hi" each time we passed, there was no interchange of pleasantries. One of "them" was on the football team and, being a husky, self disciplined lad he did well. I longed to chat with the girls but they were always either studying or hurrying between classes. One of the American boys was just beginning to star as a quarterback. One weekend, he drank a bit too much. He drove his car into a grammar school child who died not quite instantly. This interrupted the usual Senior after-school auto races for the next few weeks. The quarterback was tried and sent to jail. I tried to write for the school paper, something light to cheer us up. The editor said, "that's filler and I don't use filler."

We took a test designed to see where our interests lie. Mama said, for years, "Your father was a mining engineer. He graduated from Stanford after going to the Colorado School of Mines." In the early days at Rider's Run, I relayed Mama's information to the teachers who tried to learn more about me. It never occurred to me Mama might not be telling the truth. Still firmly believing her, I decided to try to be a mining engineer. As I took the test, I answered the questions in the way I thought a mining engineer would. What I really wanted to be was a writer but "writing wasn't a real career." So I did not fill in the little box beside "spend an hour in the library". I did fill in, "survey a riverbank for varying strata." When my English teacher got the test results, she said, "I thought you were more literary than this." I didn't score high on "engineering." I scored lower than I should have on "literary." Actually, I would have been equally eager to study strata. I always collected rocks.

One of the most miserable days of my youth came after Mama got a letter from my Palo Alto uncle. I brought the letter from the Post Office on my way home from school. I recognized the name and address of my father's brother on the envelope. I did not have the courage to ask about it. He offered to let me stay at his house, and to help out financially, " to further my education." Mama seethed with anger for two days. Basically, it was not for me to mind someone else's business. The mail was Mama's department. Saturday morning, she made me sit down at the diningroom table with writing paper and a pen. She dictated a letter to my Uncle. I "thanked him for his offer to provide lodging and financial help while I went to Stanford. However, I had other plans. Even if I did not have other plans, I would not accept his offer to, save my soul." I wrote it, word for word, but I didn't believe it. All my life I longed to be like my father, to go to Stanford, to be a writer. I expected to do so ever since I first heard how well I was doing on tests. It never occurred to me that anyone could interfere with "my future." This hope kept me going for how many disappointing years? I finished the letter, addressed the envelope and even mailed it, praying to God to rescue me.

A few days later, Mama received an antique liquor cabinet. The Pacific Grove warehouse, where it was stored since she and my father lived there, went out of business. The owners absorbed the storage charges and simply shipped it to her. She worked a medallion off the door and had it made into a pendant which she gave to me. Then, she announced "it is high time for you to go to work to help support the family. You better enjoy the rest of your Junior year because you will not be a Senior." I told Florence I was going back to Carmel even before I told Mama. On the school bus, Florence asked what I was planning for the summer. I just blurted, "I'm going back to Carmel for my senior year."

The year ended. We autographed each other's yearbooks. Florence and her brother appeared at my house. Mama was at home. I told her I was going to a party with the Rider kids. They thought I should have a proper send off for my trip to Carmel. I explained I was going there even if I had to walk all the way. Mama was wearing a clean dress, shoes, stockings, curled hair. She chatted pleasantly with the Rider kids. We went into Stockton to a new "Arabic" restaurant featuring shish kebob. We enjoyed an excellent dinner. We went to a movie. We wished each other well in my driveway late in the evening. Mama was still awake. Some cash was in an envelope. Some of my clothes were in a suitcase. She told me the stage would leave at 9:30 the next morning. I went to bed, and slept fitfully, wondering what the catch was.

In the morning I got up early and woke Mama. "Oh, don't forget to close the door when you leave", she said. I didn't. Resolutely, I carried my suitcase to the Soda Shoppe and caught the stage from Calaveras County. This time I wasn't carrying a note for the bus drivers from Mama. I rode the Monterey bus into Carmel in a sparkling evening. There was the same wonderful feeling of homecoming when I saw the Pacific, still there, still glorious, still welcoming. I went to Ellen's house. Of course, Mama telephoned her. She already found a job for me. That night I slept on the outer side of her double bed. Cold fog swam through the open windows of her room. Ellen was afraid of tuberculosis. She believed open windows were a sure preventive thereof. I read her plaque, "a wonderful being is a mother"... I felt so grateful to be there.

I became "a companion" again for a lady whose sister from Canada was visiting for the first several weeks. There was my own pleasant room, little to do, and time to visit Ellen who always welcomed me. My employer called me into her room twice. The first time it was to see a crescent moon hanging over a star. We agreed it looked like something in a children's book. The second time it was to see her sketches from a trip to Egypt. This time she and I shared a short conversation. She seemed to want to give me some solid advice. Very clearly and solemnly she said, "Never deny yourself anything. I have learned very few things in my life but I know this. Opportunities do not often repeat themselves. Never deny yourself anything." We liked each other. She put a small scarab into my hand as a good luck amulet. After the sister returned to Canada, my employer went to the hospital with a respiratory ailment. One morning, two days after the lady left me in charge of her house, she died in the hospital. Her neighbor came to tell me. She asked me not to leave before she went through my belongings to be sure I didn't steal anything. I nodded dumbly and went up to my room. I took a long bath in "my own" bathroom, dressed carefully and packed. I left the scarab on a table downstairs. I didn't want anyone to think I stole it. Ellen was peeling a small carrot for me when the neighbor telephoned. I heard Ellen say, "No, I am sure she didn't steal anything." Ellen said the neighbor's Chinese cook used to work with Mama in someone's house when Mama first came from Sweden. The cook regularly received photographs from a wife and son in China. His culinary specialty was sculptured mashed potato whales. These were always cold when they reached the table. Once, she pointed out the cook for me. Years before, Mama introduced me to the lady for whom they both worked. In fact, Mama wanted me to live with the lady in her mansion. Only two things prevented this. While her husband was "eloping" with his secretary both died in an automobile accident. The other minor detail was more pertinent. Between seventeen and thirty-four cats ran freely about the mansion while she herself used only two cluttered rooms.

This time I found my own job, almost. From Rider's Run, Papa occasionally drove us to church in Lodi. In Carmel, I lived within walking distance of Mama's church. Sunday School was where I always spent Sunday mornings. Now that I could walk to church, I did so. Roxanne's family shared Mama's religion and were very active in the church. So I became reacquainted with George's former girlfriend. She took me along to the Playhouse to help her usher. I got a job there and then, and I loved it. I could even wear a dinner dress to usher at a live performance, which happened regularly. The theatre owner's wife was a friend of the lady who died in the hospital. When she heard I was temporarily homeless, she invited me to be a "helper" at her house. I would live in a castle "dungeon" with attached bathroom, a built-in dresser and a well padded stone shelf bed. It was lovely and I loved it. I loved the big stone house and the people who lived there. I liked the girl who lived across the street and drove me to school. I even loved the big Irish Setter who lived in a wooden house between the castle and the Pacific.

Graduation Presents

Chapter 11

My new boss owned, and conscientiously operated, a little theatre. The first thing I learned was how to answer questions about what was "on." From a schedule beside the kitchen telephone, I learned running nights and ticket prices. Their daughter was not much younger than I, involved in her own school, horseback riding, and tennis. I did help her memorize Longfellow's, "This is the forest primeval." I suggested Amelia Earhart's *Last Flight* for a book report. Otherwise, we didn't even see each other for days at a time. I shared one meal in the dining room with the family. My new boss played his cello. The monk's table was too crowded. After that, I ate dinner in the breakfast nook with a textbook and the telephone. When no one was at the Playhouse, calls automatically transferred to the castle. I used the first dishwasher I ever saw. The Bendix clothes washer and dryer were squeezed into the passage leading to my tiny room. It was another case of my "boss really preferring to do her own work."

One night Roxanne brought some friends from Monterey to the castle kitchen. She chatted with the lady of the house in the dining room. Three Monterey football players and one of their girls stayed in the kitchen with me. They made lots of noise and helped themselves to some bananas which just happened to be there. The boss appeared, everyone fled, and I was asked not to let that happen again. To me, it seemed it should have been obvious Roxanne brought them in. Roxanne worked as an usher all year although she was now the head cheerleader and dating college men. She found time to smoke my cigarettes after Sunday School and after lunch in the woods across from school. Of course I smoked, once in Lodi and, frequently with Lawrence in Monterey. Roxanne restarted things by asking the temporary manager at the Playhouse for two smokes, "one for me and one for my friend here." Now Roxanne apparently enjoyed having me available when she needed a cigarette. She never carried her own, insisting her mother didn't know about her habit. Our cigarettes came from my allowance.

The head of the house and his wife were constantly active. They started a class on English Theatre pronunciation which I was invited to attend. For lesson one I was much the youngest person there. After having learned a few ways to say A, I was not included. My English class, College Preparatory, as usual, was taught by a theatrical person whom I came close to worshipping. She made us work long and hard. We memorized First Corinthians Chapter 13 because she wanted us to know more than Beowulf and Chaucer. This was well before the confusion of church and state made such assignments illegal. My mechanical drawing teacher also taught art. This gave him an excuse to avoid class except to take roll and administer tests. With no one to teach me, and no preparation, I rapidly lost any opportunity to pass the course. This was also true in my other all male, except me, class. The physics teacher was physically present but mentally engaged in talking baseball with the boys. The mock-up of a radio in front of the room was very useful. We listened to baseball games. Mama's plans for me did not include a senior year. Otherwise, this year was almost an educational disaster.

I was sick again, stuck in bed with severe bouts of coughing, using lots of kleenex. Kleenex replaced the handkerchiefs of my childhood as soon as I discovered the marvelous invention. I was so sick my boss came down one morning, picked me up, and carried me upstairs. His wife held the door to my room. They took me to the hospital and visited me there. Roxanne came, too, with two movie magazines and a cheery, "You better lay off the coffin nails for a while." She didn't stay long. I didn't either, only a couple of days.

With a date, I attended every major dance. A young gentleman from Monterey invited me to a party. Roxanne and several other people I knew from Summer School were drinking and smoking and necking halfheartedly. We didn't stay long.

This lad invited me to dinner and to the Prom at Monterey. As we were returning to Carmel we both fell asleep. He hit a tree, damaging the car and breaking off one of my front teeth. Fortunately, neither of us were drinking. As it was, an insurance investigator came to Carmel High School, borrowed an office, and interrogated me at length. He found it hard to believe we both simply fell asleep. My date was a championship tennis player. I was in my first, and only, play at the time. Each of us was exhausted, he from hours of tennis competition, me from school and ushering at the Theatre. After changing clothes quickly, then waiting in the wings, I walked on stage. Through a mouthful of fog I said one line, "That's my father," in William Saroyan's *The Time of Our Lives*. Then I changed back into the formal dresses we wore for plays. I served coffee at intermission and helped clean up the coffee service. After these activities I sank into bed, sometime around 3 A.M. No wonder I fell asleep in a car the following night—which happened to be the night of the Prom.

A friend of my boss was a dentist who sized me up as quite worthless. He pulled what was left of my tooth and, in the course of time, provided a pivot tooth. The insurance company which provided for the tennis player paid part of the bill. The dentist signed it, well knowing the dental work was incomplete. As my mouth healed the pivot tooth slipped about embarrassingly. The time came to replace the pivot tooth with a more permanently wired arrangement. The dentist was surprised when I returned to his office. He told me I would have to pay him for this most important half of the procedure. My boss and I worked out a financial arrangement. He cut my earnings to pay for hospital and dental expenses. I wound up with very little cash to pay for the cashmere sweaters I bought and wore proudly to school.

Then I got poison oak all over my body. My Prom date took me to a party up the valley. I drank too much and left the group to relieve myself in the nearby woods. On the way home I began to itch. My poor friend must have believed I was a jinx by this time. I wore calamine lotion and only scratched at night but for some time I was miserable. One Friday morning, I turned off my alarm clock, dressed and got ready for school. It was too late to catch my ride up the hill. Walking along the beach, I said to my self, "I wonder if salt water would help?" I took off my shoes and socks and waded into the cool, salty, surf. It seemed to help. All day, I alternately waded and splashed Pacific Ocean froth over my thin clothes and flaming skin. When I could see children bicycling or walking on the street above the beach, I walked home. As I entered the castle kitchen I thought, "Uh Oh, Now what?" Then, I remembered Roxanne's bragging, "Whenever I need some time off from school I just write myself a note and my Mom signs it. She never reads it so she never knows I skipped." I never learned! It never occurred to me that Roxanne usually did not tell the whole truth. I wrote a note, "Please excuse … had to stay home due to illness." Then I realized my boss lady would never sign it. Telling myself I should have asked her, I knew she would never have let me spend a school day at the beach. Hopelessly, I wrote her name at the bottom of my note.

Actually, physically, I felt better. The sun and salt water and peace of one day scoured the itch from my skin. Mentally, I felt terrible. I forged something. I was a criminal. It didn't matter if Roxanne probably did something similar much more frequently. It was a relief when I dropped off my note at the office on Monday. I saw the Dean of Girls reach for it, scan it, and head for her own office. First period the Dean sent a runner to bring me to her office. I was not really prepared for what came next. Without asking me to sit down, she closed the door. The first words I ever heard from her followed quickly. "I see here you are in the first group on the Stanford Test. You may have noticed I did not arrange transportation for you to take the test. I was somewhat surprised when you paid your $5 and squeezed into the car to take the test at Monterey. Now, I suppose you think you are going to Stanford. It just happens no one can get into Stanford without a written recommendation from the Dean. I am the Dean here and I would not recommend you for a cleaning woman's job. I saw you Friday morning. I watched you come up to the school and meet some soldier and go off with him. I expected something like this. You are no good. Get out of my office. Go back to your classroom. You will be lucky if you ever even become a lousy bookkeeper. Dismissed!"

After school, as I walked down the hill, some of the boys with cars played their usual game. After driving toward the path on the shoulder of the road, where students rambled home in wayward lines, they veered away. I held my ground while the other girls scattered, giggling, before an oncoming vehicle. One driver swerved sharply—so startled he honked his horn as his jalopy just managed not to hit me. I was still hearing, "I would not recommend you." I went straight to my boss lady who was waiting for me in the kitchen. She said, "You know what you did. Will you promise me never to do it again?"

I nodded. "I promise," I said and then I could cry. She gave me a piece of Kleenex and left me alone for a while. "It's O.K.," she said.

A few days before semester end, Roxanne passed me in the hall. She announced, "The Dean is having a meeting about the facts of life. It's in the cafeteria-only girls, 2 o'clock." When we met the Dean clutched notes which she didn't really need. Her message was, "Never put anything in writing. 'I love you' could be really embarrassing if the wrong person finds your note. If you go out with too many boys people will call you 'shop worn' ... and good luck in college. For the rest of the period she chatted with her group of elite students.

I left the meeting with a lawyer's daughter who was not going to college. She looked straight into my eyes-as straight as the Dean when she said, 'shop worn'. "Get yourself some publicity if you want to go somewhere. My Mom says 'It doesn't matter what people say, good or bad, it's free publicity. You can use it to get what you want.' All those cats are doing is giving us a lot of free publicity." This was something she wanted me to know. I thanked her aloud and wished her success in her future in my heart. Another one of the "wheels" at school was not heading for college. He was going to work at his family's stables to earn money for school. Another was going straight to Purdue to become an engineer. We dated, a movie and a prom, and I wished him to have everything he wanted from life. He, too, was naturally nice. The Dean of Girls supervised graduation rehearsal. In my Freshman year, at Lodi High School, I belonged to a scholarship society. The Dean asked scholarship society members to form a group. I did not realize one semester did not constitute a membership. I headed for the group. The Dean was not pleased. When graduation dates were being arranged, I was aflame with poison oak. I did not have a date. When I called my tennis playing friend at Monterey he pleaded another engagement and I could not blame him.

My boss gave me a graduation present—Mama. Suddenly, I was on the stage at Sunset School receiving my diploma. Walking outside afterward, I was startled to see Mama waiting on the sidelines. I could not spend my graduation night with Mama so I rushed up to her. I explained I was "going out" and walked rapidly away. I walked the long miles to the castle and eased into the old Hudson parked beside the dog house enclosure. I cried there long and hard. I was defeated! There was no more life! Always, always I wanted to go to Stanford like my father. I felt for the pin Venus sent me for graduation. It was a ruby and pearl pin from Lodi High School and I loved it. Roxanne borrowed it last week when she saw it on me. I knew I would never see it again. I cried a lot before I sneaked back into the dungeon to sleep. The Setter didn't bark. We were friends.

Mama took me back to Rider's Run. In San Jose, I made another grievous error. After lunch, several girls regularly smoked in the woods across the street from school. One of them actually told her mother she smoked. She said, "I just pulled out a pack and asked her if she would mind if I smoked." According to the girl, "she already knew but she was glad I stopped trying to hide it." A group of smokers stood together in the bus station. Still believing I was as much a person as anyone else, I pulled out a pack of cigarettes. Mama seized the cigarette pack and threw it on the floor. She stomped on it furiously several times and then decisively slapped both sides of my face. "You idiot. You complete horse's ass. No wonder you didn't get any scholarships!," she yelled. People stepped back, trying to escape her wrath. I just stood there until the line formed to board the bus.

When we completed our silent journey back to Mama's house, I closed the door to the veranda. Very quietly, I informed Mama, "In two weeks I will be eighteen years old. If you want to put me in jail, it is your privilege. I am not going to wait two weeks before I leave."

Mama nodded, "You just want to smoke. Tell you what! Pansy's at camp. You stay with the boys till she gets back. Then you can go. It's only a week." I nodded. Mama went to see Mrs. Piggee. I found a pack of cigarettes in my baggage and rode my bike down to the bridge. One spring Mama painstakingly remodelled an Easter dress from Mrs. Pigge to fit me. I walked down to the bridge, found a raft and tried to pole across the pond. The raft sank, the dress was ruined and Mama was not happy with me. The raft was gone now but a young turtle basked on the bank. It was quiet and serene. I was out of tears and the cigarette tasted awful. The slimy grass at water's edge reminded me of baked avocado. Another Carmel senior from the smoking group took me to her home for lunch. She repaid herself for a baked avocado with the topaz ring Mama sent me. I knew Mama wouldn't notice it was missing. Considering the various meanings of words like borrowing, trying on, and friends I smoked the whole cigarette. Remembering the Carmel shop where I bought my cashmeres, I remembered one sales lady who watched me try on a sweater. Embarrassed, I asked why. She blushed. "Too many sweaters have been disappearing," she said. I knew the elite always managed to look so nice because they wore each other's clothes. Now I thought I knew why. I could imagine Louella saying, "Of course this isn't my sweater, Mom. I borrowed it from Jonesy." I could imagine Jonesy saying, "Of course this isn't my sweater, Mom. I borrowed it from Louella." I could even imagine Louella saying, "Let's go adopt some sweaters, Jonesy." I thought it might be fun to watch them get caught. Then, I decided I didn't need that kind of fun. I found where the raft rotted into splinters and green foam. I bicycled home to wash the dishes Mama always left in the sink.

When I worked at the Playhouse I bought some Stan Kenton records. Mama did not have a phonograph. I took them out to Florence and gave them to her mother because Florence wasn't home. Her mother's hair was more grey but her face lit with the same wonderful, welcoming smile. I was glad to see her again and not really sorry to miss Florence. What would I say? At week's end, the boys walked with me to the Soda Shoppe. Pansy was supposed to return to Rider's Run but I dared not wait for her. I awakened Mama, said, "I'm leaving now," and heard her, "Don't forget to close the door." When she turned back to sleep I knew she was still following her "kid them along policy." The boys and I reached the Soda Shoppe before the stage did. I bought them each a milkshake. This meant I could no longer pay the fare all the way to Carmel. Mama was not subsidizing this trip. When I reached San Jose I started to walk. A car drove by, backed up and stopped beside me. Three men were inside. The driver asked, "Where are you heading?"

I truthfully replied, "To my aunt in Carmel." There was a moment of silence. Then he invited me into the front seat beside him, turned the car around and drove to the bus station. As he did so, he explained he and his friends were on a hunting trip. It was in the opposite direction from Carmel. He handed me some bills and shook my hand. "Good luck, young lady, keep your eyes open," he said, starting the car again. I took the bus to Carmel, felt the familiar welcome of the clear, blue Pacific and suddenly didn't dare go to Ellen's. I was such a failure! I remembered Roxanne told the Sunday School class a friend stayed at her house when she ran away from home. It never occurred to me Roxanne wouldn't want to have anything to do with me. She didn't, of course. When I appeared at her house, she got her mother to telephone Ellen. In total humiliation I walked to Ellen's house. Ellen already found a job for me.

My new job was as a live-in baby-sitter. I was typecast. It was logical because I was always Mama's baby-sitter. Probably there wasn't much else available in the small Swedish town where my mother and aunt originated. Mama started working for a telephone company when she was twelve years old, she said. She also said her father was a drunk who produced twenty-three children before he drank up his father's estate. Ellen spent most of her life finding ways to get those siblings settled in Canada or the U.S.. Mama said Ellen was responsible for the suicides of two brothers who went broke on their farms in Canada. I didn't believe her. Usually, Mama hated Ellen. She never hesitated to use her for lodging or jobs for me or, I suspected, money. I tried not to use Ellen. This was very hard because Ellen would peel small carrots for me to munch on. She would find me a cookie or show me a new flower from her garden. For Ellen there were many ways to show love. For Mama there were very few.

The people I now lived with were in advertising. They adopted a little girl and rented a house. I really was more of a burden than an asset because the lady was so good at almost everything. It was easier and faster for her to do things her way than to watch me do things my way. We tried, both of us. Her husband spent weekends in Carmel. He took me with them to Los Angeles to visit a college friend. I baby-sat several children, ate lots of barbecue and listened to small talk when I could. They borrowed a house in San Francisco one week. I got time off to go to the Ice Follies, which I did. I got "earnings to buy clothes," which I also did. I bought a subdued plaid skirt, a blue blazer, white blouse, red socks and loafers. The lady insisted I earned the money for these. She was amazed how nice I looked in my own unremodelled new clothes. The Ice Follies were great. The new clothes made me feel very good indeed. Shortly thereafter, they moved to the city permanently.

Two Big Hugs

Chapter 12

It was the summer after my graduation from High School. I packed a box of my things that wouldn't fit in the suitcase and left a note requesting my most recent employers to drop it off at my Aunt's house when they actually left for the city. I was very tired of being a liability, a failure, a misfit. The time had come to do what I had always dreamed of doing after I got my education. How many times had I gone outside in tears to pet Rex and promise myself, "I am going to find my own father?" Probably, hundreds of times!

I took the bus to Monterey. From there I got a ticket to Seattle. On the bus I chatted with a school teacher who recommended the YWCA as a good place to park my suitcase while I looked for a job. However, after miles of glorious scenery, when we finally reached the Seattle bus station, I caught a local bus to the docks. Here I met two young men who were waiting in line to buy tickets to Alaska. From them I learned the money I had earned that summer would not be enough to continue my trip, and I would need a passport to identify myself for travel through Canada plus a certain amount of cash to show the border officials, to prove to them that I was not going to be a liability to Canada. Digesting this news, I went to the YWCA.

In the YWCA lobby I met a young lady from the far south who promptly befriended me. I paid in advance for lodging. We found the cafeteria and I was amazed how expensive everything was. I looked through the classified columns of The Seattle Post-Intelligencer for a job just like I had seen Papa do when he lived in Rider's Run. At the desk I got directions to a candy factory located on the edge of a lake it shared with a cluster of sea planes. My new friend and I went for a short walk that evening. I loved Seattle at first sight but I still had to find a way to go north.

My first full morning in Seattle I took a bus to the candy factory, located the door with the Help Wanted sign and pushed my way in. The boss was a young, friendly, man in an apron over coveralls who worked full time at making candy. He signed me up and introduced me to a pair of young ladies seated on stools beside a conveyor belt. One of them brought me a large apron. The boss urged, "Eat all the candy you want, please." I was on the coated marshmallow line. I followed his orders, catching incompletely caramel-coated marshmallows from the continuously moving line and stuffing them into my face every so often. After work, I took the bus back into the business district and walked among the buildings—looking for a way north. I was doing this when a young man called, "Hey, you! You lost or something?" He was so honest looking, so concerned, I said, "Well, actually, I'm trying to find a way to go to Alaska. I'm looking for my father."

The young man took me up some stairs to his office, which was incredibly stuffed with newspapers and magazines, cleared some of these from a chair, and made me sit down. He handled advertising for several Alaska publications printed in Seattle. He explained he could get me as far as Annette Island free because "transportation was part of his perks." The remaining problems should really be thoughtfully considered. Where did my father live? We sat there in his office, that generous and sensible young man and I, while he helped me understand the difficulty of my situation. I'd need a good parka to keep out the cold. I'd need a few hundred dollars to live on till I could get a job. Nobody hired outsiders in September, or even until Spring. I'd definitely need a complete address for my father because Alaska was extremely large. "Please let me know if you still want to go to Annette Island next week," he concluded. He gave me his card. I returned to the Y cafeteria and put a nickel in the jukebox. "Your cool and limpid green eyes" came softly through the room. The food was so expensive.

I did go back to tell him I couldn't make it and to thank him for having offered me the transportation. In the meantime, my friend and I tried eating at other places but found the Y had the best food for the least money. She found, or was found by, two soldiers who took us to an amusement park where I rode the first roller-coaster I had ever seen. The soldiers went with us back to the Y where we listened to the jukebox for a while. Then, they left to catch their bus and we went to bed. I remembered how furious the Dean had been because I was supposed to have skipped school to be with a soldier. The two soldiers who took us out to the amusement park and back were people to be proud of. They held our hands but didn't even try to kiss either of us. Was it because we stayed at the Y? I decided I didn't hate the Dean anymore. How could I hate someone who was missing so many marbles?

I got my first week's paycheck and came to a decision. I'd work one more week so I could give the week's notice my new boss had asked for. I tried to find cheaper foods, even cheaper lodging. I met a lady who now lived in Utah but had grown up in Seattle. She seemed to think I was living as economically as possible. We had a long chat beside one of the major Seattle lakes where I had gone exploring. She was a telegraph operator-a career she suggested as a good one for me. While we talked I made another decision. I would go back to Carmel and I would go back to school. So I couldn't be an engineer or a writer. So I couldn't find my father. I certainly could not spend my life in a candy factory. I couldn't even eat a candy bar or a coated marshmallow. Thousands passed me on the conveyor belt, thousands and

I no longer regarded them as something to eat. Worse yet, I couldn't save any money to go to Alaska. All that I earned went into lodging and food. I had just enough money on hand to take the bus back home. My YWCA friend was leaving, too. She had, "taken a breather from a bad marriage and was heading back to face the music." She had been a good friend.

The homeward bound bus took us through old growth redwoods and miles of other remarkable trees. I noticed more on the way back than I had on the way to Seattle. I went first to the Playhouse where my boss saw me and broke out in a laugh and crossed the room and hugged me so hard he lifted me off my feet. He asked me to come back when I was settled. Then, I went to Ellen's, not sure of my welcome. This time, Ellen said she really had to worry about Cap who had moved into a big tent in the yard and devoted most of his time to drinking with, or without, his friends at the Ale Shop. She had more grey in her hair but she still had her inner glow and she still moved with the ease and grace of a sparrow. Ellen found lodging for me less than a block away. She sent me there right after we had some of the leg of lamb she just happened to have leftover with mashed potatoes and peas from her garden, baby carrots plus steamed carrot pudding with hard sauce. I felt beloved.

I got myself into the new school in Monterey, a Junior College, where I signed up for Spanish and Italian from the same teacher plus College Algebra. One of the girls who signed up with me arranged a ride for me. It turned out she felt better having another girl sharing a car with three boys. I was having my period this week and some of the blood fell on my sheets. Without warning, the very old landlady, a new friend of Ellen's, changed my sheets. She flew into a rage about the sheets and, when I came home from my first class, everything I owned was on her front porch, the door was locked and she would not respond to the doorbell. I carried my suitcase up to Ellen's. Ellen telephoned her and tried to explain. Turning from the phone, Ellen shrugged, "She must have forgotten women don't bleed because they want to." I spent that night with Ellen who promptly found me another live-in baby-sitter job.

This time, my bosses ran a business, had an adopted daughter and a small house near downtown. Usually, the little girl would be asleep when I came home from my night classes. I could study and baby-sit during the day. There wasn't much work and I should have been happy except for the confusion between Italian and Spanish which were so much alike I had to choose which one to drop because I was driving the teacher crazy. I chose to keep Spanish. College Algebra was beyond me. When I tried to get help from the girl who had arranged my ride, I was invited to parties. The petite, young blonde who couldn't help me with algebra sang, from memory, like a chorus girl. It was a pleasure to sing with her, even to hear her, as we rode to and from school. When she ran for cheerleader, I ran against her, to make it a real election. I got two votes. I think one of them came from her. I spent Christmas at her house with her family although I did take a scarf to Ellen and a pocket knife to George and a *How To Win Friends* book for Cap. Ellen reminisced about the times George and she and I played poker for match sticks. Cap drove into the yard and I slipped down the back stairs past the empty fuchsia pots hanging from their hooks on the porch and wondered again why such beautiful flowers had no smell. I had a terrible crush on a man who affected an English accent and tweeds and had date-raped a young girl, as I later learned. Fortunately, he didn't like me so at Christmas time he handed a bottle of perfume, (gift-wrapped) to another girl, right in front of me while we were supposed to be on a date. Someone suggested he had venereal disease. The person who said that also volunteered that, "whores have big stomachs." One Friday she gave me a ride home from school. The usual driver was at home, sick. I missed the songs we always sang as a group travelling to and from school and, often, on weekend evenings at the Mission Ranch where the piano player knew a string of songs and could play for hours without repeating any one song. I mentioned that my bosses were out of town that weekend and suggested we might study together. I went into the house with her, "sounds like a party to me," raising questions in my ears.

Suddenly, the house was literally full of people. I was helpless. People I had never met were everywhere, couples in the bedrooms, groups in the kitchen, clusters on the lawn. I came from the kitchen into the living room and found the younger sister of my new boss lady seated on the couch. A stone slab on the entry walkway was broken when a friend of my ride provider had a fist fight about my honor, or so I was told. At Christmas I had found a small package under the tree. It had my name on it and I was so curious I snipped the Scotch Tape and looked at the silk scarf therein. Later, I decided that yielding to the temptation to find out what I was getting for Christmas had left me wide open to this girl who could very well have had a party in her own house but didn't. This was a tragedy! After they finally left I cleaned up the best I could. The girl whose party it was disappeared early. When my bosses came back, they had already heard from her sister. They gave me my last week's earnings and I left in disgrace. I never went back to that college.

Meanwhile, my boss at the Playhouse created a small room just off the green room. So when I went back to usher and told him I no longer had my "main job" he hired me as assistant to the manager, gave me a key to my new room, and a card which entitled me to go to the uptown theatre free. It was like a card Roxanne had been flashing for years, only I was actually working on sets and cleaning up the makeup etc. after a play, sweeping the entry, using the addressograph for mailings, even discussing the blurbs he wrote to entice the public to come to watch a play or a movie. Now that I no longer went to class I had lots of time to go to the movies and I did. I told my boss about, *The House of Death*. "It's too gory for our house but it is a real wow," I said. The next time he booked films, he ordered, and got, *The House of Death*. I was ushering when he showed it for the first time.

"You were right. It is a wow," he beamed.

I lost my job just at the right time again. I was just getting used to the wonderful things I could now do, painting sets for a play, washing the coffee service myself, typing notices, when Mama telephoned Ellen who telephoned me. My boss gave me an advance to buy my ticket and even dropped me off at the bus station "on his way" somewhere. Mama was in a hotel in "the city." An infection she had long ignored had been spreading. Now she was going into surgery to have her leg amputated. We got into a verbal battle immediately which lasted till she fell asleep. I had some paper and a pen. I wrote my own version of the Declaration of Independence, set it on the dresser and went to sleep. Mama woke me before dawn. She was laughing at my note, telling me I was, "just like your father, no earthly use to anyone, a zero, a nothing, not entitled to be called a person." I picked up my suitcase and walked out of the hotel room, down to the street, to the nearest bus stop.

Where would I go? I thought about the University of California at Berkeley where the only brother of Florence Rider lived with his roommate, their longtime friend. I put my suitcase in a locker at the bus station and took the ferry to Berkeley. I was praying pretty hard and trying to stop crying because Mama was right. I was a nothing. I heard someone call my name, looked around in the crowd of students hurrying between classes, and found Florence's brother, Gordy. He hugged me, too, a real hug.

Gordy took me to the basement alcove, it wasn't big enough to be a room, where he lived with his friend. He began, "So how's your mother?" I found myself suddenly demanding, "Gordy, tell me. Why did Florence and Holly hate me so much? Why did they call me such awful names?"

He shoved books and papers off a chair and sat me down on it. "Didn't you know?" he asked. "Didn't you know your mother wasn't married when your sister was born? Didn't you know?"

"It wasn't me?" I asked. "You mean it wasn't me?"

Gordy nodded. His roommate arrived. They offered to take me to the movies. I said I had to catch a bus and walked briskly away, just away. When I could think I mentally revisited that room and remembered their gaunt faces—and they had savings accounts and family backing, probably scholarships. I was going back to college for real—only not just yet. Someday I was going to college. I was not going to be a zero, a nothing, forever.

The Way We Were

Chapter 13

I returned to the Playhouse just in time to join a select group of younger ballet students. Our teacher was formerly a professional ballet dancer. He was skillful and patient. Once again, I did not practice and, once again, I left the class before it ended. I felt gawky and awkward and ill-at-ease. One lovely morning my boss, Mr. Justice, found me sunning myself on the section of the theatre ramp concealed from the street. He drove me back to the castle and taught me how to drive a motorbike. I drove it several times and loved to do so. The Irish Setter remembered me. The family was spending the summer in Europe. A week later I was sniffling again at work so he took me back to the castle. He lit a fire in the fireplace and wrapped me in blankets on the couch. He gave me a hot lemonade to drink and read Henry Moore aloud until I fell asleep. While I painted the flats at work the next day he read more passages from Henry Moore. I thought my father would have been this kind of person. Mr. Justice was a grateful man—grateful to have been alive when the radio, telephone, and movies came into being. He was knowledgeable in law and literature, a solid, humorous, happy man.

When Mr. Justice booked films again, he took me with him. To this day I do not know how he could stand the cigarette smoke. He didn't smoke and I was addicted by then. One cigarette I thought I threw from the car burned a hole in the back seat. He even forgave me for this. We went to the Hollywood Bowl to hear Andre Previn play piano and to Coconut Grove to hear Frankie Laine sing. We went to San Francisco to see the play, *Magdalena* and, another Saturday, *Time For Elizabeth*. Neither play survived all the way to New York. I loved every minute of each of them. We saw a beautiful new film based on Tarzan. We lunched at the Golden Pheasant and Solari's. We dined at the Palace Hotel and looked at the Coit Tower by night and by day. We talked about more than plays and movies. He taught me the key words, "conception, detection, infection." These are still the best reasons why sex should be something you do after marriage. Not my father, of course, certainly not Mama, but Mr. Justice, my boss, talked to me about these things. It took all summer while I was painting and ushering and addressographing. He asked me what I wanted the most from life. I said, "a home and my own family—like everyone else in the world."

I was growing more alert and more relaxed, less self conscious and less painfully shy. For my birthday, Mr. Justice gave me a clear glass vase which refracted sunlight into rainbows. He filled the vase with one dozen American Beauty roses. My clothes accounted for most of my new self confidence. For once in my life I didn't wear, or even own, anything Mama remodelled. While shopping in San Francisco, in Macy's, I bought a Hunter's Green suit. I bought brown pumps, underwear, stockings, a brown cloche hat of exactly the same color as my shoes and purse. I wore these with a splashy flowered scarf and one of my high school cashmeres. I looked in the mirror and was pleased with my reflection. The blue blazer from the summer before still looked good. I was presentable wherever I went this wonderful summer. A borrowed splashy flowered skirt, made me look like an upside down multicolored tulip. It came from the green room costume box. When I wasn't ushering, I went to the movies at the other theatre.

The summer ended. I was having a cup of coffee in the diner beside the other theatre. A girl I noticed before came to sit beside me, introduced herself, and began to chat. She was so pretty and so nice. She told me she worked in a bank. She thought I might like to work there, too. When we parted, I agreed to come to the bank, to look for a job, the next day. When I told Mr. Justice, he said it was good news. His family was coming home from Europe. He was going to drive across the country to get them. He asked me to stay in my little room while he was gone and the Playhouse was closed for two weeks. I agreed. I kept the appointment my new friend made for me at the bank. My new boss said Mr. Justice gave me a fine recommendation in writing and "wasn't he a good man?" I agreed. The day he left Mr. Justice came to the bank to give me a small package. Inside was a lavender fountain pen. "Write objectively," was the only thing on the note he sent with it.

I sat behind Andrea in the bank. Each of us ran a big Burroughs bookkeeping machine. Each of us did half the daily posting for the private bank where we worked. There was a supervisor, the head bookkeeper, two tellers, a secretary, and a manager. There were some really wild parties at the drop of anyone's hat. One of the tellers used to be a WAVE. I admired her tremendously. When we went out to lunch, I met another girl who worked in another bank. She talked about advertising a room in her house as rental property. Despite my promise to Mr. Justice, I moved into the new room before he came back. Andrea and I thought the room would not still be available in another week. After Mr. Justice brought his family back from New York there was a fire in the green room. The Playhouse was closed for repairs. I didn't read the newspapers and didn't hear about the fire. One evening, Andrea and I went out to dinner together and then to the other theatre. I flashed my pass at the manager. "Hey, you, he laughed, "Your pass doesn't work anymore. The Playhouse is closed." Then, he told me about the fire and I paid for the first movie ticket I ever bought. It was to see Oscar Levant play George Gershwin's *Rhapsody in Blue.* It was worth it.

While I roomed with Marge, I found myself double dating with her and two soldiers. One of them invited me to a dance. Marge made my dress on her sewing machine. A girl I used to know at the college gave me a permanent wave. Looking very much unlike myself, I was taken to meet the young man's mother and sister. Both of them looked very much like I did at the moment. It was scary, three permanent waves, three ill-fitting dresses, and the eager young soldier. I couldn't find anything to say. The next date Marge arranged for me was someone in a much more important military category, someone quite tough. I was in over my head so I looked in the want ads and found another place to live.

This was another disaster. A high school girl from Monterey happened to see me walking home one day and gave me a ride. Then, she used me and my room as an excuse to stay out all night. While I was sleeping, she was out. I didn't know anything about this until her parents knocked on my door in the morning. There was a lot of loud noise when she and her date drove up a bit later. I found another apartment in the want ads. I bought a Revere tea kettle, some dishes and silverware and the basic groceries. I was quite happy in a tiny abode above some outside stairs. I bought flowers and put them in my clear glass vase. They caught the light between tall trees nearby. I got a bill for income tax. I expected a refund but Mr. Justice did not deduct withholding taxes and the bank did. Suddenly, I owed the IRS $200.

I remembered my father's brother in Palo Alto. I went to see him. He was friendly and polite. He gave me a handkerchief formerly belonging to his mother, my grandmother. He took me to the house my father helped build when he and the current Fish & Game Commissioner were both Stanford students. He even introduced me to this gentleman who was standing in his yard. He drove me by Stanford. I said, "I wanted to thank you for trying to help me further my education at Stanford." He shook his head. "No, not me, not Stanford, not after they railroaded your father. No, it was San Jose state." I wasn't impressed with what I saw of Stanford, a few bungalow type buildings. When I asked for the money to pay my income tax, he gave me a strange look. "I understand how a young lady could have been exploited," he said and counted out the money. I put it into a cashier's check when I got back to my bank and sent it to the IRS. His wife still didn't know how to cook and she still didn't like me.

Since I was running a machine all day, I faced a regular schedule. There were frequent pay day lunches at a real restaurant with Andrea. There were frequent pay day dinners at a real restaurant by myself, lots of fast food, weekends. I walked down to the mission ranch, rented a horse and tried to ride up the valley to visit Andrea. After a while, the horse refused to go any farther so I turned the reluctant traveller around. He trotted back to the stables like he might be late for lunch. I tried this twice with different horses, same results. I walked down to the river one Saturday and found my cousin George fishing for steelhead trout. He was not delighted to see me. I went to the movies. I tanned on the beach.

Andrea invited me to her home several times this year. We went up the valley with her father in his Packard convertible, shared a scrumptious dinner with her parents and chatted. We slept in twin beds in her room and the next day we rode for miles. She rode her Arabian stallion and I rode her Palomino gelding, Tony. We stopped to chat at the Post Office and at the store. We bought ice cream cones for Tony and Andrea and me. The Arabian didn't like ice cream. Tony loved it. At Christmas, I exchanged gifts at her house with her parents. Andrea's mother gave me a pair of Scotch Thistle silver earrings. Andrea went with me to set up a charge account at a ladies' shop. I bought a Glen Plaid suit to go with the thistle earrings. I paid for the suit in three paydays. Being in debt was so uncomfortable, I didn't even try to charge anything else. Andrea and I also bought bras, which fit properly, at another ladies' shop.

One day I met Ellen, near the bank, after I left work. She was glad to see me. We went on the bus to the hillside where Carmel High stood, then beyond it toward Monterey. When she pulled the cord, the bus stopped and we walked along a paved road for what seemed a long way. Finally, she stopped and held onto my sleeve. "Here it is. Here's my land," she said. "I wanted you to see my land. I bought it with the money they sent me when Keith died. I think I'll build a house here someday. Do you like it?" Her face was so eager, so wanting me to see something good she did alone, as usual. "I love it, Ellen," I said. We went back together and left each other near where we met. She explained, "Cap is worse, much worse. Take care of yourself." Then, she walked back down to Dolores Street.

Andrea and I walked up from the bank to the Post Office, now and then, during our lunch break. We chatted with a young Postal employee Andrea thought was cute. One day he asked me what I was doing Friday night. I replied, "I don't know." He asked me to go dancing in Monterey. We did go dancing after an excellent dinner at a famous local night spot. He was a fabulous dancer with dips and swoops and long, low, bows and necking in his car. We went out several times. I was glad Andrea was dating a forest ranger so neither of us was a wall flower. One evening, he took me to his home where we played cards with his brother and sister-in-law. I learned how to play Hearts. At the end of the evening his mother came home and we were introduced. She said, "I hope you'll come back when it's not so late and we can talk." I said, "Don't be surprised if I do." It was a line from a movie, totally inappropriate, out before I knew it. Everyone froze. I never saw the young man again. He must have hidden somewhere whenever Andrea and I went to the Post Office.

The annual Easter invasion of college and university students occurred. Andrea and I double-dated with two Cal-Berkeley Juniors. The tall one was attracted to me but Andrea more or less adopted him. The short one, who liked willowy Andrea, was more "my type." We sunned on the beach one Saturday and swam in the surf, went to the Mission Ranch and sang. We drank and parked at the beach and necked. Andrea needed a ride miles up the valley to her home. It was almost morning, and her date was asleep in the back seat. My date parked on a hill top. He presented me with a silver dolphin pin, and asked me what I wanted to do with my life. He said he heard about my "reputation," he liked me and wanted to be a friend. Was I planning to work at the bank forever? Did I ever think about going to college? Suddenly, I found myself telling him about the time Mama dated a Pebble Beach playboy. He tried to kiss her. She slapped him and walked all the way back to Carmel in high heels. My date started the car and took me home.

A few days later, I met a girl who visited our Sunday School. She was a clerk in a dress shop now. I wandered in. Glad to see someone different, but not too different, I introduced myself as being from the same congregation. She suggested we lunch together the next day. Andrea was on vacation showing Arabians in Los Angeles. When I went to the dress shop the following noon, my new friend wasn't there. I asked another clerk where she was and was told she didn't work there anymore. On a hunch, I walked around the block, came back and peeked into the shop. She was there, giggling.

Andrea and I weren't getting any younger. She and I double-dated a couple of forestry students. She dated one of them several times but nothing came of it. My landlady decided she needed more rent, advertised and found some newlyweds. My lovely, woodsy, apartment was vacated so fast I left the clear glass vase behind. I answered an ad and found a perfect landlady, a tiny basement room, and a young man. He rented another of her rooms and was pleasant and unassuming. We spent parts of Saturdays on her sun porch getting ever better tans. My new landlady was a great cook. I paid more but—she enjoyed making me lunches for work and her dinners were fabulous. Besides, the landlady was someone I sought forever, it seemed. The first evening we played Canasta with her mother and aunt. Clara said, "Her neck's dirty. Her does?" And I understood I could be at peace in her house. I went on evening walks with her and her big shaggy dog. We talked and we appreciated each other. She was a retired social worker. Her aunt was a department store buyer in the Midwest. Her aunt told us, frequently, about the evening she dressed impeccably to attend a special buyer's convention meeting. In the hotel elevator, the operator kept looking down toward her shoes. Finally, he said, "Pardon me, Madam, are you sure you want to go out like that?" Looking down, she discovered she forgot to put on her skirt. I played a lot of Canasta with those ladies. Her mother read the newspaper obituary column in a loud, clear voice every evening after dinner. She chuckled at the ages of the deceased. She must have been in her nineties.

Andrea was getting restless. Prizes, ribbons, and cups, from the Arabian Horse Shows she entered, cluttered her room. Usually, she rode for a valley Arabian breeder. When appropriate she wore a Burnoose and full regalia for various events plus lots of silver on her saddle. She really looked good on a horse. One day, she introduced me to a young man from Salinas who was very rich. He telephoned me at the bank and, after the initial recognition, I didn't say anything. He snapped, "What did you expect? Chimes?" and hung up. I disliked him even more. Andrea suggested it would be fun to save our money and go to Sun Valley for a real vacation. I was still considering "a real vacation" when she suggested we join the Navy. I went with her to the Recruiting office in Monterey. We took tests. The recruiter telephoned me. Back in his office, I learned Andrea chickened out. "She didn't seem to like men much," the recruiter said. "You'll be the first WAVE I ever recruited," he added. I said to myself, "Why not?"

Exactly one year after I went to work at the bank, they gave me a bathrobe. At a final party, they added a pair of pajamas and a check for the club car. I sold my clothes to the girl who replaced me at work. Andrea got my Glen Plaid suit. My landlady got my new coat. My blue plaid Lanz raincoat went to another friend. My suitcase contained the things I was supposed to bring to Boot Camp. I was wearing a new plum colored suit and the silver thistle earrings. Ellen signed for me, in her kitchen, because I was not yet twenty-one. I took the bus to Monterey. The soldier whose mother, sister, and I got permanent waves at the same time waited for a bus, too. We shared some coffee and a smoke. He pressed a $5 bill into my hand for "more smokes." My bus left first so there was someone to see me off when I started my new life. On the bus, I was awestricken. I wished there would be someone I knew to say, "Good-Bye," and there was. I remembered, "Be careful what you ask God for because you'll get it." Maybe those words were true.

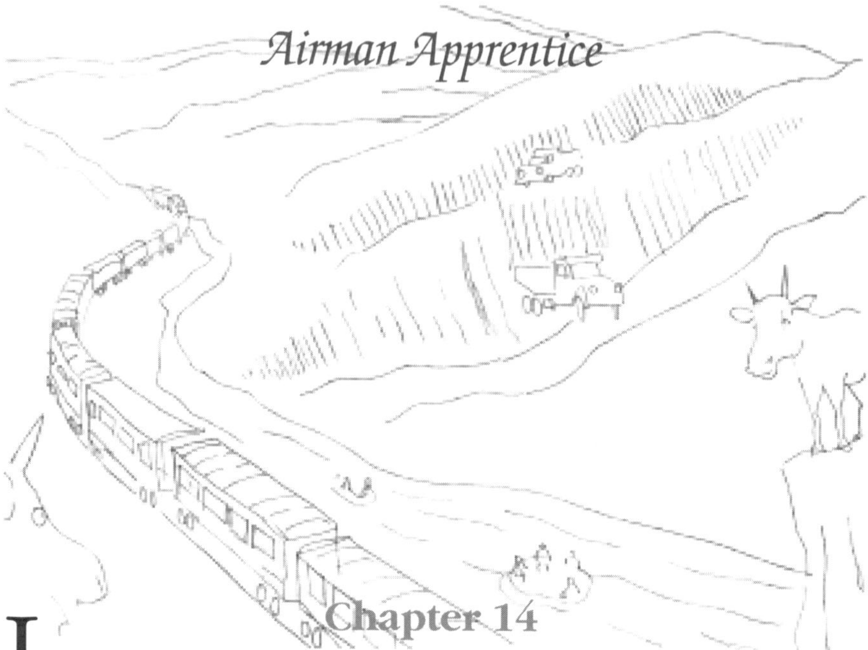

Airman Apprentice

Chapter 14

In a San Francisco skyscraper, we swore to uphold the Constitution of the United States of America. Each of us signed several documents. The WAVE officer said, "You know you're promising not to get married during the first year of your enlistment?" I laughed, "That's easy.—I'm going to stay twenty years like my recruiter." I meant it. I meant every word at the time. I expected a career in the Navy. I was looking forward to adventure and travel. We were entrusted to a thirty-four year old former school teacher who carried our official documents. She shepherded us to the ferry, then to the train where we shared a sleeping car to Great Lakes. I thought the country through which we passed was really beautiful in its fall colors.

I loved the Navy. Going to and from classes or the chow hall, we sang. There were field days and fire drills. There was a new friend, a former secretary of statuesque build, who slept on the bottom bunk. We scrubbed toilets together. Across the aisle was a pretty girl who plucked everyone's eyebrows—free. A Midwesterner hemmed my grey striped uniforms. The blues were done professionally. We marched to the parade ground to drill or to the chow hall to eat or do kitchen police. We marched to the main building to classes or to clean. I was one of two girls who read the entire history textbook. We, therefore, passed the Naval History Test with a good grade. The other girl and I showed each other the poetry we wrote in class. We took tests and more tests and physical exams. I was in a line in the gym for a review by the Commandant of the WAVES. Determined not to move while she walked between our ranks, I fainted.

I came to in the nurses' office. The next day I was interviewed by a psychiatrist. He was so pleasant. We quoted "Polonius' Advice to Laertes" to each other. He began, "There, my blessing with thee and these few precepts in thy memory. See thou character." I added, "Give thy thoughts no tongue nor any ill-proportioned thought his act." He concluded, "The friends thou hast and their adoption tried, grapple them to thy soul with hoops of steel but do not dull thy palm with entertainment of each new hatched, unfledged, comrade." I nodded. "Good for you, young lady, enjoy the Navy," he said. He signed a paper and sent me back to my group. The following day I was sent to a second psychiatrist. He read the document I brought him and snapped, "I see your aunt signed for you to join our illustrious group. Why didn't your mother sign?"

"My mother lives too far away. My aunt was right there," I replied. He looked me over thoroughly and sighed and said, "Well, keep your nose clean. Dismissed." I remembered to salute.

We went on liberty to Waukegan where Jack Benny was born. We went as a group on a bus, to a bar. There was a piano and we did lots of singing. Many Moscow Mule Cups were carried away when we took the taxis back to the base. We went on another liberty to Chicago. We lunched at the Palmer House and dined at the Old Heidelberg. I mentioned my uncle said the Field Museum was the place to go in Chicago. No one wanted to go with me and I would not leave my new buddies. I drank and smoked and listened to my bunkmate cry about the man she left behind. I worried about her. She waved her ID card at the bar tender to prove she could legally drink. Taking a rest room break, she left her ID card lying on the bar. I picked it up and tucked it away with my own. Just before we left the bus in front of our barracks, I slipped her ID card into her hand. The next morning, we were waxing the floor when we were sent for. Two officers wanted to know why I was holding her ID card on the bus. I said, "I picked it up when she dropped it and I was just giving it back to her." This was as close to the truth as I dared to go. She got an hour more of mopping as punishment. She hated me because I didn't get any demerits at all. We went from warmly chatting friends to silent bunkmates.

Everyone was expected to learn how to swim. Since I already knew how, I became part of a water ballet. The group swam in circles, slow motion, for a review. The swimming instructor glimpsed my face before we jumped off the high tower to simulate leaping from a ship. After everyone else jumped, she made me go back and do it again. I was still scared the second time. Maybe she realized I would jump from the platform all day no matter how terrified I was. She let me rejoin my group.

A short letter from Ellen included a clipping from the *Monterey Herald*. In my plum colored suit, I faced an American flag. The article noted I was the recruiter's only WAVE. He was now retired. About a week before graduation, we were told there would be no more singing. Silence would reign in the lines for chow or classes or even on the parade ground. It was sad to hear only the pounding of feet in cadence. Then, our beloved, incredibly cranky, drill instructor went on sick leave. Replacement people led us through the graduation. One of them was the young lady who didn't like my haircut. In Carmel, Andrea and I got professional haircuts at a beauty shop from two cute, young, gay men. The WAVE who trimmed my hair didn't quite know how to keep it from waving. It looked something like a Mohawk-both sides met on top like a line of surf breaking at sea. Neither barber nor officer dared give me the really short haircut which looked nice and kept my wave from waving. I was grateful for my Navy cap and the bucket hat.

We passed in review with what looked like thousands of sailors. We signed each other's programs and packed and got our duty stations. A native New Yorker invited a girl from Wisconsin, and me, to visit her in New York City. Only one of our original company did not ship out at the same time. She wrote a letter to a Congressman complaining about the food. We thought she was probably already back home. Most of us thought the food was great. I just barely fit my uniforms. There was a flurry of good-byes.

Some of us would meet at the Palmer House. The girl whose ID I picked up from the bar strolled by while we waited for a train. "Meet me at the Palmer. I have something for you," she said. I was amazed. I waited with a group until it was time to catch the New York train. She never appeared. I was sorry because I didn't want her to hate me.

We three brand new seamen apprentices went to New York City and on to New Rochelle. Mary's mother, father, sister, and brother were all crammed together in a tiny walk-up apartment. I shared a double bed with Mary's sister. The Wisconsin girl shared a double bed, also rented for the occasion, with Mary. Mary's mother ironed baskets of clothes while she watched professional wrestling on television. I thought Mr. Justice would have loved TV and the riotous wrestling we didn't have time to watch. Mary took us to Rockefeller Center by commuter train. We were walking along, looking up, when the only black girl in our company strolled up behind us. She cracked, "Small world, eh?" She lived in New York City. We could only chat for a few minutes. Mary took us to Bloomingdale's. We met some of her friends who still worked there. We lunched in a coffee shop with another of her friends. We strolled through Greenwich Village. At night, I held onto Mary's brother's arm while we walked through Times Square. He took us to a nightclub. New Rochelle trees dropped lustrous golden leaves at my feet when I caught the commuter train back to the Navy. I thought I saw Robert Redford in Grand Central Station. I could have been right. We were on the train with some Notre Dame football players.

It was raining in Memphis. I was assigned to Aviation Electrician's Mate

School. I was a few days early. I reported in and was taken to the WAVE barracks. I stowed my gear and headed for chow hall. There was a girl from my class at Great Lakes, a girl who went to church there with me. She did this just because I was the only one who signed up for Mama's religion. Sabrina impressed the Navy Chaplain with her common sense. He smelled the smoke on me and couldn't hide his disgust. Still, Sabrina and I attended his meetings all through boot camp and I was glad to see her again. The next day her bunkmate arrived. We three shared a cubicle in an old wooden barracks. Around midnight there was a Fire Drill. Afterward, a very young, slightly tipsy, officer berated us. We were supposed to clear the building in three minutes. It took us forty seconds too long. I murmured, "Comes the revolution, we'll have fire drills every Saturday and really cut down the time." An older WAVE heard me. She immediately assigned me the scrubbing of the bathroom sinks up where she lived. She told me a fire was not funny. I scrubbed diligently. She was right.

On Navy insurance forms I listed my father as my beneficiary with "somewhere in Alaska" as his address. I was pulled from my class one day and sent to the insurance office. Here, an officer informed me I could not do this. The Navy would not be responsible for finding out where my father lived. I thought, if anyone could find him, they could. Wrong again! I started to write Ellen's name and was asked, "Isn't your mother living?" People were staring at me. How could I tell them I didn't want Mama to profit from my death? I made out the forms to Mama and wondered what I would have to do to become an adult.

I was the only WAVE in my class. We mustered in front of a long, low building every morning to hear the Navy Regs. Among other Marines I met, as we headed for our various classes, was "Straight Gouge." His specialty was tiny lists of answers to quizzes. I pretended not to know about them even after one of his fellow Marines was pulled from class for using one. Not only didn't I see the Marine again, I never heard what happened to him. One of the girls in the barracks got a dishonorable discharge. This was after she became too pregnant for anyone to believe she was just obese. A Marine from Pittsburgh kind of took me under his wing. I heard jokes, but they were clean. He didn't mind when I rattled on about the Amps looking for Ohms.

Sabrina and her friend attended a different aviation school. The friend got romantically involved with a Marine whose friend dated Sabrina. A third Marine went along. The girls introduced me to their dates and to the third man. Together in the chow hall, we shared a really good Thanksgiving dinner. The third man invited me to accompany them into Memphis. At a night club in a major hotel, we danced and drank and chatted. He was from Pennsylvania and Camp Lejeune, in training to be an aviation mechanic. Sabrina's friend announced she and her Marine were getting married. We walked back to the WAVE barracks where each pair held hands and talked.

At the end of the evening, each man kissed each woman good-night. I sang in the bathtub till someone yelled, "Shut-up."

Every evening that week we three couples met at the chow hall. After dinner we walked together to the Wave Barracks. We held hands and talked till the lounge closed. It was agreed we three couples would go to Mississippi next Saturday morning for a wedding. Sabrina and her boy friend would be Maid of Honor and Best Man respectively. I would pass Norman standing with the Marines, for their muster, before morning chow. Wednesday or Thursday evening I said, "Why don't we get married too?" Norman agreed, "O.K. Let's get married when they do." Melissa, the Bride to Be, frowned when we told her the good news. Then, realizing the fees would be split, she didn't argue. It turned out Norman was also too young to get married in Tennessee.

My "something old" was my grandmother's handkerchief. I carried it with me since my uncle gave it to me in Palo Alto. My "something new" was another handkerchief from Sabrina. My "something borrowed" was a penny from Melissa. My "something blue" was my WAVES uniform. We caught the Greyhound bus from Memphis to Senatobia, Mississippi on Saturday morning—all of us in dress blues. We breakfasted in a cafe near the Presbyterian church. Norman couldn't eat any breakfast. After the ceremony, I couldn't eat any lunch.

We stood solemnly in the church while a minister performed the ceremony. Norman slipped a "gold knotted," as a rope is knotted, ring onto my finger. I slipped its mate onto his finger. It was a double ring, double military wedding in a church and it was between meals, as it were. We took another bus back to Memphis, returned to the Hotel Peabody, and we three couples drank and danced. My period began right on schedule. I discovered Norman didn't know how to dance beyond a very basic two step. I decided that wasn't enormously important. I prayed in the church, and before, and after the wedding itself. I prayed for this marriage to work. I prayed to be a satisfactory wife.

Sunday morning we walked around Memphis. We found a special little park with a plaque containing a poem. It ended "Art thou a mourner, rouse thee from thy spell. Art thou a sinner, sins may be forgiven. Each morning gives thee wings to flee from Hell, each night a star to guide thy feet to Heaven." Once, when Mr. Justice and I were talking, he said, "When you are really in love it will be like bells ringing. It will be like sirens and you will know it and you will be very happy." Once, one of the men who helped out when Andrea was showing a horse told me, "You're going to be involved with several men. They won't matter because the one who loves you will love you so much. The only place he'll want to be is wherever you are and he will be so lucky." I remembered also the young man who thanked me for not going out with him. The girl he turned to for comfort turned out to be, "a most satisfactory wife." I read the poem and remembered these things. I tried to be worthy of such a young and tender husband. The third man happened to be a Marine training to be an aviation mechanic.

Monday, I did not meet Norman at the chow hall. There was a message at the barracks for me. I walked over to the hospital this evening and several other evenings. Norman endured an appendectomy. We spent our "honeymoon" in the hospital, Naval Air Training Center, Memphis, Tennessee. Later, we looked for housing in an office on the base. It featured a large sign. "The difficult we do immediately—the impossible may take a little time." We found a room and moved into it. We ate in a small nearby cafe. One breakfast was marred when I remembered aloud Mama said my father's table manners were terrible. Norman's table manners were terrible. How was it I never noticed his dancing or his manners until after we married? Then I felt contrite because how much did table manners, any manners, matter? He showed me the letter from his mother, "I can understand how you happened to get married. You were away from home so long and you got homesick." I heard from Mama too, "I got your letter back from the Navy. I thought you were in Ecuador." She enclosed an old letter to me. It was forwarded to Great Lakes before being returned to Rider's Run. I smiled about Ecuador. Mama habitually sent letters asking for money, and, just as habitually, I ignored them. One day, I sent a postcard, "Gone to Ecuador on noon plane. Will try to contact you later." This actually worked for more than a year. Now I wrote to tell Mama I was married.

Norman graduated with his class from the base and was sent to North Carolina. I moved back to the barracks, missed two periods and started to bleed heavily. One morning I fainted in the middle of Navy regs. I woke up in the hospital. Norman borrowed money from Navy Relief to come and hold my hand while I lost a baby. When I saw, "spontaneous abortion," on my chart I thought it meant I was responsible. When I understood, "spontaneous", as I certainly should have immediately, I felt better, but not much better. We got a liberty for me and went into Memphis. We walked around the little park. We looked in the shop windows where I found my butterfly dress for the times we went dancing in Memphis. His shoes were professionally shined where they were shined before. Finally, we just sat and held hands in the fog near the bus station. We were too poor to get a hotel room. He went back to North Carolina. I went back to the hospital and, then, to the barracks. It was June 6, 1950.

I was in Aviation Electrician's Mate School when a messenger came to take me back to the hospital. A very official looking doctor held out some documents for me to sign. "You have ten minutes to decide whether you want to stay in the Navy or not. You probably don't remember but back in September you signed an agreement not to get married during your first year. You did get married and you did have a miscarriage. Now, we can pretend you never had a baby and you can stay here, and probably never get back with your husband, or we can pretend you are still pregnant and give you an Honorable Discharge. I would take the Discharge. Just between us, it looks like we're going to war. You might not see your husband for a long time."

The trouble was I really loved the Navy. I loved learning about electric circuits and the wiring for guns in aircraft. However, I couldn't very well let Norman get involved in a war without my being somewhere in the picture. I said, "Well, I suppose I could join the Reserves."

"Oh, no," he said, "If you're supposed to be pregnant your baby would have to be eighteen years old and you would be too old by then." He typed, "Not recommended for reenlistment," on my Discharge papers and gave them to me to sign.

I took the bus to Memphis and left my footlocker in a locker. I located the Western Store Norman and I window shopped only a day before. I went in and bought myself a pair of cowboy boots, jeans, western shirt, and straw hat. Thus outfitted, I headed for North Carolina on the bus. I was no longer an Airman Apprentice. I was a wife. The cowboy clothes were in honor of Andrea. I was not ready for house dresses.

North Carolina One

Chapter 15

While we were stationed in Memphis Norman applied for, and received, commuted rations, to pay for off-base meals. He asked me to do the same. I never got around to it. Now retroactive commuted rations increased my discharge pay. Therefore, I brought enough money to buy pots and pans, sheets and pillowcases. I bought these and many other useful items we needed for the furnished apartment Norman found. He signed up for the only furnished apartment available through the base. He didn't like it. It was actually most of the attic of a two story brick building dating back to the Civil War. It was half a block from a big steepled, white church with a gigantic Magnolia tree. And, of course, it was on Church Street like Mama's house in Rider's Run. The view from the livingroom window was of the Neuse River. I loved the apartment, the views, the stairs. The wicker furniture was painted before our time but the paint never dried, ever. When Norman's Marine friends came to visit us, they left with black stripes on the backs of their shirts and pants.

One of these friends was Melissa's husband. He came, with or without his other Marine buddy. He would drop in to chat for a little while. When there were four of us we played Gin Rummy. I made spaghetti dinners and hamburgers. Melissa's husband was increasingly miserable as time went by. Finally, he stopped coming at all. Melissa used him to pay off some of her debts before she divorced him. Boxes of dried corn and sausages, fragile pink serving platters and candy dishes, came from Norman's parents in Pennsylvania. I put a fallen magnolia blossom from the churchyard in water in a pink glass candy dish. I thought, "I know what all these Marines have in common. They came from Pennsylvania."

On the bottom floor, the landlady's apartment was next to one shared by a Colonel and his wife. On the second floor, two Staff Sargeants lived with their wives in their two apartments. We lived on top. In the summer, we kept fans going and windows open. In the winter, well! The landlady explained, "Heat rises," every time I asked for more heat. Our thermometer seemed to be stuck on fifty degrees and I wore several layers of clothing. While ice storms were breaking tree limbs in the church yard, I went to bed. Fully clothed, except for shoes, I covered myself with all the blankets under all the coats we owned. I got up now and then to walk around. Then, I fled back to bed to watch my breath floating in the room and read. In part of the attic was a storage area. Here the landlady kept the sombreros and serapes she brought back every midwinter from Mexico. Here also were books, her deceased husband's books, English translations of Horace and Ovid, Aristophanes and Euripides. With her permission I read one after another of these books. I finished *War and Peace* not long after the last of Norman's friends transferred, leaving us without Pennsylvanians and, therefore, without friends.

One of the ladies underneath us worked as a photo engraver, something Mama said she did in San Francisco. She and I tanned once in the backyard. The landlady caught us and informed us we were not paying to use her backyard. One cold day, I heard a scream, jumped from bed and ran downstairs. My new friend burned herself. "I tried to use the pressure cooker like an ordinary pot," she explained. Her husband brought a doctor. She was swathed in bandages when I brought her the tuna fish casserole originally intended to serve Norman and me. I made something else for us. She brought me the dishes two days later on her way back to work.

I was expecting a baby when we went to Pennsylvania for Thanksgiving. It was a long bus trip over poor roads in winter weather. I did not want to take any chances on another miscarriage. I need not have worried. When we reached his parents' home, Norman sat down in an overstuffed chair. It was as though he were a ship approaching a safe harbor. I tried to help with the serving and dishes wherever we went. We went to the homes of several aunts and uncles, grandparents and not one friend. When we did see a former classmate of Norman's, they stood beside the friend's car. They talked interminably without Norman's ever introducing me. Each relative's house contained enough overstuffed chairs so Norman could rest comfortably between meals.

The meals were always feasts. Thanksgiving dinner was a composite of offerings from aunts and uncles. Long tables were planted from the door of the front room through the livingroom through the diningroom to the kitchen. Counting nephews and nieces there must have been forty people for one meal at the grandparents' house. Leftovers went back with various sub-families. After dinner Norman sat with the men and I washed dishes with the women. When we made our expected calls on the uncles and aunts Norman sat with the men and I worked with the women. My mother-in law and her sister, Aunt Cecily, who lived nearby, tested me. While we did the dishes, one evening, Aunt Cecily started telling dirty jokes. Grandma told one. It was my turn. I remembered a joke the Marine from Pittsburgh shared one morning before Navy Regs. There was an elderly gentleman back in the old country with three marriageable daughters. The first, Nasturtium, had a dowry of one Dinero. The second, Diefenbachia, had a dowry of two dineros. The third, Wisteria, had a dowry of three dineros. A potential suitor inquired why poor Nasturtium would bring him only one Dinero. The old man replied, "She's just a little bit, not much cross-eyed." The second daughter was "just a little bit, not much, bowlegged." And dear Wisteria was "just a little bit, not much, pregnant." I thought it was a clean, humorous, satirical joke. Grandma and Aunt Cecily may not have understood it. They gasped. I told myself, "There's one joke which got a decent burial even in its native state of Pennsylvania." I remained an outsider. We took the bus back to New Bern with a new blanket and a bottle of perfume from another aunt. I cried when I found the perfume tucked inside the blanket. It was the only thing for me. Everything else was for "the house." The only thing I asked for, being given a choice by one of the aunts, was a pressure cooker. This was a treasure I really used.

I took back a memory, too, of Norman's father coming home, parking his car in the garage and going upstairs to take a bath. He came downstairs to sit in the overstuffed chair in the livingroom and read the newspaper until dinner was ready. All of this invariably happened without any verbal exchanges His work on a cement mixer soured him. Shortly after we returned to our attic I had another miscarriage, all by myself, in bed. It hurt as much as the first- without the drugs from the hospital. Norman was most considerate. I did all the cooking and dishes and was always up and dressed when he was around. There was no change in our routine. Norman went to the base housing office with a question. He returned to the landlady with the answer. By legal agreement, we paid by the half-month, not every two weeks. The landlady tried to squeeze an extra two weeks rent from Norman! We went "home" for Christmas to another feast with the great-grandparents. We came back to snow on the streets of New Bern. It wasn't as high as Pennsylvania snow. The people we passed on the street were enjoying it. By spring, I finally carried a baby more than three months for the first time in my life. I walked slowly and moved carefully. I really wanted a child. The landlady met me on her porch while I was getting the mail. "I want you to tell your husband the baby you're expecting is making it necessary for me to raise the rent. You'll be using more water for diapers and such. I'll be needing ten dollars more every time. He's got another stripe now so you can afford it."

Norman heard the news with equanimity. Two days later, he took me several blocks away to a big apartment. There was no view, no character and no neighborly feeling about it. It was just a square box with a bed, a table and two chairs. There was a closet and a linoleum rug, stove and refrigerator. I hated it instantly and forever. It wasn't even near anything nice to look at. Actually, it backed up on a freight yard. The walls were windowless, windows painted over. We moved. The rent was also more than we expected. I found myself ironing the uniforms Norman formerly sent to the laundry. I stood at an ironing board which was the right size for me. I listened to baseball games on the radio and ironed khaki shirts and pants Norman called trousers. I wore a solid purple maternity dress. I bought it in the small town near the Navy base in Tennessee before the "spontaneous abortion". It was purple because my child was royalty to me, royalty to be clothed in purple, of course.

Norman hated the dress as much as he hated the cowboy outfit I wore on the bus to North Carolina. Aunt Cecily provided dresses from her three bulging closets when we went to Pennsylvania. I wore them with the same attitude I felt toward Mrs. Piggee's castoff clothing remodelled by Mama. This was "something for now," as Norman said about everything he never intended to repair or replace. I did intend to repair and replace but I was learning not to say so. For months, I walked slowly and made no sudden movements. Going for walks and reading the newspaper were Norman's recreational outlets. Maybe if he pointed out something he noticed as we walked... My child was going to have a father. In fact, when I wrote to my uncle in Palo Alto, I very clearly stated, " This isn't going to be my child or his child but our child." My uncle in Palo Alto must have decided it was safe to let me have my father's address. After all, I was married for almost two years. He sent me my father's address immediately and I wrote immediately, basically the same thing. It took a while to get a reply. After a couple of weeks, when Norman brought word he was going overseas, I sent another letter to Alaska. This time I said, "If you want to do something fatherly, send me a typewriter, because I want to write." I used the address of Norman's parents as my return address. We would be Pennsylvania residents. We lived in the new apartment less than three months. I was so glad to leave it.

Norman was happy to be going overseas, especially to the Mediterranean on a carrier. He rented storage facilities for our belongings and we took the bus to Pennsylvania. His parents were not happy to see me but everyone tried to make allowances. I caught his sister sticking her tongue out at me. I waited endless hours for her other brother to finish using the bathroom. Even before my stint in the Navy I never believed the bathroom was a place to read. Now, with a fetus knocking about inside me, I needed it more frequently. The hours he spent combing his hair and polishing his teeth gave me real pain. Once, I went next door to use the neighbor's bathroom because I couldn't wait any longer. They made such a joke about it. I planned to use a jar in the basement next time. There was no next time-for which I was extremely grateful.

Norman bought a camera set with a flash unit and took pictures of everyone before he left. At the train station he hugged everyone in the family. He remembered to give me a quick peck on the cheek. Everyone cried, except me. I thought this was a real opportunity for Norman. Norman was going to do something he wanted to do.

Every day I wrote a letter to Norman. It was terribly hard because nothing ever happened. His mother canned fruit and the kitchen was hot. She made fruit pies and the kitchen was hot. I helped when I could but her own system evolved years before. It worked efficiently so I watched a lot. I helped her dust twice a week. A slag concentrator from a nearby steel mill put a quarter inch of dust on the radiators. The anti-macassers, tabletops and lamps became grey with dust. Grandma ran the vacuum sweeper regularly. She cooked prunes for Grandpa and many delicious meals for everyone. Norman's sister, Lisa, was in grammar school. Norman's brother, Darren, was in the high school band. They were going to New York City for the Macy's Thanksgiving parade. We visited the soon to be great-grandmother and found her on her knees, scrubbing the kitchen floor. Another day, we found Aunt Cecily doing the same thing, everyone too busy to chat. The day my first letter, ever, from my father came I was knitting some baby booties. "Dear Kid," the note said. "Buy yourself a typewriter. Glad you're having a baby. Enjoy it. Love, Your Dad. P.S. Ran into a big moose by the store the other day."

I just sat there, in the rocking chair by the new television set. I read and reread the note scrawled on a lined yellow notebook page. I counted the bills which fell from the envelope. Then, I went to the kitchen to find Grandma. I asked her if she would go with me to buy a typewriter the next day. "A typewriter? What in the world would you want a typewriter for?" she queried. "My father just sent me some money to buy a typewriter. Would you go with me to buy it, please?" I replied. She said, "Well, I guess so. I don't have anywhere special to go tomorrow so let's go buy a typewriter." We did. I got an Underwood because my father used an Underwood in Juneau. Mama mentioned this to Mrs. Piggee when I was all ears so long ago. I got a portable because it was lightest in weight. I carried it the long way home, shifting from hand to hand, now and then. Grandma pointed out the ladies' shop where she said cashmere sweaters rotted in the windows because who could afford them? I hoped this wasn't true. I promised myself, if anything happened to the baby, I would never forgive Grandma or Norman. I was here to make things more convenient for him, not me. I carried the typewriter up to the room which normally belonged to Norman's sister. While I was there she slept on a daybed in the sewing room. No wonder she didn't like me.

A thin box of typing paper and a bottle of cleaning solvent came with my new tool. There was no clear spot to set up the typewriter. It didn't matter. What was I to write there and then? I wrote my daily letter to Norman, and an exuberant Thank You to my father, in longhand. Almost a day later my water broke-exactly when the doctor predicted it would.

North Carolina Two

Chapter 16

I read a frightening story in Grandma's *Reader's Digest* about a bus full of children. They were rescued from a snowstorm in the Midwest. Within days, Grandma told me which bus to take to Indiantown Gap Military Hospital. At the bus stop it was starting to snow. Thick snowflakes spiraled to the ground, faster and faster, beginning to pile up. This was the first snowstorm I could remember. I was afraid I would slip on the icy ground. The bus delivered me to a squat, rambling building with a wooden entry ramp. Inside, I met my doctor. I was still praying to make my way back "home" safely when the doctor came to my alcove to examine me. He told several funny jokes before he told me when I would be seeing him again. I was grateful for his sense of humor. Grandma was setting the table, usually my job, when I came back safely.

When my water broke, Grandma was up in her sewing room. Norman's sister, Lisa, and I were playing Parcheesi at the kitchen table. When she saw what was happening, Lisa ran upstairs. I thought I better not move for a while. Grandma called the next door neighbor who worked the night shift. Lisa carried my preloaded overnight bag to his car. I walked through the yard to the alley with one of Grandma's old sheets between my legs. The neighbor maneuvered me into the back seat and Grandma into the front seat beside him. He sent Lisa back to the kitchen. After he carefully cleared the blind alley, the young man at the wheel floored the gas pedal. I hung onto a strap on the side of the vehicle and was properly terrified. As we came to a stop at the hospital entrance, the young man's face broke into a smile, "Hey, we got you here! We made it!"

"You are some driver," I said with sincere admiration. Grandma said, "Let's see if you can go that fast on the way back. Grandpa will be expecting his dinner."

A nurse was at my elbow with a wheelchair. She pushed me into the hospital while Grandma and the neighbor headed for home. The baby was born after a short, relatively painless labor. I asked for anything there was to make it bearable. This was before natural childbirth with husband's help became popular. I never heard of such a thing. I assured the doctor I was an absolute coward and he proceeded accordingly. I never wanted to tell a child, "I went through Hell to bring you into the world and you are going to be somebody." Mama used exactly those words to me on several memorable occasions. I was drugged only enough so I could be helpful. I was alert enough to see the doctor hold up the newborn. I heard his first cry and, "Looks like it's a boy. What do you think it is, Mom?" Then I fell, gratefully, asleep.

When I woke up it was very dark. A noise awakened me. What was it? I was cold. My eyes became accustomed to what little light there was. I was in a metal bed, like a cot. Beside me was a heavy metal basket on wheels. In the basket was my baby, crying like a puppy, in a whimper which brought me upright. I maneuvered myself so I could sit up and lift the baby into the bed. There I laid him beside me and shared my light weight blanket. I felt weak. I closed my eyes to rest. Lights snapped on. A nurse, who must have weighed two hundred and fifty pounds, reached over the basket. With arms like telephone poles, she seized the baby, and plunked him back into the basket. "You'll overlay him. Leave him alone. You'll overlay him," she insisted. She glared at me for a moment before she turned out the light and left the room. Of course, the whimper came again, only stronger this time. This time I felt a new strength, cold fury. I put the baby back at my side even as the nurse's heavy footsteps died on their way down the hall.

When she made her rounds again, the nurse moved the baby again. We didn't speak to each other. We were at war. In the clear light of a very cold day I learned two things. The radiator in my room at this ancient military hospital was out of order—complete with ice crystals. Moreover, there was a blue shading all over the body of my brand new, totally perfect, baby. He was cold. So was I. I fought the battle of the baby basket for five days. The doctor came in each day to examine us and, apparently, was pleased. The nurse brought bottles and diapers and watched while I changed the diapers and refused the bottles. I decided to feed David myself and I never regretted the decision. Lying beside me, he could escape the creeping cold and so, in a real sense, could I.

On the third day, Grandma and Grandpa appeared, held the baby and made cooing sounds. On the fifth day, the neighbor brought Grandma. She assured me she brought extra money. She could not believe me when I told her the total cost for this baby would be $12. This was the same price as the double wedding rings Norman bought at the PX. I signed the paperwork in the hospital office while Grandma stood by. I pulled $12 in cash from my wallet and gave it to the nurse at the desk. She said, "Thank You. Enjoy your baby," and we walked out. Grandma stuffed her money back into her purse. I carried David proudly, and gratefully, into the temporary cold outdoors. David was no longer blue.

There was a bassinet in Lisa's permanent, my temporary, room, a pile of baby clothes and no extra space. The relatives came to see the new baby. While they were there, he slept in a baby carriage in the front room. The baby carriage was bought for Norman and passed down through the family as nephews or nieces arrived. It was incredibly heavy and hard to maneuver. Norman sent toys from the Mediterranean including a plastic Pluto, soft and pliable and fun. He sent rubber ducks and a pair of stiff leather baby shoes from Turkey. He sent me french perfume from the aircraft carrier's PX. I knitted and read Reader's Digest and washed baby laundry. Norman wrote his parents he was going to buy a car when he came back. In another letter he asked me to get a driver's license. He knew how to drive the APUs of his squadron but needed a way to get a driver's license. I discussed this with Grandma. Grandma never nursed a baby. She did not approve of my doing so. Norman's plans for a car gave her a perfect excuse to put David on a bottle. She began to take the baby to bed with her and Grandpa for an hour, or so, every evening. I could hear them cooing. After she brought him back to the bassinet, I could hear the louder noises of their love-making. I wondered about Lisa and her brother. Sound was magnified in the old wooden house. When Norman came back, we could hear the Grandparents and they could hear us. I thought about the families all over the world who lived in one room. I wondered how Grandma could be so insistent breast feeding was abnormal. Weren't they part of the same process?

Norman was gone for several months and, meanwhile, Grandma made several things clear. She was not going to be my baby-sitter. I neither desired nor intended to leave David alone with her for ten minutes. She was not going to store anything in her semi-empty attic. We would have to take everything involving the baby with us—which was the final excuse for a car. We would have to pull baby furniture etc. back to North Carolina on a stake-bodied trailer. This would be attached to an, as yet, nonexistent car.

So I took driving lessons. I telephoned a number in the yellow pages. A young man appeared at Grandma's door. David was sleeping in the baby carriage. Grandma was already getting her coat so I knew David was going visiting. I met and introduced Grandma and the driving instructor. There were several lessons, once each week, while David got lots of fresh air. Grandma required me to take him out in the baby carriage every day no matter what the weather was like. How I longed for the day I could decide what to do and when and how. The driving lessons went well until it was time to take the test. I drove the entire course with the instructor first, then, with the policeman. I completely forgot to use turn signals until we approached the starting point again. Of course, I failed. The policeman said, "Not to worry. For some reason this is where everyone remembers turn signals." The following week I remembered to use the turn signals. I passed the test and the instructor suggested we practice parallel parking on the way back to Grandma's house. I hit the gas too hard and backed into a telephone pole. The instructor insisted insurance would pay for the damage. He said it was nice to know me. The driver training car sped from Grandma's house while I was taking my first steps away from it. Grandpa was in the living room when I came in. I already knew it took him two tries to get his license years before. Now I gushed, "Well, Grandpa, you and I have something in common. It took me two tries to get my license but I got it!" Grandpa didn't say anything. He just frowned.

Norman came back to Pennsylvania, a little fatter and, to my consternation, no more worldly wise than ever. He sat down in the overstuffed chair near the TV and held David when Grandma handed David to him. He handed David to me when Grandma left the living room. He took me along to buy the car because I could legally drive. He got Grandma's permission to withdraw money from their joint savings account. The account was his alone while he worked in a box factory after school. His mother kept his passbook for him. At the beginning of his senior year he quit his job. He told his parents he intended to have some fun the last year of his education. Meanwhile, in a little box, he saved enough money so he could go to the Prom and other events. When he was accepted by the Marine Corps he made the savings a joint account with his mother. Now, still under age, he asked her for some of his money. Reluctantly, pointing out, "It was supposed to be for your furniture," Grandma gave him money to buy a used car.

He telephoned the salesman from whom Grandpa bought his used cars. The salesman brought a maroon Pontiac sedan to Grandma's front door. I got into the driver's seat and we went out into the rolling hills of Pennsylvania. It was a huge, heavy, hulk of steel which I pushed and pulled to maneuver. I missed a turn the salesman wanted to make. Norman made me stop the car and slide over so he could drive. Much more smoothly, to the relief of the salesman, Norman drove to the showroom. We signed the papers and became "owners." In fact, the cars Norman bought were always Norman's personal property. I drove to the driving test area where Norman immediately took, and passed, the test. He drove to a junkyard where he found a trailer he could make useful enough to carry our gear. Within the week we visited all the relatives. We even went way out into the country for chicken and corn soup with an aunt and uncle. Then David and I were in the front seat of the Pontiac heading for North Carolina.

I did about one tenth of the driving and it was not easy. We rolled up and down hills towing a trailer from which a high chair projected. David slept a lot in the fresh air from an open window. Norman hated my driving most enthusiastically. I drove only when he was exhausted. Coming down a hill near Hertford a trailer tire blew. Sparks flew on the highway as the car jerked from incoming to outgoing lanes. When we finally stopped, my knees were like jelly. I shook Norman awake. Since David slept most of the day he, and I, were awake most of the night. We found a small upstairs apartment in Hertford "For Rent, reasonable." The landlady reminded me of the retired social worker in Carmel. I felt deep gratitude for not having to pull the trailer any more. Norman had no trouble selling it at a profit. I was putting small household items in their places in our new apartment. The new landlady sent her black maid to help. The maid was sure vinegar didn't belong in the bathroom so she carried it back to the kitchen. I used it to clean and planned to clean the tub with it. The third time I couldn't find it, I sent the maid back to the landlady with thanks. I was not prejudiced. The girl was right. Vinegar does belong in the kitchen. Later, it occurred to me she probably cleaned the whole area just before I got there. I liked being my own boss.

Three Marine couples from the nearby base lived near each other in Hertford. Each man drove a car to and from the base every working day. Norman spent long parts of Saturdays and Sundays washing and waxing the Pontiac. David tanned nearby in his playpen. Otherwise, he sat in the stroller we bought in Hertford with dimes we collected for some time. We left the huge baby carriage in Pennsylvania. I did not miss it. Eventually I met the wives of the two other Marines. For a while we played cards on Saturday nights. One couple was from Pennsylvania. Norman invited them to dinner. I was glad he wanted them to come to our cheery apartment. I kept the big fan on the floor by the playpen where David stayed cool. In the kitchen, sweat poured down my face while I pressure cooked beef heart. I mashed potatoes with butter and milk. Dried corn simmered on the stove. There was Jello and watermelon in the refrigerator for dessert. Half an hour before the couple came I moved the fan to the dining area. We possessed no serving dishes. The couple came and I served dinner on four plates. The girl picked at her plate and cut things up. She ate nothing and said she just wasn't hungry. The man picked at his plate. He said they really must go home because it was so hot in our dining area. Norman walked them the few steps to the door. We had dinner with the baby. I put things away. Never again did I make a Pennsylvania Dutch dinner in North Carolina in the summer time.

The landlady commended me for "eating cold French Toast left over from breakfast as a way to save money." I didn't tell her I liked cold French Toast with jam. She baby-sat with David, for nothing, when we went out to the base to dine and dance with the other couples. She even baby sat when we went out to play cards with them. One couple was from New York. We left their house early one evening because the beer and the hot day made him uncomfortable. He was starting to repeat himself and his wife was embarrassed. The times we went to the base were best, more formal, not too close. One night the girl from Philadelphia who actually hated beef heart, considering it inedible, confessed this weakness. We spent a couple of hours chatting in the ladies' room at the base. The men we left behind were still chatting at our table when we returned. One of the girls drove David and me to get his checkup and shots at the base. According to her speedometer, she was travelling ninety miles per hour. I asked her why she drove so fast. "Oh, I don't want to get messed up in an accident, disfigured or maimed. I want to die right away," she explained. I clung to the arm rest and to David and prayed.

I went to the local dentist who filled my mouth with hardware and chatted on the telephone. Meanwhile, the novocaine wore off and my jaw ached. The great grandparents came to visit us. Great Grandpa smoked cigars and drove a Buick. He was on his way to see the new crop of Thoroughbreds in Kentucky. Mine was his wife's nickname because Norman couldn't keep his hands off her knickknacks when he was a child. She said, "Don't touch it. It's mine," so often he decided Mine, must be her name. Mine told me Great Grandpa started making annual trips to Kentucky years before. The first time he left, she looked out the window. A strange woman sat in the front seat beside him. Forever afterward, she made sure she was the woman beside him on all his trips. He went for a walk while Mine and I were chatting. When he came back he told us about a fish fry the Democrats were having. He knew how much the barber charged for a haircut and which teams were playing softball next weekend. Great Grandpa was retired. Early in our marriage, I asked Norman, "What do you want to be someday?" he said, "Retired." I said, "No, I meant what about your life? What would you like to be?"

"Retired," he said, with feeling. He meant it. Great Grandpa's life was good with "Mine" to take care of him. Did I want to be like "Mine," taking care of Norman? I didn't know the answer yet.

Norman took lots of pictures of David and the car. He drove the car to Nags Head where we played in the sand. We went to Roanoke where we watched *The Lost Colony*, In Virginia Beach we window shopped. Sometimes we bought hot corn on the cob and souvenirs. Norman took pictures of me holding David in a standing position on a pedestal at the Wright Memorial. Kitty Hawk winds were strong enough so David would have been blown from his feet unless I held him. In Norman's wallet he carried a picture of me before David was born. He said, "One of the guys on the ship said you looked like Gene Tierney." I frequently wore one of the hats I made from rug yarn with a pattern idea from a neighbor. She came to talk to me while I aired the clothes from the closet on clotheslines. I remembered Mama did this in the years when she was such a good housewife and mother. The winds at Kittyhawk were much stronger, strong enough to have really aired the closet's stuffiness from the clothes. I only tried this method once. I made yarn purses, too, when I wasn't knitting for David. We often parked in a nearby field, with several other cars, to watch a movie.

Southern California

Chapter 17

One evening we took David, in his stroller, to watch a softball game. On our way back, Norman said, "It's time to reenlist or get out. What do you think?" I knew the other two couples decided not to reenlist and were already packing. "It's your decision, Norman. You have to decide," I insisted. I intended to be a twenty year WAVE. He said he wanted to be a twenty year Marine. I expected him to stay. It was a good life for him, working on or around airplanes all day, everyday. He became a crew chief in his squadron. When he tried for Officer Candidate School he was turned down. At the time, he said, "It was because I married so young." I sewed the stripes of a Staff Sergeant on his shirts. I still ironed his uniforms, sweating puddles from my elbows onto the floor. I listened to the feats of Alvin Dark and Roberto Clemente as described by Red Barber on the radio. I listened to the political campaigns, too. I ceased to be a Democrat when party big wigs refused to allow Estes Kefauver to withdraw his candidacy. I was ironing at the time and so angry I almost burned the collar of Norman's shirt.

Another week there was another home game to watch from the bleachers. The sun poured blessings on our little family. There was another, "Should I stay in or get out?" Again I said, "It's your decision, Norman. I can't decide for you." Finally, he told me he decided not to reenlist. I told him I thought it was the right thing to do. In my heart, I hoped it was. We said our good-byes to the other two couples as each left. Norman bought another trailer to carry our worldly goods to Pennsylvania. Again, I drove about one tenth of the way. Grandma was not glad to see us. She didn't pretend she was. She knew about an apartment we could rent and a possible job at a foundry. We slept at her house one night because it was so late. Norman rested in the overstuffed chair and made appointments by telephone. He did take the foundry job but the apartment came from a want ad. I kept David out of Grandma's knickknacks and washed the clothes from our trip and peeled vegetables for dinner.

Norman came back with a job, saying his military service gave him a kind of priority. He could start at a "decent salary" at once. The apartment would be, "all right for now." At nightfall, he drove the car and trailer into a grimy neighborhood near the railroad tracks. Our new home originated as a warehouse for the foundry. I didn't see how forbidding it was until we were moving in. The only entry was on the second floor atop a flight of wooden stairs. The pole railing terrified me when it moved while I was clinging to it. Inside was a closet-like area for boots and coats etc.. Another thin door away from the winds sweeping across the tracks, was a kitchen sink against a wall. One enormous room was empty except for an aluminum dining set, a wooden dish cupboard, and two sagging overstuffed chairs. The second room contained a bed and dresser. Everything was scarred and worn and extremely dirty. The shower was in an enclosure near the entry, a door away from the sink. The kitchen sink was where teeth were brushed and dishes washed and David got his bath. The windows were frosted, painted shut so the viewless view was unavailable. I thought being able to see the railroad tracks, even, would have been an improvement. Our worldly goods looked almost lost in those big, dismal rooms.

Grandma and Grandpa came to see us just once, to bring something inadvertently left at their house. Grandma said, "It's very nice. I'm sure you'll be happy here." They left the cold apartment in less than five minutes. The worst thing of all was—Norman promptly formed the habit of stopping at Grandma's house on his way home. He cleaned the foundry dirt from his skin in her bathtub. Of course, he stayed to chat for a while. The dinners I made got cold while I wondered if a piece of steel flattened him at the foundry. I was cold in New Bern. Now, I was cold with a baby to keep warm. Grandma must have spread the word. Nobody came to visit us.

I tried to write. I got out my typewriter and wrote short poems for the *Daily News* and they were published. I used my maiden name and, of course, none of the family noticed anything unusual. Although each household paid for daily newspaper delivery, who read more than the headlines and the want ads? Now and then, someone must have read the sports page. Long before this, I promised myself I would never get a divorce. I kept reminding myself of the promise. Norman got into the habit of dropping in to see Grandma even on weekends. He stayed a few hours whenever he went to get gas for the car on Saturdays. It was hard to carry buckets of water down those external stairs to wash the car on Sundays. Norman managed to do so. He kept the car shiny until the winter really closed down. From Chief Pontiac on the hood to the shiny rear bumper the car must have known it was loved.

One Sunday, Norman looked up from the Funnies and said, "Let's go to California." I almost cried. We packed and departed as quickly as we could. Norman read an ad about an Aviation School in Los Angeles so we went there as soon as we pulled into the area. Norman learned he was not qualified to enter the school. However, his military service instantly got him a job at an aircraft factory. I was tanned and strong from two weeks of holding diapers outside the car window to dry. Every night I washed them in our apartment sized washer. I did more than one tenth of the driving and felt more confident as the miles increased. We had a flat tire, on the Pontiac near Denver, and, on the trailer near Tahoe. We stopped in Sacramento to see Venus—without warning, of course. How could I know where we would be and when? She was not delighted to see me. After a short conference with her husband in their garage, she asked if we could come back later. It seemed they were about to have dinner. I said, "Oh, we just stopped in on our way. It was good to see you." She blushed and we departed. I was getting used to people not wanting to admit they knew me. The next stop would be Rider's Run.

I was literally sitting on the edge of my seat in the car. Years before, I decided a pack of cigarettes per day was my limit. When David was born I stopped smoking until one of the uncles brought cigarettes as Christmas gifts. This evening I was chain-smoking. The one thing I knew about Mama, for sure, was her capacity for doing or saying the unexpected. Expecting Norman to follow, I practically ran from the car into the kitchen. Mama was there. She held the baby and smiled at him while I laid out things to change his diaper. My room was now the boys' room with a set of bunk beds near the shower enclosure. Mama cooed over David while I made the bottom bunk. While I changed the diaper she went outside. I made the top bunk—pulling grimy sheets and blankets into shape. The boys watched me. I asked them where Pansy was. Each said, "I don't know." This was incomprehensible till I realized Mama told them what to say. Followed by the boys, I took David and the diaper bag back to the car.

On our way we passed an organdy dress on the dining room table. It was still in various stages of construction. I noticed a baby grand piano in another corner of the same room. Norman was still sitting in the driver's seat chatting with Mama. I said, "Where is Pansy?" Mama broke into tears, "Oh, she ran away with a soldier and got married. I wanted her to finish high school. I called her boy friend's mother. He was such a nice boyfriend. I made her a wedding dress. You come and see it."

"Who plays the piano?" I asked.

"Pansy does. She left that, too. The boys play your violin. Come in and see the dress I made for Pansy's wedding," Mama insisted. Suddenly strong, because somehow the jelly in my knees melted, I said, "Can't, Mama. Tell me where Pansy lives now. I want to see her." Mama's face became crafty and I shuddered. "Oh, no, can't tell you. It's too far. You couldn't find it. I'll tell her you were here."

"O.K., Mama," I said. I got into the car beside Norman and waved at the little family. Norman's face was red. He started the car. As we pulled away, he said, "How could you treat that nice lady like that? She told me you were a slut and it looks like she was right." My head was spinning. I thought of explaining, "She's just a bit angry because I wrote to her after David was born. I told her I didn't go through Hell to have him and he didn't have to be some one if he didn't want to." I didn't say anything. I didn't even smoke. My mouth tasted awful. I thought, "I should have had a drink of water at Rider's Run. Poor Pansy was only sixteen years old when she ran away from Mama! God help her and the boys, those poor boys!"

We made two more stops on the way to Los Angeles. This time we were close enough to telephone Andrea in San Francisco. We were close enough to arrange to meet her at the ladies' hotel where she now lived. We found a motel, unhitched the trailer and got cleaned up. We met her roommate in the lobby. Andrea hung a coat, of the same fabric as mine, over her shoulders. "We still have good taste," she remarked. She took us to a nightclub, with tables as close together as those in Greenwich Village. We listened to a jazz band. I took the opportunity to thank Andrea personally for the silver brush and comb set she sent to David. We ate and drank and talked. It was so good to see her again! Then, she took a taxi home and we drove back to the motel. I was still sober enough to pray the Pontiac over every hill. I knew those brakes were getting worn.

We went to Carmel to see Aunt Ellen and I did not call ahead. Norman parked in front of her house and I ran up the chalk steps to the porch. I looked in the lantern for the key and it was there! So I rang the doorbell and Ellen came to the door, wiping her hands on her apron. She hugged me! Just one big hug can make such an enormous difference in a person's life! She hugged me and held me at arm's length and this time Norman didn't sit out in the car. He came to join us, carrying David. We stayed for roast beef and fresh peas and angelic mashed potatoes and chocolate cake. Ellen told us who moved away and who died. George and Cap were out, Cap at the Smoke Shop, George working at a gas station. After a good chat, I changed David's diapers and we drove away refreshed. I did not compare Mama and Ellen for Norman and I was glad he didn't either. We headed for Los Angeles with high hopes for the future.

Then we learned Norman would have to take some high school classes before he could begin to become an engineer. For two weeks we stayed in a shadeless motel with inadequate and very expensive laundry facilities. Norman found his aircraft factory job and I found a day care center. I got a job of my own in the Bank of America. My first day at work, the manager informed me he owned an apartment we could rent. Norman and I went to look at it after work. It was the bottom floor of a two story adobe, small but shaded by a big tree. It was cheap enough so we could afford it. The day care center was in a lady's home and it looked clean, though bare. At the bank I would run a bookkeeping machine again. Two dollars would be extracted from my pay envelope, every payday, for social activities. I didn't appreciate the deduction because I didn't expect to be socializing and we were very short of money. During the weekend we moved from the motel.

Then, my own private Hell began. The adobe floor got wet from beneath and became slimy on top when it rained. The night was filled with cockroaches which swarmed over David and woke him up. When I got out of bed to care for him, they crunched underfoot. By day, they were invisible. I put insect repellents everywhere. It was so damp I found it hard to breathe, then almost impossible to breathe. It became impossible to sleep because the cockroaches kept David awake. Norman heard David crying and me trying to breathe. Once or twice, he reminded me he had to go to work in the morning.

We tried various escapes, like Drive-In Movies. The small Drive-In Movies we occasionally attended in Hertford would have been lost here. In Los Angeles, one could drive for miles in any direction to buy a loaf of bread. After driving another few miles, one could get in line for a movie. Once there, the one going to buy popcorn would need a good memory to find his way back to the car. In Los Angeles he belonged to the car -lock, stock, and barrel. Norman washed and polished his car on weekends. I cleaned house as much as possible, scrubbed green mold from walls, tried to exterminate vermin. I cooked and baked and did the washing in our portable electric washer. We washed the larger items at the laundromat, a half hour drive from home.

At work, I met a girl who appeared on Queen For a Day. She spent most of a year vainly waiting for her prizes to arrive. Another girl used the adding machine at her desk. She determined how long it would take to pay for a home smaller than the one we lived in. It was almost as baldly nondescript as ours in a neighborhood where all the houses looked exactly alike. I sent a postcard to Mama to let her know we arrived. I still wanted to hear from Pansy. She wrote back she was coming to visit us. Just what I needed! I was washing a Pyrex cake pan, drying it and putting it back in the oven to dry completely. Norman came home through the mud. He didn't look happy as he changed rain-wet work clothes. I chased a bug out of David's play pen. The play pen kept him above the greasy, wet, uncleanable floor. I slept very little, thankful it was Saturday.

Norman went out to wash the car early Sunday morning. A moment later he came back in-sputtering. I went out to see why. At first, I didn't see anything on the street where Norman always parked his car. Then, I thought, "What happened to the car? Where is it?" I walked gingerly through the muck covering the yard. I found the car. I could have stepped onto the roof. It was parked unwittingly, for weeks, right over a sink hole. Overnight, the hole, and the car, sank! I thought it was hilarious! The first real belly laugh I had for years!

In those days Norman never got excited or furious or what one could call emotional. He wasn't emotional now, just kind of surprised. He called a tow truck which lifted the car to the pavement. He parked it farther down the block. The tow truck company must have notified the city because the hole where Norman's Pontiac sank was promptly filled. Meanwhile, Norman decided to go back to Pennsylvania to try to get into Penn State. He thought it might be tuition free since he was a native Pennsylvanian. He heard Cal Berkeley supplied free tuition for native Californians. He assumed his home state did the same. I gave my two weeks notice at the bank the next day. The manager said I was a trouble-free tenant and he would miss me. I knew I would not miss him. We suddenly realized we never saw Los Angeles. We went to Olvera Street to browse the Mexican shops and to the train station to admire the architecture. We drove past the home of Milky Way, around Grauman's Chinese Theater and the Hollywood Bowl. We drove on Santa Monica Boulevard, to Malibu, miles along Sepulveda Boulevard. Norman brought the trailer, still with most of its original contents, from behind the house. On the morning we left Los Angeles I forgot two Pyrex cake plates getting dry in the oven.

Flowers For The Table

Chapter 18

Every payday of his working life Norman bought a savings bond. It was just something he did. I kept my last paycheck instead of giving it to Norman "for the house." With this money I bought cigarettes. In Arizona, I bought Navajo earrings and a small wool rug for beside David's crib. I purchased various other earrings in Texas and Louisiana. Outside El Paso I ordered real Texas tamales which came from a bag in the freezer with a famous label. So much for the "homemade tamales" on the sign outside. In Shreveport, the oysters came from a large can from a commercial cannery. So much for "local seafood delicacies." I remembered the oysters, clams, and fish slices on a seafood platter in Morehead City, North Carolina. They were worth the long drive from Hertford! I did a little more than one-tenth of the driving this time for two reasons. Norman was more comfortable with David (who was bigger) and, we took the southern route with fewer mountains. We stopped in Columbus, Georgia, to visit my father's sister.

My Palo Alto uncle decided it was safe for us to communicate when he gave me my father's address. She wrote spicy, entertaining letters which made me giggle. I loved her from the first paragraph of her first letter. Now Aunt Martina wore a brace to support what remained of her chest after cancer surgery. The note she sent with David's christening dress mentioned neither cancer nor surgery. Nor did the letters she sent later. What she said was, "One day I just couldn't get up in the morning so they put me in the hospital. Now, I'm out again raising hell with the grandchildren." Her son and his friend were playing ragtime on the piano and drums when I rang the doorbell. She flung open the door and held out welcoming hands. "Sorry it took so long to answer. We've just been burying a chicken-family pet, you know." Norman looked shocked. We were there in her small, cozy, living room less than half an hour. Norman insisted he wanted to leave the city while it was still daylight. I just sat and listened to Martina and her son at the piano and her son's friend at the drums. Her face was grey. I longed to stay there absorbing courage and street wisdom and great love. The words they occasionally interspersed with the notes were casual but full of gentle meaning. It was soul music before soul music was a category. Norman was bored. I felt like I was trespassing on some of their last moments together and like they didn't mind my being there. My Aunt Martina provided a home for her mother until she died, She provided a home for her husband until he ran away with another woman. She provided a home for two sons through college and a daughter through high school. Now, for a few weeks, there was time just to do something she loved to do. Until recently she played the piano very well. Now she listened. It was definitely not fair but she was making her exit a triumph. I learned later, she died that same week. I was so grateful to have met her.

Once again, we pulled up in front of Grandma's house in the Pontiac, pulling a trailer. When Grandma opened the front door, she said, "Now, I'll never be able to go to California. Why did you come back?" I said, "Norman decided to go back to school." Norman finished getting out of the car. Grandma hugged him and cried. I took David into the kitchen. "So, son, why did you come back?" Grandma queried as they joined us. "Oh, she got sick," he said. I was amazed. Then, I thought, "From his point of view, he's telling it like it is. I better remember this."

Norman unhitched the trailer in the back alley. We went to Philadelphia the next day to find out about Standard Evening High School. The College Preparatory Course Norman ignored in high school was available at night. All the math, physics, chemistry, biology, and English literature classes were available after work. He enrolled there and we went to look for an apartment. Norman sat in the car while I inspected three apartments from the *Philadelphia Inquirer* For Rent columns. The first two were both too small and too expensive. The third one looked too small to me. Then, through the car window, Norman started talking to the landlord on the sidewalk. I was explaining to the landlady that we didn't have our own basic furniture. The landlord and Norman came up to join us. Norman made the deal and paid the first month's rent. One of the landlady's tenants was moving out. He needed to sell a day bed. Norman bought it, drove back to Grandma's house and arrived just in time for dinner. He asked me not to tell his family he planned to attend night school so I didn't. We moved to Philadelphia the very next day. We would live three blocks from Temple University for four years. For two years Norman went to Standard Evening High School. For two years he attended a branch of Penn State. By day, he worked as an inspector for a company which manufactured fork lift trucks.

Norman bought furniture from Sears Roebuck on the installment plan. I chose a white-painted bedroom set which I really liked. Norman chose an aluminum tubing dinette set which shouted "cheap" but at least it wasn't "used." The stove and refrigerator came with the apartment. I used the portable washer for David's clothing and we took heavy items to the laundromat. Again, Norman sold the trailer after we unloaded it. There was very little closet space so I kept my footlocker, as Norman kept his. There was no storage room for my WAVE shoes. Sadly, I put these solid black walking shoes out by the curb. I changed my mind. Those shoes were comfortable. I noticed, when I carried out an armful of grey striped uniforms, the shoes were gone. The uniforms were removed just as rapidly. Norman parked in front of a small grocery store down the block. The next morning his battery was dead. The store lights were never turned off. He deadened three batteries the same way over the years.

In the want ads were lists of baby-sitters. I located one two blocks away. She agreed to keep David five days per week with three other children. On the second day, she told Norman David was too much for her. However, she knew a lady, with no other children to care for, who would probably care for him. And so it was Norman who found David's baby-sitter. He spent part of each afternoon chatting with her and her husband before bringing David home. Norman left for work every morning before I awakened David. I got David up and ready to go out into the world. He hated to leave the apartment. The sitter gave him a pegboard table, with colored pegs for Christmas. Each morning David grabbed a handful of pegs to take with him, clutching them in one small hand. We rushed along the lovely shaded neighborhood street, one of David's hands in one of mine. David's other hand carried green, red and blue wooden pegs—every morning of the week. The pegs were in his pockets when he came home.

Rushing to the subway, I felt guilty for not being at home with my child. Grandma didn't go out in the world. She took in laundry and did housecleaning for one regular customer while the children were in school. She was always there for them. I felt like I was robbing David. Norman did nothing, said nothing, to make me feel better. One day, Norman stopped to pick up his car from the repair shop after work. By prearrangement, I went to get David. The sitter's home was quiet and orderly. Over a cup of tea, she told me how much she appreciated each day with David. What a joy his constant questions were, what fun his discoveries in her house and garden! I realized this lady was a much better mother than I could ever be. Gratefully, I stopped hating myself for short changing David.

I sent my usual Christmas cards to all the relatives. A card came from Mama's youngest son. He was going to school in Sweden while living with Mama's distant relatives. He looked happy in the enclosed snapshot. Mama wrote her other son was living and working on a ranch. Pansy was divorced and remarried with children. Cap kicked Mama out of Ellen's house again and Mama was thinking of going back to Sweden. My father sent me some cash inside his card. My Palo Alto uncle was second mate on a freighter. Whenever his ship docked at Chester, he came to visit us. Invariably, he telephoned. Norman drove down to the port to bring him back for dinner. I sent pipes and tobacco packets to my father and pictures of David, of course. David's pictures went to my Palo Alto uncle also. He gave me a kimono from Nagasaki and a wicker picnic set from the Philippines. He said, "You seem to be a competent mother. It looks like you're doing a good job." This was right after David upchucked all over the back seat. His apparent ability to understand David was rarely ill impressed me. They got along together—my uncle and my son.

Lisa and her brother came in his used roadster to share a Sunday dinner. Lisa inhaled too much exhaust from a faulty tailpipe, so she slept on our bed after dinner. Her head was still aching when they headed home. When Norman's parents and Lisa came, in their car, our visit wasn't much longer. We tried so hard to do everything the way his mother did. In an awkward hurry, Norman forgot to screw the top on the saltshaker securely. Norman and I stuffed a turkey for Thanksgiving. The turkey was not quite done when we served it. Grandma started to cut her slice and remarked, "Oh, God! This is raw!" She grabbed a salt shaker. As the first grains fell onto her plate, the rest of the salt followed. After we roasted the turkey another hour, it tasted very good. This followed our dinner of dried corn, mashed potatoes, cranberry sauce and pie. The ice cream was also good. So were the leftovers. Almost effortlessly, Norman acquired a perfect excuse to go home for the holidays, all the holidays.

Norman's Marine Corps experience always got him an instant job. I walked into a bank in Los Angeles and found a job and an apartment. Now, in Philadelphia, I wasn't sure I wanted to work in another bank. I looked in the want ads, found the names of two large banks, and headed for the subway. I got off at Greengarden Street and walked along North Broad Street. It was fall and the trees were lovely. I stopped in front of a very interesting building with a new car showroom on the first floor. Unfamiliar looking cars were scattered about. There was a bank nearby but I didn't go nearby. I went into the showroom. A friendly looking man sat at a desk near the door. I inquired if there might be a job in this building. He looked me over carefully and smiled, "for you, anything." He took my hand in his and led me upstairs to a kind of loft. He knocked on a door and we waited for it to open. He said, "This young lady is looking for a job and you're looking for a title clerk. I was just thinking, maybe you don't have to look any more." Then, he bowed himself out backward. My new boss and I laughed. He handed me an application and pointed out a desk and chair. I filled in the application. He read it quickly and carried it with him to the bookkeeper. He introduced me to the staff. He told me to be there at 9 A.M. weekdays, starting Monday. I could expect to work till 5 P.M. with half an hour for lunch. The bookkeeper pointed out where he stored the lunches he brought to work. I worked for my new boss for four years. Near the end, there were two months when we thought we didn't need each other. I worked for a Ford dealer where I found more toil and less independence. I returned to my job and even more independence plus a raise I never told Norman about. Why should I? Norman was quietly getting rich on savings bonds.

Being an automobile title clerk was fun. Running the Post Branch Exchange telephone system was fun. I enjoyed handling conference calls with people in London and nearby New Jersey. I gathered statistics from reports for the senior partner and typed letters for the junior partner. I did the paperwork for as many as twelve deals in one day when times were good. I handled as few as three deals when times were not good. When times were bad I worked part-time for a relative who ran a magazine about beer. I did invoices, warranty applications, license and title applications, and leases. I bought clothes, which I really enjoyed wearing, from Macy's and Gimbel's. I wore high heels made of suede and alligator, hats and gloves and my white fuzzy coat dyed brown. I undertook dental work and bought myself glasses. We acquired dishes I enjoyed using. I conquered the turkey with stuffing etc. with a new cookbook. I sang David to sleep, very quietly, every night while Norman studied at the kitchen table. There was no social or intellectual life but we felt we were working for something. I was very careful not to have another baby.

The evenings were almost all alike. I rushed home, made dinner, did the dishes and the laundry, bathed David and softly sang him to sleep. Norman picked up David after work, studied, ate dinner, studied, read the paper and went to bed. In the subway entrance near Temple University, there was a small shop. Every Friday, I bought a bouquet of cut flowers for the table from the same friendly clerk. One Friday, I also bought an Agatha Christie book. When I came home I knew we would have leftovers, requiring little time to heat and serve. I sat down at the table with the book. I was five pages from the end when Norman came home. When he left the factory, his car would not start. He arranged to have it towed to a repair shop and repaired. From the repair shop he called the sitter. We had no telephone and he decided not to bother the landlady with a message for me. He enjoyed his usual chat with the sitter and her husband when he picked up David. It was quite late and dinner was not on the table. Norman didn't explain anything. He just glowered. I got up, set the book on top of the refrigerator, and got dinner ready. Wordlessly, we ate dinner and went about the evening's activities. Before I slipped into bed I finished the book. Norman was already asleep. We never discussed this aberration. It never happened again. I was even more grateful for my job, at which I could be me, most of the time.

One morning, the young man whose key let me in, the car buffer, wasn't there when I arrived. I walked into a coffee shop in our building and sat down at the counter. A young waitress came up. I said, "A black coffee, please." She snapped, "Why don't you wise up?" I took the cup, with a grateful smile, when she brought it and drank it all. This was despite the unusual blackness as of the bottom of the pot at the end of the day. I carried my cup and the bill, with the requisite coins, to where she was waiting at the cash register.

She said, "I know you. You work next door. When are you going to wise up?"

"I have no idea," I replied as I headed for work. A few minutes later, I told the salesman about this encounter. He said she was probably on drugs. We never met again.

Weekends in Philadelphia were fun—probably because we spent many of them in New Jersey. When we first got our apartment I wrote to my WAVE bunkmate, who came from New Jersey. I told her ours was a home away from home whenever she wanted it. Probably the address she wrote in my Blue Jackets Manual was no longer valid. She never replied. I wrote to Mama to tell her we were back in Pennsylvania. I also invited her oldest son to come to stay with us and go to school. I thought I should try to rescue him. There was no reply. Before winter we strolled the major streets and admired the wooden pipes on the sidewalk. These carried the city's water supply when Benjamin Franklin walked there, and were now being replaced. We passed the same Fire Sale signs on the same buildings week after week. We went to see Van Gogh originals at the art museum. Some winter weekends even going into the city proper was an adventure.

In the spring and summer we got into line, and stayed in line, for half a Saturday. Going to Tom's River or Atlantic City or Beach Haven one solid line of cars stretched countless miles. We took a boat between Beach Haven and Atlantic City and back, several times. We walked the boardwalk and bought hot corn on the cob. We saw the diving horse building. We swam at an Exclusive Club. This meant we bought a family membership for a nominal fee which entitled us to use a large pool. We swam there twice. Norman couldn't swim but he kept his eye on David while I swam. One summer, when we were visiting Grandma, the grandparents went swimming with us at a nearby public park. Norman was supposed to be watching David. I was across the pool when I looked toward Grandpa. He sat on the edge of the pool, with his legs in the water, chatting with Norman. While I watched, David slipped his fingers from the pool edge where he was hanging. Very quietly and efficiently, Grandpa saved David's life. As he began to sink through the water, Grandpa reached down. Casually, he pulled David up to the surface, then onto the pool deck. I blessed him from the bottom of my heart, very quietly and very sincerely. Norman never knew it happened.

I found the address of one couple we knew in Hertford, telephoned and accepted a dinner invitation. We parked in front of a two story brick dwelling in a sea of identical two story brick dwellings. The interior looked like it came straight from the Sears catalog. There were silver serving dishes and delicately patterned plates in a china cabinet and, later, on the table. These people left the Marine Corps just before Norman did. All the furniture matched and everything was new. Their child played with a plastic cow, among many other things. Looking for something to say, I asked where the cow came from and received specific directions to a specialty store. When the couple came to our house for dinner, David possessed his own plastic cow. It was years before I saved enough Green Stamps for the silver serving dishes. My silver flatware came from Grandma's hand soap coupons before David was born. I didn't like her cooking. Whatever it was lacked flavor—too bland. She didn't like my cooking either but, this time, I used serving bowls. She could select the quantity of her choice. How do you explain you don't buy a lot of dishes when you don't have space for them? Where do you get the spare money for a breakfront or a china cabinet? I didn't try. We never met again. When Norman noticed I was not sending the couple Christmas cards, he did-every year.

At last Norman finished Standard Evening High School. He took summer courses and then more and more classes at Ogontz. He formed the habit of watching basketball games at Villanova while David and I listened to the radio. One weekend he went to State College. While he was gone David tried to stand up on the seat of his tricycle. Losing his balance, he cut his forehead on the radiator on his way down to the floor. Blood was everywhere. I grabbed him and carried him to the street in front of the house. I stopped a slowly moving car. The Temple University Hospital was two blocks away. I held David in my arms while the driver took us there. Closing the car door behind us, I wholeheartedly thanked the good samaritans. The only time they ever laid eyes on us, they gave us a helping hand. I pushed our way into the Emergency Room. We sat there for hours. Exhausted looking nurses and doctors came and went. A knife victim lay on a stretcher. He knocked the tubes from his side with one thrashing swoop of the free arm, I called out, "Nurse!" A nurse came from behind a desk and reattached the tubes in the bloody body. I said, "My son hit his head. It's bleeding." She said, "Wait your turn." I couldn't see anyone having a turn.

Finally, a young intern came up to me, looked at David, and said, "Your first child? How can I tell?" I didn't answer. He set David on a nearby table and gave him a shot. Quickly, he stapled stitches in a gauze-swabbed arc. Then, he handed my screaming child back to me. It was very fast, very efficient, but it took so long to get started. I carried David home to bed. I was still up when Norman came home. He told me his rich uncle and aunt were financing a mobile home. We would live there for the next two years, or so, while he attended Penn State. He intended to pay these relatives on the installment plan. I should give my boss two week's notice. "David was in the hospital at Temple tonight," I started to say. "Oh, fine," said Norman as he headed for the shower.

One Bottle of Pills

Chapter 19

Foreign Car Distributors imported foreign cars for sale to other dealers and to our own customers. Some people picked them up overseas at the start of a European vacation. When we got a Studebaker franchise the Jaguars and Sunbeams and Anglias were moved to the shop for a while. Andrea wrote me she bought a Hillman, drove it for a few weeks and enjoyed it. She lost about $400 when she returned it because she decided she couldn't afford it. I was glad she tried to own a foreign car. We kept a picture of a Kharman Ghia in a desk drawer to be brought out and shown to special customers. When the Studebakers failed to sell no matter how carefully they were buffed, the Porsches and Hillmans reappeared. The senior partner wasn't happy but I think my boss was relieved. Several more foreign cars fit in the show room when the American monsters went back to the factory. Thanks to a thriving shop full of Lithuanian mechanics, loosely supervised by a Brazilian Muslim, our customers came back. Most of them never left us.

I loved my job. We were like family, including the black man who came regularly to adjust the odometers. This applied to the few trade ins we didn't wholesale to dealers. Regularly, dealers came up from southern military bases to buy "dogs" for sale cheap to people like Norman. Norman did not realize how fortunate he was to know his father's dealer. We were like family, including another black man who came regularly to regroove tires to match odometers. We were like family, including the little black girl whose father converted one of our "dogs" into a working car. He agreed to weekly payments. Every week, at exactly the same time, she ran upstairs to put some bills in the bookkeeper's hands. We were like family, including the two men I saw only when they came to sign something for the bookkeeper. For years, they manned the paint booth behind the shop. We were like family, including the man who moved and buffed the cars and delivered them almost anywhere. He wore a chauffeur's uniform when the cars were being photographed or on TV. The bookkeeper and I were allies. We kept the sales manager, and the one or two salesmen who worked the floor, relatively honest. The sales manager formed the habit of not including the invoice in the package he handed the customer. I used the list price and the true discount and, frequently, his worksheet didn't. He endured me because I did a complete paperwork package on time. I would not forge a customer's name, no matter where the customer forgot to sign it. Theoretically, the salesman would have to call the customer to get a valid legal signature. Actually, the salesman would take the offending papers and bring them back later, mysteriously signed.

The bookkeeper gave most of us cash on payday when we endorsed our checks. He carried the bank deposits and insisted it was no trouble to do our banking for us. He was such a calm, kind, genial person. I thought he was saving himself the trouble of wrinkled or mangled checks from someone's pocket. When I left he gave me an electric alarm clock. The resident mouse raced across the office. In any crisis, such as this, the bookkeeper remarked, "In the excitement the conductor rang up the right amount of fare." On the subway, we used coins in slots on posts to get from here to there. Was fare handled differently on a Philadelphia bus? I never knew. He was telling a joke to the parts manager. It was a joke I heard many times before. Thoughtlessly, I started to add more information. He stopped cold, looking stricken. I felt remorseful for the rest of my last day. He was a true friend and I hurt him! So much for rewarding the years of banking he did for me and for the new clock. So much for the telephone calls he made to keep in touch when I worked for the Ford dealer. So much for his jokes which I memorized and relayed to anyone who would listen—for years.

Norman drove to Grandma's house with our bedroom set in a rented trailer behind the Pontiac. It was going to replace Lisa's bedroom set. When he came back, Norman sold the dining set and day bed with a want ad. He packed what was left of our gear in another rented trailer. He patiently waited for me to give the apartment a last look and bring David. Our landlady and her husband sold the house. They were moving next weekend. The bookkeeper told me he would be leaving for another job in a week. The senior partner was retiring. The junior partner was looking for greener pastures in New Jersey. He expected to make more money, at less risk, working for someone else. It looked like we were a linchpin holding things together. Even the forklift factory where Norman worked was being sold. Actually, the economy was in another cycle. We weren't holding anything together except our marriage. Norman didn't like my new electric clock.

We stopped at Grandma's house and visited several relatives before we pulled into State College. Norman moved our belongings into a pink trailer one space under the trailer parallel to the highway. Behind us were a fence in poor condition and a dilapidated barn. Field Daisies and Yarrow, Queen Anne's Lace and Fleabane thrived between the fence and the barn. In season, there were always plenty of flowers for the table after the insects were brushed away. Another trailer was parked beside ours, then, two with their sides facing us. Three seemed to climb up the hill across from our hill. In the center was a wash-house with coin operated washers and dryers. Across the highway was the main mobile home park of which ours was a branch. Norman got an instant part time job with the park management. His first assignment was to help set up our trailer and those near it. Well before his classes began he became very helpful to the management. He spent spare time chatting with the manager whose hobby was hunting the abounding deer in the area. State College was famous for hunting and fishing.

Norman drove me into State College while we were still incompletely moved into our new abode. We wanted to take advantage of an arrival time earlier than most new students. I went from automobile dealer to automobile dealer. There were several but no one needed a title clerk or switchboard operator. I filled out an application at the University. I was assured there really were no openings but they would call me when one developed. Norman drove me all the way to Bellefonte to the State Unemployment Office. A very nice young man assured me there were no jobs. He suggested I should, "forget Unemployment because the State is out of money for Unemployment." Norman drove me back to the trailer. He said, "Thank God for the G.I. Bill," and left me to move things into their respective places. I remembered a friend of a friend who drove across country solo. She said the worst thing was being, "alone in the desert at night." I remembered the time near Indio, California when a wheel left the trailer we were towing. It rushed into the desert. The last time I saw it, it was heading for infinity. This is how I felt just then. Except for the scenery, I felt very much alone in the desert. It was even quiet—very quiet.

We were several miles from a shopping district. The small store near the park charged astronomical prices. A young Naval officer lived in the trailer below ours for two days. His wife appeared and his housing was upgraded. He sold out to a student whose wife already worked in town. We only glimpsed each other from time to time. In the trailer above us, next to the highway, there was a lot of activity. Twin brothers were moving into the area. We got the one with the wife from Germany. The other side of the street got the one with the wife from Canada. Both hunted and fished, studied engineering on the G.I. Bill, and spent a lot of time together. Frequently they drove to the part of the state where they originated because the hunting was better there, or the fishing. Each brought a young child.

I was trying to break the clods on the ground beside us. No provision was made for lawns. I felt closed in when we were inside the trailer. Our apartment was small but there was room to move about. Here it was like a cabin cruiser—the one my cousin showed me long ago. One could touch the table with one hand and the stove with the other hand at the same time. There was no need to stretch to do so. It was pink outside, fake blonde wood inside. A three-quarter size couch crossed the front end. Then, at a right angle, came a window, a set of grillwork shelves, the stove with overhanging cupboards. At the other right angle from the couch the side door came between a chair and the dining table. Another side door was between a closet and a bunkbed crossing the rear end. From this, at a right angle, a bathroom with a shower, toilet and sink was squeezed. Then came the bed with cupboards above and below it on the side away from the doors. A propane tank was attached to the front below the living room windows. A license plate was attached to the rear where there were no windows. Above the dining table was another window.

It was brand new and incredibly cheap in construction and appearance. Although I would never admit it, even to myself, I hated every inch of it. I did not hate it because it was pink like Mama's house in Rider's Run. I did not hate it because of the ugly aluminum and plastic dinette set, the sleazy pink couch and chair. I did not hate it because everything we brought with us did not fit. It did. Only I did not and it was only fall. In the winter, there would be mud, snow, dull grey skies and nothing to look at but trailers.

We owned _The Outline of History_ by H. G. Wells. I remembered this author cited famous books as sources for historical material. Norman went to check out the library. He left David and me at home but I sent a list of books with him. A year or so before, I began reading children's books, from the grocery store, to David in the evenings. Norman brought books for David along with the books I listed for me. While I was digesting *Plutarch's Lives* by day, David was mulling over *The Velveteen Rabbit*. He kept wanting to hear a score of favorites from the library over and over again. These were in addition to the piles of Golden Books and Doctor Suess he already knew. We got Field Guides to identify the wildflowers proliferating behind the park. In another Field Guide, we looked up Goldfinches and Robins when they appeared. Sometimes, Norman took us to a movie on the lawn outside one of the ivy-covered halls. I loved the Stuart Frost watercolors in the Hub where we got a rare milkshake.

I did not love the way Norman saved money. He trimmed David's hair to a G. I. cut with antique clippers. David would begin to scream when he saw the clippers and continue to scream throughout the entire procedure. Norman could have used the clippers anytime as a threat of punishment. Instead, when David didn't answer him (because he did not hear him) Norman struck him on the head. David pleaded, "Just not on the head, just don't hit me on my head. Please don't hit me on my head," while Norman pounded him. Then Norman hit him on the knees. Tears streaming down his face, David claimed, "That didn't hurt." Norman hit him again-hard. When I tried to stop him, Norman grabbed my arm and twisted it. I soon learned to just cower in a corner until the emotional storm was over.

One day, I walked through a hole in the fence behind us. I looked closely at the barn slowly falling apart behind a farm house. Inside, there was an old farmer in clean well-worn overalls. He asked me if there was anything in the barn I wanted to buy. I surveyed the rotting harness on the walls and a broken farm wagon. Stacks of hay bales were drifting apart with age. On one wall hung two tennis rackets without strings. He noticed I was eyeing them. He offered to sell them at "twenty-five cents each or two for fifty cents," with a smile and a wink. I bought them and had them restrung at a sports shop for $5 each. David and I tried to bounce a tennis ball on the rough ground for a while. We collected spiders in jars for a while. Finally, a park employee gave David a dog and a doghouse. The dog attracted other dogs and got sick and died. We missed him. Norman brought home a box turtle with one foot crushed by a car. It thrived on raw hamburger and lettuce. We called it Peg Leg. We could always hear it coming.

For a time, Norman drove a truck for a paving company. In a rain storm he slid off the road. The cop who found him gave him a ticket for driving too fast for conditions. He worked in a cannery processing green beans from our area. The girl from Germany had a fight with her sister-in-law and discovered me. We became real neighbors, she with her three year old—me with David. We drank coffee in each other's "dining rooms." She showed me the set of demitasse cups her mother sent her, one by one, at intervals. She played classical music on her phonograph. She was well educated, pretty, sophisticated. I gave some money hoarded from my last paycheck to her husband to buy a rifle for Norman. This was to make hunting with the twins possible. I spent most of what was left for a fishing rod for Norman. Norman tried to go hunting, shot a rabbit, and cleaned it behind the trailer. I put it in the freezer section of our tiny refrigerator. I couldn't eat it. So it stayed there while we ate unchewable but cheap "filet mignon." Norman caught fish (catch and release). David and the neighbor's child, Ludwiga and I, walked around the fishing area and talked. Ludwiga got English translations of newspapers from home. She taught me about poor Jews bottled up by Syrians at a port on the Gulf of Aqaba. For Christmas, I bought a copy of Ann Morrow Lindberg's *A Gift From The Sea*. I gave it to Ludwiga.

In the spring we acquired lawns to rake and mow as the mudholes of the winter disappeared. The twins and their families went home for the summer and I read. My father sent me some money and I bought a red, sleeveless sweater for David. It was much too big. I thought he would grow into it. David was asking questions in a downtown store. The storekeeper laughed and said, "Don't ever stop him from asking questions. He's a real thinker." We survived the first year. Norman eased out of engineering and into accounting where he was much more comfortable. I tried to write and Ludwiga was amused. I remembered when Venus and I tried to write. Her story was about a farmer and his wife. My story was about a safari. Venus was impressed and I loved her for that. Ludwiga just giggled.

I sent Christmas cards early and received cards from Andrea and Venus and the Justice family. I felt so lonely all of a sudden. We went to the Great Grandparents for Thanksgiving and to Grandma's house for Christmas. Grandpa recalled the tricycle he bought and took to David in Philadelphia. Then he took it back to the store because David already owned one. Norman sank into an overstuffed chair wherever he happened to be. Grandma asked me what Norman might be able to use for Christmas. I said, "Atlantic Monthly Magazine—for English." He got shaving gear. There seemed to be such a big gap between Norman and engineering. He tried. I even asked Ludwiga's husband if he could help. One evening, the two men gossiped in our trailer while Ludwiga and I gossiped in her trailer. So much for help in engineering. Her husband shot a pheasant. We were invited to her house for a special meal. I was so hungry and the pheasant was so small. I made something with tuna fish when we came back from the "dinner," still hungry.

One day I was called to the office to accept a phone call from Mama. She was in Philadelphia on her way home from Sweden with her youngest son. She was coming to see me, she said. "Please don't come," I pleaded.

She hung up. I waited, sitting on the steps of the trailer. David used his squirt gun to spray bugs on the lawn. I waited for two days. A week passed. Mama neither came nor called. Norman said his boss told him his wife really loved hunting. Norman's gun and fishing rod were taking up space in the closet. Norman socialized with his boss while the twins went hunting or fishing. Norman got food stamps. I decided to stop eating one meal a day, usually breakfast. Ludwiga and I argued about something trivial. She stormed home from our kitchen. I tried to read Shakespeare while Norman was studying. I began to read aloud, "As the bee stings." Norman asked me what was wrong. I sent him to get a medicine for periodic pain—something I heard about but never used. The next morning, I took David across the street to catch the school bus. He was having a terrible time in the first grade, being teased about the big red sleeveless sweater. He hated school, hated being teased. I took a few of the pills, like peanuts, with a cup of coffee. David was gone. I was talking to myself aloud and, suddenly, I couldn't stop talking to myself aloud.

I remembered, later, walking to the wash house in the middle of the day. I took all my clothes off and put them in a washer. I remembered going back to bed right after Ludwiga's husband came to the wash house. He asked me if he could help. Of course, I said, "No." I remembered later, pulling on my breasts to make them bigger. I was so unsatisfied with myself because Ludwiga was so pretty, so sophisticated. I remembered leaving Norman asleep and taking David's little world globe outside. I was sitting on the step and looking for Sputnik in the night sky. I remembered at Christmas Grandpa and I were in the living room. He said, out of nowhere, "I'm never satisfied." I remembered Norman saying, "You've been in bed for two days. Are you going to get up today?" I remembered saying, "Yes." I remembered also looking for clothes in the trailer closet. Norman was waiting to take me somewhere. Nothing fit and I couldn't find anything to match anything else. And I remember hugging David so hard he winced because I knew he wasn't going along. I wanted him to remember I loved him.

I even remembered the sycamore tree in front of the doctor's office where we went for David's regular checkups. Only now Norman was opening the car door and controlling my elbow. The doctor looked concerned. He gave me a shot and Norman took me back to the car. The window was open and I remembered enjoying the wind in my hair. I remembered the hospital and another shot and a glass of something I spilled intentionally. I thought it was poison. Why else would someone in white hand me something to drink? Then I was flat on my back and someone in white was holding up three fingers. He asked me, "How many fingers?" We were in an ambulance and I was strapped down. My mouth would not form the word, "Three." I was mildly surprised. I couldn't move my fingers to indicate, "Three," because they were strapped to my body.

Next time I woke up, two student nurses were giving me a bath in an ancient bathtub. I passed out.

This Christmas, I was one of many patients in a large ward who received a tiny package from a charity. Mine contained lipstick and a comb and I was grateful. There was one night alone in a totally bare room with bright lights. The glass window walls were for medical observation. Two student nurses unlocked the door and gave me a massive shot of something in my hip. With, or without, the student nurses, I sang—college songs, movie songs, Broadway songs, popular songs. I danced my way into the shock treatment area and was ordered out. In the observation room, someone died from heart trouble. Later, I saw the supervising nurse crying. Norman came and we sat stiffly in the waiting room. Another weekend, the aunt and uncle who financed the trailer came to visit me in the asylum. I loved the nurses, the nurse's aides, the doctors, even the cooks. I was moved into the area where people waited for other assignments. I befriended a diabetic and we walked through several inches of snow, in high heels, to two dances. Someone pointed out the deaf girl, who lived in this hospital all her life, using sign language. She was discussing something with a doctor in a lively manner. My quota of pills was decreased at regular intervals.

Norman came to get me for a "home visit." On our way to the trailer, we barrelled down a mountain road. Norman said, "You know you had a nervous breakdown. Our doctor in State College sent you to the best, not the nearest but the best, psychiatrists in the state. Did my relatives visit you?" I said, "Yes, thank you. How is David doing in school?" Norman said, "Fine, as far as I know." David was skeptical. I didn't try to touch him. Nothing was changed. Norman and I sat on the couch. Every once in a while I left the couch to go to the bathroom.

Within the week I found myself seated before a group of three psychiatrists of whom I knew two. The third, a young lady, gently asked me if I wanted to go home. "Oh, yes," I said. They conferred while a student nurse walked with me back to the ward. That was all. Later, I was sitting on an examining table, fully dressed. One of the psychiatrists hit one of my knees with a small hammer. He said, "Nice reflexes. You definitely have nice reflexes," and beamed at me. The following day one of the patients assured me, "They will never let you out if you don't do the puzzles." As Norman drove toward the trailer, he pointed out I was released early because the hospital was so far away. I was grateful for this. I remembered asking the Filipino doctor to pierce my ears, in his "spare time." Of course, he did not. Norman asked me what I wanted for Christmas. I was amazed when Norman stopped at a jewelry store in a small town. He helped me choose a pair of golden earrings. I wore them back to State College.

Parenting

Chapter 20

We used the same table for meals, and study, and things which didn't land on the couch. On it was a bulky letter from my father. The letter contained $2,000 in grimy $100 bills. I handed them to Norman without comment. Dad's note said, "Dear Kid. Get something for your house. I love you." I wrote a Thank You without mentioning my recent "vacation," as Norman referred to it. People at the school David attended finally noticed he was having trouble. Norman and I took him to a hearing specialist. He mystified and delighted us with a variety of tests performed with a tuning fork. An eye, ear, nose, and throat specialist operated on his eustachian tubes. Suddenly, David could hear clearly. He needed glasses, too. When he got them he asked more questions than ever. Another improvement was the disappearance of the hair clippers.

A day or two after my "vacation" Ludwiga knocked on the door. She invited us to watch television on her new TV set. Actually, David and Norman and Ludwiga's husband watched TV. I sat grimly facing the set while being studied by Ludwiga as another American curiosity. I didn't invite her to our trailer. We packed things in boxes, including the Halloween cat and owl costumes I made for Ludwiga's son and David. We went to the auditorium at Penn State University. David and I sat in the balcony while Norman, in cap and gown, marched to "Pomp and Circumstance." He received his Bachelor of Science in Accounting Degree. David wanted to see his favorite cow in the dairy barn afterward so we went to the barn. Other young families celebrated in other ways. I was really grateful for the G. I. Bill because it was the only way most of us could have been there. Then, Norman spent two weeks sending resumes and receiving negative replies. The only positive reply came from a company whose supervisor loved hunting and fishing. Norman listed those as his favorite hobbies!

Norman led a professional mobile home mover from State College to Erie. He drove into a driveway, got out and started to walk toward what looked like a barn. The hayloft was being used as living quarters. He was met by an elderly couple who pointed out our "spot." The professional movers arrived and set up the trailer. It was sandwiched between two trailers, each one car width apart. This was it—the whole trailer park and all the management.

Norman and I got groceries and settled down. He went to work. I took David to a grammar school just a few blocks away. He was assigned to a school bus route and enrolled in the first grade. I was delighted there was a bus because we lived two blocks from a major highway. This was well travelled by airline passengers. A small international airport was located one house and one heavy barbed wire fence away. Norman took me to a family practice doctor who read the prescription Norman filled after I left the asylum. He looked aghast. This doctor completely eliminated the pills in three visits, two weeks apart. I noticed, first, I could see much better. Then, I didn't have to put my feet down so hard when I walked. Then, there were a few things to laugh about once in a while. The doctor laughed, too, when he said, "No more pills for you, young lady. How does it feel not to be a zombie?" It felt great and I was glad to admit it.

Norman took David and me to a get-together hosted by his supervisor's boss at the boss's home. The women were my age but much better dressed and much more at ease. At least, I thought they were more at ease until I was getting David ready for bed. I tried to remember what we talked about. There it was—the boss's wife owned "two drawers full of white gloves, just white gloves." She came from Pittsburgh and thought the Pirates were terrific. She wondered why Norman's hobbies were hunting and fishing. He didn't "look like he knew one end of a fishing rod from another." The boss's house looked like it came straight from the Sears Catalog—inside and out. And what was so good about a Manhattan? Or two Manhattans? I thought a Grasshopper tasted better. I was glad Norman's supervisor knew how to make one for me. I didn't think we would be going back to their house. I distrusted their insistence we sell the trailer and "move in somewhere closer to us so we can visit." To me, the evening was a colossal waste of time.

The grandparents told us about a "$500 insurance policy soon to mature. Since Norman has his own family now, we are going to keep the $500." They told us this before my "vacation" when I was trying not to eat too much. I was saving Norman the expense of one meal a day. They did send him a graduation card. Norman's graduation present to himself was his second used car. The car came as a surprise to David and me. Norman traded the Pontiac sedan for a Plymouth sedan which was actually easier to drive. The car payments reduced our income back toward the poverty level. Norman reminded me I promised the doctor in State College I would drive again. As it turned out, his supervisor really loved hunting and fishing and was still looking for someone else who did. So Norman began to come home for lunch and I began to drive him the two blocks back to the highway. I walked back to the trailer to wait for David's school bus to bring him home.

Next door on one side was an elderly lady. She drove away to work before Norman did and drove back after Norman did. On the other side was an elderly couple whose daughter was a waitress. She supported them because her father used to work for the company which just hired Norman. After twenty years with the company, two days before his scheduled retirement party, he was fired for unsatisfactory job performance. I believed this immediately. Someone whose wife owned two dresser drawers full of white gloves couldn't be too concerned about abstract virtues like loyalty.

Our first weekend after unpacking, Norman took us to the airport in the car. It would have been such an easy walk. However, we were on our feet for several hours. Norman admired airplanes from the observation deck, airplanes going, coming, being parked, gassed, inspected, loaded and unloaded. I admitted to myself, at length, airplanes are not intrinsically fascinating. Who could say such a thing to Norman who missed the North Carolina flight lines with his whole heart? Under his supervisor's watchful eye, Norman was doing menial paperwork which he hated. It was hot in the trailer. The night our second child was born, we spent an evening at the airport. We ate blueberry pie at the airport restaurant and went home to bed. At 2 A.M. I awakened Norman. He carried the sleeping David to the back seat while I found and brought my overnight bag. I was so glad the doctor freed me from pills. I was sure I would ask for something to separate me from pain when we reached the hospital.

Somehow, I expected Norman to be in a hurry. He wasn't. The hospital was almost diagonally across the city from the airport. We managed to reach every stoplight on the completely deserted streets while the stoplight turned red. Invariably, Norman came to a complete halt and waited for the light to turn green. When it did, Norman accelerated slightly and just kept the car going till the next stoplight. I considered asking him if it was my turn to drive. I stopped driving those two blocks at lunch every weekday after I became heavily pregnant. It was like Norman didn't want to reach the hospital. We finally did. I stood at the counter beside him while he brought insurance cards from his wallet and signed papers. The result was a very short period in the labor room together. Norman announced he really needed to make arrangements for David and departed. Again, I was alone in a labor room. The grandparents came to get David and take care of him for a couple of weeks. They dropped in to see their new grandson in the hospital, and me. Bruce was quite comfortable in a crib in the nursery.

While David was visiting Grandma and Grandpa, they reminded him about the tricycle they brought to Philadelphia one Christmas. They returned it to the store because Norman bought his first. David rested his hand on a part of their back fence. So did a bumblebee-as he very shortly, and painfully, discovered. He held his own among the many relatives. He could never understand why a cousin of Norman's, who was supposed to be retarded, was always greeted the same way. "Now, don't you go upstairs and steal any of Grandpa's change on the dresser," Grandma said. He entered the house like everyone else did, through the kitchen. I remembered having questioned the procedure myself, aloud, before David was born. Grandma's reply still stung, "Oh, he's retarded, you know. He doesn't think like we do." From his facial expression, anyone could see he felt exactly like we would. Anyone could see the effect of such a greeting, anyone except the ones doing the damage. David was glad to be back home.

I persuaded Norman to join a church because we needed to be part of something. The pastor asked me if I would return to the church whose Sunday School sheltered me through turbulent times. I really believed I would not and said so. I thought God was otherwise occupied the last year in State College. I knew He could have kept me out of the insane asylum. I decided to try a religion which made no effort to help ordinary people like me. I wanted one with a hierarchy to make sure there was a lot of distance between God and me. Fortunately, we didn't have to drive far to the church and we were admitted after a remarkably short time. David was coerced into joining the choir. He resisted every time there was a rehearsal because he missed *Gunsmoke*. As a recent Penn State graduate, Norman went straight into the hierarchy, an almost instant deacon. I sat beside Norman in the balcony for adult Sunday School, every Sunday, wearing one of Aunt Cecily's dresses. The oldest deacon was the teacher. The lessons were pure politics, simple and galling. They were so far from the humility I associated with Christ, I seethed inside. The new baby gave me an excuse, for awhile, to just stay home on Sunday mornings. Two things I thought I learned: if you want a bigger home, have enough children so you have to move to make room for them; if you want a different wardrobe, get too fat or too thin to wear out what you have. We could leave the trailer now, after just two years by the airport, because there was another child. Norman asked someone at the church if he knew where we could live. It just happened the deacon was moving out of his home for the same reason we were. So Norman found a house which looked like a box inside and out. We soon learned it contained less storage space than the trailer. There were four real rooms with real doors. Although we still took our laundry to the laundromat, it was much closer to our house. The laundromat owner was friendly. The furniture was old but sufficient and Norman bought a used television set. His supervisor discovered there was no work for Norman, "in the new system." Norman asked someone at the church, another deacon, if he knew about any available employment. The day after he left his first Erie job, he started his second Erie job.

The house which looked like a box was built like those on either side of us. On the right, lived a gardener who drew plans for his garden. He worked on it all year and gloried in its perfection. He and his wife shared a small yapping dog which stayed on its side of our common fence. Frequently, it let us know it was there. On the left, lived a grandmother who baby-sat her granddaughter. This child threw things over our common fence so we could throw them back. Usually, we found them before our dog did. Our dog was a beagle and we loved him. Norman insisted he was an outside dog. During the bitter winter, in his doghouse way back in the yard, he froze. He got sick. Once again, Norman and David took a sick dog to the vet and came back without him.

Our landlady and her husband were carefree Polynesians. They kept cutting our monthly rent payments every six months until I asked them to stop. We were paying ridiculously low rent. Norman never saved to upgrade our way of life. Norman's bonds were for his retirement. Certainly, the landlord and his wife should receive a proper return on their investment in our house. They were shocked when I said this but I meant it. Norman was already buying his third used car on the installment plan. I didn't even pretend to drive this one. Two years after Bruce was born, I woke up at 3 A.M. and awakened Norman and David. David asked me if he could have a peanut butter sandwich so I made one for him. While he munched on it, I wrapped up Bruce and grabbed my overnight bag and Norman started the car. Again, he drove like a caterpillar to the hospital. This time my water broke as we entered the office, A wheelchair appeared and I didn't see any of the family till the next afternoon.

Norman took a rare two day vacation to stay with the boys while Honey and I were in the hospital. Insurance companies no longer insisted on a full week's stay for maternity patients. Norman's insurance was provided by his employer, of course. Meanwhile, I finally got my girl! Oh, it was great, now and then, to mother David and Bruce. I really didn't know how much I wanted to be a girl's mother, to have my own daughter, till there she was!

A dour new minister replaced the friendly old man who let us join his congregation and baptized Bruce. He came into my hospital room unannounced. I was gratefully patting my newly flat tummy when he appeared. He saw where my hand was and grimaced. He withdrew the hand already extended to shake hands with me even while I was reaching for it. Undiluted disgust was on his face. Inside, I swore I would never set foot in his church again. Of course, I did go back to church for Honey's baptism. Afterward, I began a gradual withdrawal—so gradual Norman didn't even seem to notice.

Grandma mailed commercial birthday cakes to Norman for years. The year she stopped doing so I made a cake, telling David it was a surprise. When Norman came from work David met him at the front door. "Surprise! Surprise!" he shouted. David did this every time I told him there was a surprise in the offing. We purchased a car with foot pedals which David rarely used. Now it became Bruce's toy car. Honey got her own rocking horse. She rode it passionately. She spent so little time crawling, even less just walking. When she was running around the yard one day, she figured out how to exit the premises. By lifting the latch on the gate, she could explore. She ran at her usual speed across the street to visit her friend, Karen. Karen's gate was like ours. Before anyone knew it, the girls were racing about the neighborhood. They went down to the minipark where a policeman found them. I was still searching the house for Honey when I heard a knock at the door. There she was, holding one hand while Karen held the other hand, of a puzzled looking policeman. I thanked him while Karen's mother came dashing across the street. They never opened the gate for themselves again. No one punished them. The cop just talked to them both—seriously. I thanked God—seriously.

Bicycles In The Living Room

Chapter 21

Norman went bowling every week and, in the spring, he got on the company golf program. One day, as I assembled the laundry to take to the laundromat, Norman spoke up. He remarked Honey would probably be our last child. I was "getting too old, past childbearing age." I responded to a fight over toys just then so I didn't answer. Later that day, when we gathered the family and a cooler of picnic items, I left my sandals in the car. I remembered a sunshade for the baby on my back. I forgot two things. The trees shading the spot where we kids entered Carmel beach did not exist in this part of Presque Isle. Moreover, it was at least a year since I went barefoot, even on asphalt. Norman was wearing his wingtip shoes. I could never get him to try on sneakers or loafers. While the sneaker clad boys ran ahead of us, Norman and I each carried one end of the cooler. As my left foot hit the broiling sand, it stung. My right foot burned. Suddenly I dropped my end of the cooler. I explained as I ran back to the car, "it's too hot, have to go back for shoes. Sorry." Norman picked up the rest of the cooler and remained silent for the rest of the day. Since Norman was usually silent, the children enjoyed the outing.

Norman was employed as a full time accountant. This required another two years of accounting courses. Naturally, they were in the evening. David was used to spending time with his father when Norman wanted company to the gas station. Bruce was used to staying home with me. The grandparents brought Lisa, with her new movie camera, to take endless pictures of Honey and Bruce. They ran around the lilies of the valley in the side yard. They somersaulted on and over the lawns in front and back. Lisa graduated from high school with a business major. She was able to use her business courses for less than a month. Afterward, she spent a lifetime as a seamstress in a clothing factory. Fortunately, she enjoyed sewing. She sent fantastic dresses for Honey to be photographed in and, incidentally, to wear to Sunday School.

Another occasion when Honey could run in dizzying circles in a dazzling dress was the wedding. We received engraved invitations to a formal wedding ceremony. Lisa's brother was engaged to an office worker from his high school graduating class. Grandma's letter announcing the engagement mentioned the wedding was on short notice because they were so much in love. We wore our best clothes to the event. I even wore one of Aunt Cecily's straw hats. Honey looked like a Shirley Temple doll with her natural blonde curls. Having lunched with Grandma and driven to the church immediately, we were still somewhat late. Grandma's rule was, "Never leave the dishes when you go somewhere. What if you died?" Norman even helped wipe some of the dishes, a memorable event.

A member of Darren's high school band led us to front row seats. The church was decorated with white lilies ribboned in green. When the bridal party appeared, Darren was in his black graduation suit. Leona wore a high-waisted, full-skirted, pale green satin gown. A long green veil floated from her pillbox hat. Grandma looked as close to radiant as I ever saw her. Certainly, the bride and groom looked very happy. After they whirled away in Darren's new used car, we went back to Grandma's house. We stayed overnight before returning to Erie.

When David joined the Cub Scouts one of the neighborhood ladies supervised the group. Some deacons at the church helped with the Boy Scouts. We attended Scout ceremonies regularly. David went to Scout camp every summer. Norman would drive down to the camp for Parent's Day. The first year, David pleaded to go back home with us. The second year, and thereafter, he barely managed a short visit with us. He went all the way to Star Scout before the Assistant Scout Master moved out of the area. I sewed many badges on his ceremonial scarf, many patches on his shirt. He was most proud of his mile swim and lifesaving badges.

Another deacon told us about the thrills of camping! Norman rented a tent-trailer for our first vacation as a family. He bought a Coleman stove and other vital equipment and locked the house. We were heading into his home town almost before I knew it. I was astounded when we pulled up in front of Grandma's house. We stayed there just two days—long enough to visit all the relatives. Then we hurried off to a camping area outside Washington, D.C. Norman and David loved camping. Joyfully they left me at the campsite with Bruce and Honey. They went to get wood for the fire, fuel for the Coleman, gas for the car. I got to wash diapers, bathe the children, and prepare the meals. Norman grilled hamburgers or hot dogs. I got to wash the dishes, pack things away, shower, and fall into bed. This was long after Norman and the children fell asleep. I got to stay with the children while Norman and David chatted with fellow campers. I did not love camping! Every year, I hated it more. Finally, we went to Shenandoah National Park. There I carried Honey on my hip. I wore a backpack containing a day's required diapers, etc.. In one hand, I carried a box of crackers for her and Bruce to munch on. Bruce held onto my other hand. Norman and David were leading the way. I was listening to a forest ranger pointing out wonderful things in the park. Honey was old enough to run around. She was also young enough to get tired and have to be carried. I loved Shenandoah, the big ravens, the wonderful trees, the all day hikes we took. I finally learned. Norman didn't know how to help me. For him the concept of digging in and bearing a hand did not exist. It never would. I bought a whale carved from basalt at Michie Tavern. Near Monticello, I bought some silver dogwood earrings. At the end of the first of two weeks, Norman headed back to Grandma's house. He enjoyed his vacation in the large overstuffed chair in front of the TV set. And we owned a TV!

This became the pattern of our vacations. We would camp somewhere near Washington, D.C.. He would drive to the Capitol, to see the Smithsonian, the Lincoln Memorial, or the cherry trees. We went to Gettysburg or Lancaster or Hershey. There was always plenty of time to sit in Grandma's house and to visit the relatives. Every two or three years, Norman bought another used car on the installment plan. There were always car payments. Whenever he brought home a different used car, I asked why he never paid one off. I suggested he just drive it for awhile with no encumbrances. He assured me the idea was ridiculous. The credit cards he applied for when he graduated from college were never paid off. It was like he was married to the concept of debt.

He handled the checking accounts and paid the bills—all of which he accumulated. Every Friday night we went food shopping exactly like his parents did. He pushed the cart like his father did. When I selected something he didn't approve, he lifted it from the cart and put it back on the shelf. Sometimes, I would plead for whatever it was, grapefruit, for instance. At first he would let me buy whatever it was. Gradually, he began to put away, back on the shelf, items he approved for years.

When Honey was growing too big for her crib, Norman decided it was time to move. He discussed this with his fellow deacons—as he did most things. He got another job. We attended a party at his new employer's house. There were several couples and I enjoyed helping serve the chicken divan. The boss's wife was down to earth, educated, smart. I would have loved to talk with her. She was too busy running the party, of course, and I looked so cheap in Aunt Cecily's cast-off dress. We went to a Christmas party. Norman's new supervisor asked me, in front of Norman, how I would feel about a transfer from Erie. I knew Norman would never leave Erie. It was so close to Grandma's house. I said, "He would have to be tricked. The only way he would ever leave Erie would be if someone tricked him into doing so." We were drinking and I could see the other people at the table believed I was drunk. I wasn't. I just knew Norman much better than they did. It was a hypothetical question. The supervisor transferred soon after the party.

Grandma and Grandpa and Lisa came to visit us at Easter. We took the cooler and some raw chicken parts, a potato salad, and a Jello dessert to the beach. I never grilled chicken. The grilling idea was Norman's. Neither of us realized the chicken must be precooked. So, after an hour or so Norman served the grill-blackened chicken legs. Grandma tried to cut the one on her plate. She exclaimed, "it's raw! The chicken is raw!" We brought hot dogs for the kids so it wasn't a tragedy. There were enough hot dogs for everyone. We never cooked again for the grandparents. We were at their house every Thanksgiving, every Christmas, and for years, on both sides of every summer vacation. The arrangement was just more convenient for everyone.

Good Friday 1964, a major event occurred. We were listening to the news. Actually, Norman and the children were watching the news on television. I was listening from the kitchen while I served dinner. I heard, "Hundreds of people are dead or injured," and went to look at the screen. Then, there was something about calling the Red Cross. David said, "There's a big earthquake in Alaska." Norman nodded. It was so! I tried to call the Red Cross. The line was busy every time I tried. Finally, I went across the street to the Ham Radio Operator's house. I knocked on his door. When he answered, I asked him if he could get a message through his radio to my father. He shook his head, "There's no way. Maybe, in a week. There's too much confusion. Keep trying the Red Cross." I did-for days. The newspapers showed pictures of devastation—stores sliding into great caverns where sidewalks broke off. Other pictures showed the effects of tidal waves. We were members of the National Geographic Society. I joined when David was three years old. Honey loved the magazine and pored over the pictures for hours. When the Alaska Earthquake Issue came we devoured it. Mama sent me a picture of my father standing in front of his upturned, and mangled, cabin. The clipping from the *Seattle Post Intelligencer* was sent to Mama by one of her friends. I wore it out.

Most of the kids David knew rode bicycles. Even the much younger only child across the street owned a bicycle. He rode circles around David when David played in the mini-pool in the mini-park by the laundromat. David scraped his foot on the bottom of the pool. Waiting for his foot to heal so he could go back to the pool gave him thinking time. He brought bicycle brochures to support the arguments he devised to convince Norman he needed a bike. Norman owned a bike when he was young. When he was very young he got his first paper route—bringing home money to help support his family. When Norman suggested a paper route for David, I vetoed the idea. I wanted David to know how to play. Play was something Norman's family never seriously considered. Toys were manipulated. David got plenty of these. Play for him was lying flat on his stomach and drawing, swimming, or Scouting. At school, there was a group of friends. The School District tracking system broke it up rather abruptly. David was kept behind a full year. I was irate. I swore I would try to help him. I began to really talk to Norman about the disadvantages of living in Erie. I relayed everything I heard about the scandalous school system. I talked about going to Chicago or Albuquerque, or even back to Philadelphia. Norman snapped, "O.K. you go back to Philadelphia if you love the subway so much." This is why, when his boss suggested a transfer, I already knew the answer.

Norman quickly reached the point where, if he suspected I wanted something, he wouldn't get it. I didn't push for a new bicycle, didn't even mention it when Norman made David beg. Then, one evening Norman looked up from the newspaper and smiled, "Let's go look for a bike tomorrow, son." I didn't say anything. I was familiar with the Schwinn brochures David pored over in the room with the bunkbeds and Honey's crib. How joyful he was when he got into Norman's car on his way to his first real bicycle. About two hours later, he came into the kitchen for a glass of water. "What happened? Didn't you get your bike?" I asked. He nodded sadly. I went to the front window and looked at the green peppers growing in the window box. I saw the bicycle Norman was removing from the trunk of his fourth used car. It was big and old and very heavy. Probably after an accident, someone repainted it the color of green seaweed. I went back to the kitchen and told David, "It'll be all right. Maybe he just wants you to learn on it." We both knew better. David nodded. He went to get the bike from Norman and park it where Norman said to park it—behind the house. Norman came in smiling, "Ten bucks! It cost exactly ten bucks! Good thing I saw the notice in the paper. There were lots of bikes at the police station but this one was the cheapest!"

I never knew what brand the bicycle was because I never went near it. I know it wasn't a Schwinn because it fell apart at the first opportunity. David was hurrying down a hill which intersected with a road. This time, this once of many times, a car was coming. I got a telephone call from the driver who ran into him. Norman and I went to see David in the Emergency Room. We were told he seemed to be all right. However, the doctor suggested we watch him at night. With his kind of head injury, there might be projectile vomiting. Together we left the Hospital. Norman started the car with, "Why the Hell were you going down the hill?" I said, "Shut up, Norman." Since no one could remember my ever saying "shut up," before, Norman did. He ate his dinner and went bowling. I put the other kids to bed earlier than usual after dinner and the dishes were done. Then, I sat on a chair beside the couch where David lay covered with a blanket. He seemed deflated. I read, Run Silent, Run Deep aloud until he was really asleep.

When Honey started fussing, I brought her to sit on my lap in the rocking chair. At last, she, too, slept. When Norman came home, we went to bed. The rocking chair was just the right size. How often I rocked Honey to sleep. Once, when she couldn't breathe lying in her crib, I sat there all night, holding her and praying. In the morning I woke up, still holding her, only now her breathing was clear and free. In absolute silence, I thanked God.

I thanked God again when David did no projectile vomiting. He came into the kitchen in the morning all ready for school. A week later, Bruce came into the kitchen from the backyard. He was using an old branch from a lilac bush like a walking stick or a cane. I thought he was being funny until I noticed how knobby his knees looked. When Norman came home we returned to the hospital. I left David in charge of Honey in the back seat of the car. Norman and I led Bruce up the ramp to the Emergency Room. This time Norman did not grumble about dinner getting cold. A doctor in the Emergency Room took Bruce's temperature and looked at his knees. He called for a wheelchair to take Bruce into the hospital proper. A nurse asked, "Hey, weren't you in here last week?" I nodded.

Bruce had Rheumatic Fever. He was in the hospital for some time. Norman and I visited him there. David and Honey sat waiting in the car in front of the hospital. After Bruce came home, I very quietly reminded Norman how many hours David spent taking care of Honey. I told Norman David deserved a bicycle of his own. This time, I added, it better be a new, red Schwinn with several different speeds and good brakes. Norman waited till there was a sale. David chose the bike he really wanted, a red ten speed (with good brakes). It was not the least expensive model. I was there, with the other kids, checking out the Bike Shop. We helped make sure Norman bought what David deserved.

Not much later, Norman asked me if I didn't "think it's time to have another baby." I thought about how hard it was for David to retreat into the background. When Bruce came home from the hospital, Norman moved him into David's slot. Helping polish the car, going on errands, going along to the barber shop became Bruce's prerogatives. When we lived in State College, Norman cut David's hair with an old pair of clippers. David screamed so loud the neighbors always knew about the haircut before they saw it. Bruce never endured a similar experience. The worst thing he suffered was taking a pill every day for the next several years. Bruce called it, "Moratic Fever." David went to choir practice and Scouts while Honey and Bruce stayed home with me. Norman's suggestion about another baby drew a reply he should have expected, "not just now."

Leave it to Norman to find a way to use David's bike! Norman took David to get a work permit. David began to caddy as soon as the golf season started. I reminded Norman it was a few years since I got a present. I remembered aloud there was a lady's Raleigh at the Bike Shop. It was used, shiny black, and cheap. He bought it. We now stored bicycles, for safe keeping, in the living room. I wrote a story for *The New Yorker* called "Bicycles In The Living Room." They sent me a rejection slip. I even sent my autobiography to my father, in installments. He wrote back, "Most people don't write their biographies until after they have lived a little."

One reason I started to write again was, with three children, we needed a bigger house. Norman's fellow deacon just happened to have another house his family outgrew. It was a house he needed to sell because he was already living in a much better one. I loved the tree house, the big dog house, the flowering bushes in the yard. Between the time I first saw it and the time we moved in, all but the tree house disappeared. They even dug up bulbs from the side gardens after we moved in. I would go out to water the garden after hours in the house using our first real washer and dryer. To take a break from vacuuming our own carpets I would walk around the yard with Honey. Each time I went outside I found another set of holes someone dug to remove some plants. There was a back fence and a side fence but no front fence. Besides, the bulb-snatcher knew exactly what she was doing. What I thought of the deacon and his wife was not at all Christian. I made my peace with God when Honey woke up breathing free. After our night in the rocking chair, I consciously suspended judgment. I was quite ready to believe, "All things work together for good to them that love God." Only, why was the deacon's wife so cheap?

Ours was a two story house. At first Honey would not go upstairs unless someone, usually I, held her hand. Her friend, Karen, and she loved to bounce down the stairs in Karen's house. One day, Karen fell down the entire flight of stairs and got a concussion. Our warnings, and the fact that Karen couldn't play with anyone for a while, made Honey worry. In fact, when we first moved into our seven room, plus full basement, dwelling, Honey clung to my skirts. She would play in the kitchen, or any other room, as long as I was there. She would not be alone. Grandma was the first to use our new telephone. "Does she hang onto you when you leave the room?" Grandma asked. I admitted she did. I didn't mind. Gradually, she got used to the house.

Of Schools and Fish

Chapter 22

David always loved Science. He loved it so much he walked, or bicycled, miles to get lumber for the Science Fair Projects. With plywood and nails he built a weather station, a way to compare weights and measures, a gravity machine. These were big and crude and not at all pretty. Each of them demonstrated what he was trying to demonstrate. I watched him toil patiently for hours and was proud of him. Still he was kept on a lower track, which limited his school friendships and access to what he yearned to learn. Almost daily, I pleaded with Norman. Repeatedly, I begged him to look for a city with more opportunities. He ignored me. Norman bought another used car and took the family to the annual Air Show. This time I seized a chance to fly above the city in a DC-3. It was fun, unsettling to the stomach, but strengthening to the heart. Now I knew I was not afraid of flying. Having one less fear was important to me.

Every morning I got the mail from our front porch. I always riffled through the junk mail looking for something not predestined for the garbage. One morning there was a card from Grandma. It wasn't Easter or Valentine's Day or Christmas or Thanksgiving or even Saint Patrick's Day. Any of those brought quantities of cards. I ripped open the envelope as I entered the living room. It was a birth announcement. I didn't take the junk mail to the garbage. I sat down in the rocking chair and read what was on the card. And I read it again. I remembered Holly and Florence hissing on the Rider's Run school steps, "You filthy Nazi pig!" I remembered Florence's brother at Cal-Berkeley, "Didn't you know? Your mother wasn't married when your sister was born!" Honey clambered up on my lap. I read aloud, "Just to let you know … a girl was born … weighed … mother and child doing well … proud grandparents." I actually wrote a reply on the announcement. I actually wrote "Are you trying to tell me the bride wore green to her wedding because she was pregnant? Are you trying to tell me I sat through a church wedding when the bride was already pregnant?" I crumbled up the announcement I wrote all over. Then, I put it, and the junk mail, in the garbage. When Norman came home I didn't mention the announcement. I was afraid of what I would say.

The next holiday we visited the relatives, including Aunt Cecily. I asked her why no one seemed to notice how soon the birth announcement followed the wedding. Aunt Cecily chortled, "Lambie Pie," she said, "Those kids gave Norman's family a wedding! Hereafter, and no matter what, they can do no wrong. You didn't give them a wedding. Remember?" I remembered—a lot. En route to Grandma's for Thanksgiving we almost demolished the car. Norman's foot slipped from the gas pedal. The front wheel struck some ice and veered off the road. We were safe, but I refused to return to Grandma's house for Christmas, pleading unsafe road conditions. It was very strange to have Christmas in our own home—but it was also fun. Norman sat in his own overstuffed chair and watched TV without the winter time driving.

David studied in his own room. His favorite entertainment was always drawing. He would lie on his stomach and cover sheets of typing paper with people and airplanes. I kept typing paper available. Bruce also laid on his stomach, near the TV, driving toy cars. He parked them and maneuvered them on the floor around the furniture. Honey was more sedate. She sat on the living room floor. She went through her favorite *National Geographic* magazines so often their covers came off. She loved the picture of a Thai Princess in native costume until it was barely recognizable. Bruce also drove pretzel can lids around the house and running through the yard, making appropriate car noises. One could hear Bruce coming whether as a truck or a police car or a racing vehicle. I always read to the little ones when Bruce came home from school for lunch. His lunch would be ready and we would eat together. Then Honey and Bruce would sit, one on each side of me, while I read. These were books David accumulated plus new ones we got at the grocery store. Their favorite stories were the same ones David loved. David memorized the word "beautiful" as "be you fa till." He was in school for a while before he changed the pronunciation. Bruce's word was "igertent" which became "ignorant" after he called Honey, "you igertent baby," a few times. Honey's word was "elefanut." The *Saggy Baggy Elephant* story was long known as "the Saggy Baggy Elefanut" until she outgrew it. Bruce would run back to school with lunch in his pudgy body and, at least part of a story.

Norman wore suits, white shirts, and wingtip shoes to work. The suits were regularly cleaned. The shirts were professionally washed and ironed. The shoes were always polished, always on shoe trees when not on his feet. Honey was fascinated by the shoe trees. When I sent my father my new address, he sent me another $2,000. His note read, "Get something for the house. I love you, Dad." This time, at last, I did not give Norman the money. I put it in the bank in a savings account in my name only. Then, I went to the local state employment office and took some tests. While I was there, I looked in a book for the academic rankings of several local colleges. After that, I went to the college with the highest ranking. It was then a men's college which recently began to admit women. I took tests at the college. The results indicated I could still be in the first group at Stanford, still in the top one per cent.

Honey was going to school soon. She already knew how to print all the letters and her own name. When Bruce started school his teacher told me I should not have taught these things to him. I still dared to teach them to Honey. I would have taught each of them how to read. There was too much pressure from the media at the time. Being personally, and pointedly, discouraged when Bruce entered school, I stayed discouraged. Honey was as prepared as I dared to make her. Now it was time to prepare Norman.

Each individual in the family was entitled to one dinner out per year. This happened on or near his, or her, birthday. It was a family custom. We were all in the car en route to my birthday dinner at a restaurant. I said, "I'm going to college this semester."

Norman snorted, "You? You're going to college?"

I replied, "Yes. My father sent me some money and I'm going to use it for tuition. I can take classes while the children are in school."

"Oh, I guess a couple of sewing classes would be all right," Norman said.

To my complete surprise I found myself saying, "You know what you are, Norman? You are a spoiled brat. You not only did not take a college prep course in high school. You took eight years out of our home life to get into, and go through, Penn State. Then, you took more years of accounting classes afterward. I am going to college because it is my turn, because I earned it. I earned it all those years of watching you." Bruce started coughing loudly. The subject was closed. We were silent throughout dinner—as usual.

The television set was in a corner of the living room. The dining room was arranged so only Norman could see the TV from his place at the table. Every evening, Norman watched the news while we ate dinner. Dinner was always ready when Norman came home. Dinner was always ready when Grandpa came home—a family custom. I would rush through my meal, listening to the news. The children ate silently, also listening to the news. If the TV were strategically placed, it would block part of the front window facing the street. A line of stately trees grew between the sidewalk and the street. More trees lined the side fence. Near one of them a purple martin's house was supported by a fence post. One day the deacon who used to own our house dropped in. He expected me to give him the purple martin house. I remembered the bulbs dug from the garden after we moved in, after we legally bought them. I assured him I would not think of disturbing the purple martins. Along the back fence two pear trees thrived. I made pear pies in season. No beverages were served at the table. Years before, in State College, David was intimidated by Norman. He could not help spilling anything at the tiny table. Norman would say, "Don't you spill the milk." No matter how hard he tried, his elbow or his hand would send the milk flying. I solved the problem by serving no beverages at the table. There were no beverages at Norman's table for years, except Norman's coffee. This was my addition to family custom.

I pleaded for a home with a fireplace for years. I never got one. The deacon moved into a house with a fireplace. Unfortunately, he liked it so we never "inherited" his third house. At least, now each child could claim a separate room. Bruce always felt cheated because his was so small. I washed the dishes and smoked. The rest of the family moved into the living room after dinner. Because I was going to school, I used Green Stamps to buy a tiny desk and chair. These faced the kitchen window overlooking the driveway.

Bruce was in the Cub Scouts. Honey took tap dancing lessons in a mother's basement with one of the neighborhood children. Honey wore holes in her shoes before I realized she needed new tap shoes. Just after she got them, the mother in charge moved away. The lady who brought over a pie on my first day in the new house told me she was moving away, too. Otherwise, we kept the same neighbors for years. Down the block lived a happy family with seven children who took a family vacation every year. I asked Norman if we couldn't go to Canada sometime like they did. Norman insisted, "Oh, their family lives there." One day, I asked the mother if they were Canadians. They came from Arkansas. They travelled to a different part of Canada or the U.S. every year as a learning experience for their children. Their Pa wore work clothes instead of suits but they could afford real vacations! I was impressed.

Honey hated school. She wore the same department store clothes the other children wore. She never missed a meeting of the Brownies. She played with the two youngest of the four girls across the street. A boy from the large family and his friend played with Bruce. She chalked lines on the sidewalk to play hopscotch with, or without, the others. The boundless patience she demonstrated when she decided to shoot hoops brought tears to my eyes Every day for some time she would get David's basketball. She stood in a certain space relative to the hoop attached just above the garage door. From this chosen spot, she would toss the ball until it went through the hoop. The ball was huge in proportion to her size and weight. She never cheated. She never gave up. She practiced in a half circle from the neighbor's hedge to our back porch stairs. She stationed herself at point after invisible point in a half circle on the driveway pavement. After she made a basket she allowed herself to move on to the next point. When it snowed, she finally gave up. I suspected her class at school threw hoops one day and she missed the basket. She decided she was not going to miss next time the class threw hoops. I also suspected she never got a chance to show her teacher, or her class. I could have told them how great she became at throwing a basketball through a hoop. She also ran. On our side yard sidewalk, she marked off exactly the height of Wilt Chamberlain, in chalk. Then, she practiced running long jumps until she could, and did, jump this distance. She found the right size rock and printed "Today I jumped one Wilt Chamberlain." She wrote the date and put the rock on top of her brick and board bookcase under the windows in her room.

Honey hated school. I got a note from the teacher. I went to the school and listened to the teacher tell me Honey was not socially oriented. The teacher suggested tests. Her report cards marked, "works well with others, poor." However, "works well by herself, satisfactory." She was teased going to school. She was teased coming home from school. I could not understand it. Honey was such an outburst of joy, an animated spark, a leaf whirling in the wind. How could anyone not love her? Norman signed all her report cards. David was not doing well but he was taking a college preparatory course. His teacher suggested private art lessons and I nagged Norman into providing them. Norman took him to the weekly lessons after school. In fact, the car became almost useful with Scout meetings for all three children. Bruce was a straight A student from the first day of school. He worked well with others, worked well without others, never tore his pants on a nail. He never was brought home by a cop, never even got stung by a bee. However, Bruce and Honey and one of their friends went racing their bikes. They tore up and down the hills created by trucks off-loading snow in the winter. These formed quite satisfactory mountains for young people to storm up and coast down into what they called, "The Pits." One day, Bruce hit a rock with his bike, skidded to a stop and landed on his chin. An edge of one of his incisors broke off. Bruce formed the habit of smiling so his lower lip would cover the bottom part of the tooth. Another day, Bruce and Honey and the neighbor boy were racing their bikes in front of our house. They called, "Look, Mom" so I was intently watching. Bruce made too sharp a turn and slid, on his knees, to a stop. There was something so funny about the way Bruce slid, I broke into laughter. Later, I was cleaning the wound and coating it with Tincture of Merthiolate. Bruce tried to understand why I laughed. No matter how hard I tried to explain, he couldn't believe I could laugh when someone got hurt. Years later, watching "Bloopers" on TV, it might not have been so hard to explain. It wasn't because he was hurt. It was the way he left the bike.

Gradually, furnishing and equipping the house, I got curtains (with Green Stamps) for Honey's room. The pattern was Charlie Brown and Company, "The Psychiatrist is In," and "Psychiatric tests 5 cents." The winter storms made our line of massive spruce trees sway in the wind, terrifying Honey. I would sit up in her room, beside her bed, and read a textbook until she was really asleep. Honey was held back a year in school—thereby losing the only friends she acquired the first year. This time, I didn't say anything to Norman about moving to a city with more opportunity. I pleaded for a city with decent schools. Norman would not hear me. I decided to try to become a teacher. I dreamed of eventually trying to create a child-friendly school. It would be a place where creative people like David and Honey would be welcome. Bruce and Norman came from the same cookie cutter. Both were content as long as meals were on time and not too "exotic." They were satisfied as long as beds were made and clothes were clean and nobody ever said anything controversial. This was my department—to not make waves—for five years, which included some graduate credits in Summer School.

Honey wanted a birthday party because she attended birthday parties for the four girls across the street. I bought invitations which she printed and delivered. The dining room decorations were chosen and put in place. Honey chose the cake at the grocery store. On the special day, one of the guests, a school friend who often played in our yard, failed to arrive. I telephoned his mother. I told her hers was the most beautiful telephone voice I ever heard. This was true—she worked for the telephone company. I also asked why her son wasn't at our place. "Was he ill?" She chuckled, "No. He just doesn't want to go to any more birthday parties for girls. I'm sorry but right now he's being macho!" I thanked her and told the assembled guests. They played tag on our side lawn for a few minutes before they went home. This was Honey's only birthday party. David and Bruce received the annual dinners at a restaurant and cake at home.

While David was caddying, he often stopped for an ice cream cone on the way home. Several times, someone driving by honked his horn and, startled, David dropped the cone. His next birthday, Grandma sent a card but no $5 bill. "You're old enough now not to get any money for your birthday," was written on the card. Just above was Hallmark's printed, "Because you're such a great grandson." I gave David the $5. For this birthday, I nagged Norman into getting a small TV set, after which David's grades plummeted. He was carrying doubles sometimes, saving for a really good bike. I put salve on his blood-striped shoulders. He kept the money envelope straight and inconspicuous in his top dresser drawer. When he finally got the bike he really wanted, it was defective. It repeatedly required a replacement part which was hard to get and expensive—so he couldn't use it. Years later, he learned all the bikes of this year's model were recalled. I was there when he heard the news. His face lit up with relief. "It wasn't me," he said, "Oh, God, I always thought it was my fault the bike didn't work." I knew how he felt.

His next project was a fully stocked aquarium. He set it up in the part of his room farthest from the window overlooking the driveway. This area was unshaded and terribly, cruelly hot in the summer. His discus died, one by one. None of his fish lived very long. I got a downstairs tank to put where a China Cabinet would be. A few fish lived there for a while. Every three weeks I cleaned the fish tanks but still the fish did not live long. Another, smaller, dining room tank held tadpoles a friend of Bruce brought to us. Then there were salamanders from the same source. The State College Box Turtle lived under the dining room aquarium. Peg Leg was a member of the family for fifteen years. Norman got around to buying the cabinet a decade after he died. David got more art lessons from another teacher and begged me to let him go to Technical High School. I wanted no wife of his to face those bitter years when Norman was doing high school after graduation. I wanted him to go to college to learn the things about Science he seemed so eager to learn. I said, "No." Norman made no attempt to encourage, or to discourage, him in any direction. Why?

College Two

Chapter 23

In the fourth grade Bruce started to take clarinet lessons from a teacher at the elementary school. He took additional lessons from a teacher who worked for a music store. When she reached the fourth grade Honey took clarinet lessons from the teacher at school. She took guitar lessons from a teacher at the music store. The store sold all kinds of musical instruments and sheet music. Bruce stopped off for his lesson on his way home from school. I walked with Honey, carrying the cumbersome guitar, until we were a block away from the music store. At this point, she habitually took the guitar case in one hand and the music folder in the other. She said, "Pretend you don't know me." I would walk beside her to the heavy door which led to the basement lesson cubicles. After opening and holding the door for her, I would whisper, "Have fun, dear," and close the door. Sometimes, I would run home. Who would have noticed? The streets were deserted. Most people were watching TV.

The first year David attended Junior High, he got into an after school touch football game. He covered the few blocks home on foot, supporting his right arm at the elbow. The orthopedic surgeon said it was a greenstick fracture. We became familiar with orthopedic surgeons and ace bandages. One final appointment remained when David played touch football again. This time the doctor did not ask for permission to complete the break. The left arm was cleanly broken. Gradually, they healed. A friend of his stuck his foot through the side of a fish tank. His wounds also healed. One of his teachers inquired, "Do you ever use your head for anything but a hat rack?" This was in math class, I think. At least once each week, we gathered in David's room and sang show tunes from my memory. We sang, "Oh, What a Beautiful Morning, High Hopes, It's A Grand Night For Singing" before prayers and bed. It was a time to be together—without commercials. Norman usually just stood there waiting for this nonsense to be over. As Honey and I acquired homework the group sings gradually ceased. With Norman's third Erie job and fifth used car he learned, from someone at work, about Cleveland and Buffalo. These cities, as well as Niagara Falls, were remarkably close to Erie. We went on Saturday drives to the Cleveland Art Museum and the Cleveland Natural History Museum. We went to Niagara Falls in the U.S. and Canada and home by the Canadian side of the Niagara River. Invariably, Norman made several circles of the U.S. city of Niagara Falls. Invariably, he refused to ask directions or to admit he was lost. We browsed the shops and admired black squirrels, giant greenhouses and the flowers within them. We walked through Fort Niagara and Fort George. I loved to revisit the Iris on Japanese silkscreens in the Cleveland Art Museum. Honey loved the owls tethered outside the Natural History Museum. Once Norman even took David to a professional baseball game in Cleveland. The rest of us enjoyed the Natural History Museum. I bought a seal carved from basalt in Upper Canada and Moroccan leather purses in the World of Shops. At Niagara Falls, Canada, I bought leather earrings for Honey and me. These purchases led Norman to complain I "never bought anything but trinkets." He was making monthly payments for another used car.

Bruce and Honey were close. They both belonged to the band-in elementary school, then, in high school. I always bought the instruments for Honey. Eventually, she owned a French Horn just the right size for her. She owned a piccolo, cornet, two flutes, and three clarinets—one at a time.

Honey got back into Scouting as a Cadet while she was still in the Marching Band. She went with the Cadets to Washington D.C. She was one of three Cadets at her leader's house making Christmas decorations. She was also one of three scheduled to lay a wreath at the Tomb of the Unknown Soldier. This never happened because the group ran out of time. She sold peanuts and cookies. I bought whatever was being sold by the Scouts, or the Band Boosters, whichever family member was selling it.

Early in September, I took the bus from the foot of our street to the college. I got my schedule and my books. Suddenly, I was running up the steps to my first class, Speech aka Public Speaking. I lost my footing and scraped a two inch length of skin from one shin. It hurt a lot but I kept going at the same speed. My counselor recommended Speech as a good way to find out if I really wanted to go to college. I was afraid. It was so long since my last school experience. I didn't know anyone. I didn't want to know anyone. I just wanted to do something with my life besides the dishes. The first day, the young, balding, stoop-shouldered, teacher pulled his ear and scratched his head. He rubbed his nose. He showed twenty total strangers there are a lot of things you can get away with in public speaking. It was like a heavy wet cloud was fork lifted from my shoulders. My speech about ranching in the sea was based on a *National Geographic* article. Afterward, a serious young man asked pertinent questions. I answered them in front of the class like I knew whereof I spoke. I brought a mini-Haibachi to class for a talk about Tokyo's Kanto earthquake. Speech class was over much too soon. I loved it.

Two department heads, grumpy old men, with worlds of respect for each other's character and knowledge, won my heart. I took miles of notes in Political Science and History—writing as fast as they talked. Other students would borrow my notes to clear up a point after class. It was like I was living in a desert and now I could drink. My Freshman English class began with a blank piece of paper. The teacher politely requested a "sample of your writing technique." I wrote, all period, about the Viet Nam War and why I believed in it.

The very next class surprised me. At break time a tall, gangling, young man confronted us. He said there was only one reason he was in this classroom. He wanted to stay out of Viet Nam at any cost. He was belligerent about it, expecting to be attacked for what he was saying. He said, "Look at the thousands of sudden scholars all around us. So many people can't be wrong." I said, "Right has nothing to do with numbers. Two wrongs don't make a right. Neither do fifty wrongs. You can't argue quantity in this case." He was so serious, so involved, so scared. He said, "How about several thousand Chinese soldiers on little ponies coming right at you shooting?" He struck home there.

My second class of Freshman English was in another classroom. This teacher never believed I should not have remained where I began. My first teacher read my essay and wrote several complimentary things on it. Then he carried it to the Department Head and to the Sophomore English teacher. Entirely without further input from me, it was arranged for me to transfer to Sophomore English. I was inclined to agree with the Sophomore teacher so I did the homework for the first (Freshman) book. I also did the homework for (and attended) the Sophomore English class. Neither teacher ever knew this, of course. I was grateful to get a B at semester end.

My last English class was Creative Writing. The teacher was about my age and remarkably open-minded. One of the students wanted to write for sports magazines. He was not at all interested in literature as a dramatic event. To him the process of actually catching a fish by outwitting it was enough reason to write. His goal was to sit down at a typewriter, after the event, and share it. His expected audience was anyone having not yet outwitted a similar fish. He put up with my constant questioning for two whole days before leaving the class in disgust.

The rest of the small, but active, class was less intent on process than product. We wrote short stories prodigiously. These were mimeographed by someone working his way through school. Then we read them aloud and hashed them over in class. Short stories poured from my father's gift typewriter. "Views from the Kitchen Windows" described the events leading directly to my cousin's funeral early in World War II. At semester end, this was the story chosen for me to read aloud at our class farewell party. In a dimly lit bar, after a really good lunch, I listened to everyone else's final selected production. My turn was last. I spilled tears onto the pages as I read. Everyone was respectfully listening. At last the story ended. We shook hands with each other. I took the bus home. I got an A in the course. When I tried to sell the semester's output I got a group of rejection slips. The other time I mentioned World War II was in Political Geography. I began a report on Japan with, "Of course, everyone here remembers World War II." Everyone looked blank except the teacher. He laughed.

Available job projections indicated there would be a demand for Social Studies teachers in five years. Expecting to become a Social Studies teacher when I graduated, I followed a straight line of expected courses. In the beginning, I wanted to go to college full time like Norman did at Penn State. I was twenty years late in getting started. Norman chortled, "You want to go to school full time? Who's going to do the housework?" There were no illusions about the housework. I ran Norman's house like Grandma ran her house—a family custom. All meals were on time and we never ate a TV dinner. All beds were made, all floors were swept, dishes done, clothes in order, all the time. Afterward, I sat at my little desk in the kitchen and studied.

I always went to Summer School and I took all the evening classes I could. I felt guilty when the Scouts or the Band scheduled something I couldn't attend. I worked with, tried to work with, Upward Bound students as an unpaid volunteer for "experience." The black students were suspicious of what they considered an old lady but tolerant enough to accept me. There was the great joy of hearing an earthquake expert lecture. In the Nuclear Age, it was amazing how unpredictable even the Alaska Earthquake of 1964 was. I also went to New York City as a chaperone with this group. We saw the Rockettes and "True Grit" in Radio City Music Hall. I sat beside a black teacher who led a strike for higher teacher's salaries a few months later. The last time I saw her she was standing almost knee deep in fresh snow, holding a picket sign. I was proud of her.

For a while I tutored a high school kid who sniffed model airplane glue and lost much of his sight. He went to an Art History class, taught by a campus legend, and took occasional notes. We used his textbook plus my own notes from having taken the course a previous summer. I wrote down what he said in reply to test questions we could expect in the classroom. He handed in the result and gave me a note from the teacher. "You got an A because you are an artist. He got a C because he doesn't know the material. Don't argue. For him, that's a good grade."

Too much of my "College Fund" went to buy musical instruments for Honey, Scout cookies, and other essentials. There wasn't enough money left for my last semester tuition. I asked Norman for a loan. Norman explained, "I can't come up with so much money on short notice." I didn't mention the years of accumulated Savings Bonds in his strong box. He didn't want me to succeed. I prayed a lot before I asked him to co-sign the National Defense Student Loan I got through the college. I was surprised when he did. My years of Spanish, a pure joy, World Regional and Political Geography and Biology came to an end. Term papers on the then thriving economies of Lebanon and Japan came to an end. In Human Anatomy and Physiology, my teacher was a statistician by nature and training. Every morning of the summer class he told me how many points I still needed to graduate Cum Laude. With Honors? Me? With Honors!

Norman took Honey along when he bought his used motorboat. One Saturday morning, Norman drove us to the dock where we boarded the new used boat. Norman started the engine. Smoking and sputtering, swear words, various shifts, later, the craft sprang to life. Another shift slowed it down. More swear words and it gently eased forward. It struggled out to mid channel before it completely quit. David peeled off his outer clothes down to his bathing suit before he dived into the oily scum. He seized the rope dangling over the side and pulled the boat back to the dock. The plastic Indian astride the decking above the wheel looked just exactly like Norman did. It was complete to the folded arms across his chest. Norman drove us home.

The washing machine expired. With Norman's permission, of course, I called the repairman. I was standing by the machine as he took it apart. He looked for a small part, in vain, for some time. He pointed out it was a wonder the washer worked at all. Something vital to balancing the tub was missing. I said, "It seemed to be overloaded no matter how much, or how little, I put in." He nodded, "This model had that problem from the start. I'm surprised this machine lasted so long." I asked him to write down what he said so I could show it to Norman. For several years, Norman snapped, "You overloaded it," every time I suggested repairs. I felt so grateful it wasn't my fault. I always knew it was not overloaded. Now, there was proof! Norman didn't even read the repairman's report.

Poor Norman! The last week of Finals I didn't defrost the refrigerator. It was the only thing I just didn't do on schedule. I did not have the minutes it took to completely empty the refrigerator and freezer sections. There was no time to put pans of hot water on the shelves or to remove those pans after the ice melted. I could not wash the refrigerator and replace the food. The ice was thick and Norman wanted something from the freezer section. He took an ice pick and began to defrost—his way. When I came home, trudging up the hill from the bus, Honey ran to meet me. "We got a new refrigerator. Daddy took the old one to the dump," she explained. Norman was starting to move foods from the boxes on the floor, where he stored them, into the new machine. I made sudsy water and began to wash the interior. He stopped what he was doing. He demanded, "Where the Hell did you learn how to clean out a refrigerator? The same place you learned when to defrost one? "Exactly," I snapped. "We're going to a Marriage-Counselor," he told everyone at once. The refrigerator was new, on sale, with warranty and I really appreciated the way it defrosted itself.

We went to the Marriage Counselor. When I found out who it was, I thought, "Well, maybe this time a woman's voice may be heard." Wrong again! My Sociology teacher appeared to be open minded in class. In his office, he was a mere man who could be, and was, impressed by a business suit. The shiny wingtipped shoes, white shirt, and conservative tie went straight to his heart. (Norman never wore a tie or a shirt I bought for him). His ties were so ugly! His socks were so sleazy! I was so tired of the Saturday night card parties when his buddies from his latest job played poker. The kids and I stayed out of sight and I couldn't study because the kids could neither watch TV nor sleep.

The Marriage Counselor remembered me from class and said so. Norman said, "She studies all the time. I mean always. She always studies."

I tried to clarify. "I only study after I wash the breakfast dishes, make the beds, clean the house …."

"The teacher interrupted, smiling at Norman, "What else does she do?"

"Nothing," Norman complained.

"Is she available for sex?" came the question.

"Oh, yeah," came the answer.

"How is she with money?" asked the counselor. "She never buys anything but trinkets," came the reply. Norman folded his arms.

I cooperated. For three sessions Norman complained. I agreed to "do better." Norman paid for these sessions. They were expensive. Three were enough. When the questionnaire came from the company for which the counselor worked, I threw it in the garbage. As a Marriage Counselor, this one was not a sterling example. Q. If marriage is a two-way street, when does Norman leave the parking lot? A. Never. He's still polishing his latest used car-or his boat or his golf clubs or his shiny wingtipped shoes.

Meanwhile, David graduated from high school. Ralph Nader was guest speaker at his graduation. Norman bought a suit for David—a family custom. I gave him a Bulova watch. He missed the prom and had no date for graduation night. His friends gave a party and they brought him a plate full of small pastries. He got a yearbook but no class ring. He wouldn't ask for one. Norman wouldn't ask him if he wanted one and I couldn't afford one.

All this time the war in Viet Nam was going on. I changed my mind about the war. Actually, David changed my mind for me. While the protests began, he would ask me to, "Just look at that," on TV. I would be delivering clean socks or otherwise cluttering his room. Norman was for the war-gung ho! My Freshman English teacher and his wife fled to Canada. Not much later I was assigned a term paper for an English History class. The term paper was returned full of red marks and, "See me." When I did see him, he explained he heard about me from the Freshman English teacher. He said, "I am going to take this opportunity to make it possible for you to graduate from college. Take this book and follow the sample at the end-slavishly, like your life depended on it. I want this paper back along with the one you are going to make the right way." I did as I was told and he was right. I got an, "A plus - Good Conscientious Work" on the reconstructed term paper. He was right about everything else he said, too.

We fought the war about Viet Nam in our house, quietly and devastatingly as Norman's side began to lose. The only son of my Palo Alto uncle stopped by to visit—without any warning. Having never seen nor talked with him in my life, I was surprised. He appeared to be much more interested in Norman, the ex-Marine. They chatted about the luxury car he was delivering to the east coast from the west coast—a lifetime opportunity. I invited him to dinner. He refused. I asked him to come into the house and sit down. He refused. I asked him if he wanted something to drink. He wanted water. I brought some. Then, for a couple of hours, our little family stood in the sun while they talked about cars. Finally, he left, never to be heard from again.

Another dog tried to live in our backyard and got a disease. He may have brought one with him. Norman took him to the vet and returned without him. One of our dogs ran away. We kept four chattering finches and an angry parrot in our living room. They were near the organ I bought with Green Stamps for our first Erie home. No one played the organ. Norman began to read library books. Norman and I were barely speaking to each other as my graduation approached. Bruce and Honey attended David's graduation with Norman and brought him home. I didn't want Norman to attend my graduation from college. He said, "It only took me four years to get through Penn State. How many years is it taking you to get through your rinky-dink school?" The answer was five years because so much of it was part time. If the kids came, Norman would. I graduated alone. Why not? I was alone in the Labor Room three times.

College Three

Chapter 24

David enjoyed two good seasons as a caddy. Then, someone insulted him at every stop along the course. The players who might normally have restrained their friend's remarks were also inebriated. He was carrying doubles on an unusually hot day. Finally, David set down both golf bags and walked over to his bike and came home. Unaware of this, at the time, I kept sending David back to try to caddy. The caddy master invited him to come back to caddy school. David still felt like he committed the unforgivable sin. He signed up for college without my helpful counsellor. I gave him my father's typewriter and bought another one for myself. No one helped him choose courses so he started with everything basic. I asked about his English class. He said, "There's this really old lady who keeps asking dumb questions so nobody can learn anything." He was miserable. In the mirror I recognized a, "really old lady who asked dumb questions." I wondered how many young people I offended in my classes. Norman habitually slid into his chair at the dinner table and asked "Did anybody get a job yet?" Then, he stared at David who turned red and looked away.

Once I stood for two hours waiting for a bus which never came. The next regularly scheduled bus serving the college arrived exactly on time. I asked the driver, "What happened to the last bus?" "Oh, it was too cold. He never left the barn," came the reply. Twice that year Norman and the kids came to pick me up. Norman waited till I paid my fare and seated myself on the bus. Then, he parked in front of the bus. If I did not immediately notice him he honked the horn and waited for me to disembark. Where were we going? Home. What was the occasion? I was invited to substitute in a suburban high school history class. The arrangement was for the last half of a semester. The teacher for whom I substituted held this post for years. Volumes of carefully handwritten lesson plans, in meticulous order, cluttered his desk and cabinets. The Juniors I faced really considered themselves adults. They insisted they wanted discussion groups. I tried discussion groups. They ran away with the class. My practice teaching was in the seventh grade of a Junior High. I yearned for the days in 7H and 7G and my remarkably patient mentor. I recalled the moment he left his customary post just outside the door. He came into the class I was "teaching," walked up to the class clown and thrust him into the hall. We heard the distinct sounds of a paddle hitting home. That particular class gave me no more trouble. As an occasional substitute, I could usually get one of the students to operate the film projector. Meanwhile, I figured out what to do next. Here there were plans and textbooks and eager students who considered me just another relic. For three months, I tried to be a full time High School teacher. Only one of all those kids regarded me as a person. He already had a D- on the teacher's roll when we met. He hated History with his whole heart. He preferred to consider various means of self-destruction rather than face having to repeat the class. One day, he asked me if I would please give him a D. In return, he proposed to make a paddle for me in his favorite class, Wood Shop. "You need a paddle, Mrs. You can't be a teacher without a paddle. How about if I give you a paddle of your own and you give me a D of my own. Huh? Please." I gave him the D. The paddle was beautiful, soft brown wood, smooth enough to brush across my face. I already knew I would not be invited back. I had no friends among the teachers. All I did there was grade papers and try to teach. I saved every penny I earned and paid my student loan in full. I also paid tuition for

Summer Graduate classes in Arab and Black History and banked the rest. The classes were great. I missed those awful kids. I never even thought of using the paddle.

Meanwhile, Norman formed the habit of asking me to drive Bruce to the dentist or to get the weekly groceries. His seventh or eighth used car was a station wagon. I still renewed my driver's license annually. I took Bruce to the dentist on the seat of my bike and got groceries with David's old red wagon. It was good exercise. The needs were met and I couldn't be responsible for higher insurance costs. This lesson I already knew. After graduation, the weekend evenings became available for Bridge so I took lessons from a professional. This Grand Master gave lessons at the YWCA, at her home, and at the new Bridge Club in our neighborhood. I drove the family car to the top of our hill every Friday to play with the same elderly lady. She was so addicted to Bridge she would even play with me. At scheduled tournaments, involving points, more experienced players snapped her up. Most Fridays found her trying, vainly, to teach me how to count cards, bid, and play. Either you have card sense or you don't. I don't. I tried but I could not fathom Bridge. After a year or so, I dropped out. However, during the year, I backed out of a parking spot. Waving at the Bridge players waiting for my space, I drove right into their car. The damage was slight but the insurance costs went up and Norman was irate.

I read an article, "The Navy Takes Care of its Own," and thought, "Why not?" I talked David into volunteering for the U.S. Navy. He did. Then came my turn to be irate. After David went to Boot Camp at Great Lakes, the college sent him another grade report. The only class he passed, every one of which was "required" and "basic," was gym. This final report replaced his D with an F, thereby making him a total failure. In all the years since then, the alumni have requested funds for various projects. I have immediately deposited their requests in the garbage. I thought the changed grade report the meanest thing anyone ever did to anyone anywhere. This was mean in the original sense, petty, small-time. I still think so.

Norman told the marriage counselor, "She won't even get dressed up to go shopping in the Boston Store." I thought this was hilarious. The only unusual thing about the store was the brass tubing which relayed messages over our heads to the bookkeepers upstairs. Just before Christmas, Bruce and Honey, Norman and I, went shopping in the Boston Store. I was wearing my canary yellow jeans and green sneakers with a loose brown pullover. The kids were in jeans and sneakers with pullovers and Norman was in a business suit. Bruce saw a toy and showed it to Honey who loved it instantly. I led her to another aisle to look at something she was not interested in. Norman and Bruce bought the toy Honey loved. It then became a matter of hiding a huge purple plush mouse from an inquisitive child. We managed. I let Honey lead me back to the toys while Norman took the purple mouse to the car trunk. Honey was properly surprised on Christmas morning.

David enjoyed shovelling snow at Boot Camp. I trusted God and the Navy to give him a start in life. Norman figured out the annual income taxes. As was his custom, he handed me a pen to sign the tax form. He complained, "We wouldn't have to pay so damn much taxes if you didn't work." By then only occasional substitute assignments were coming my way. The city bus schedules made last minute assignments difficult. If I needed to cross the city, I might be late, so I decided to buy a car. I knew the kind of car I wanted. I asked Norman to take me to the outskirts of the city to a foreign car dealer. In the dealer's lot, I found what I was looking for, in fact, two of them. The dealer saw us looking and came out rubbing his hands together. I went straight to the point, "How much are you asking for this one?"

"Four hundred dollars as is," he said.

"Done," I said, "Will you take a check?"

"Sure," he said.

Norman looked thunderstruck. I went with the dealer to his office, wrote him a check and agreed to come back the next day. Norman came into the office and suggested I drive it home with him behind me. I agreed. Soon the little red Fiat was visible from inside our kitchen. It bucked and coughed when I drove it from the dealer's lot but I loved every inch of it.

When the four of us were all inside our house and taking off our coats, Norman exploded. "What in the Hell did you think you were doing out there? You paid $400 for a hunk of junk. That damn foreign junk heap won't last six months. You didn't even ask the salesman to let you drive it first. I really can't believe anyone is so stupid." Thoughts of Norman's *nine* used cars flew through my consciousness as did the volumes of monthly payment coupons. I got the gasoline bills in the mail and the credit card bills and the repair bills. When his car wasn't parked at work it was leaking oil in our driveway. I didn't say a word. When Norman's car was comfortably parked at work, I checked out my new motor vehicle. This charming red automobile was my very own, the only car I could think of as mine. I drove it to the karate lessons all of us were taking at my expense—without Norman. When it rained, the water from the pavement gained entry through the floor boards. It sloshed warmly about our bare feet and we sang together. My own car was so much fun for *two years*! Two years was, incidentally, about as long as Norman kept some of his gas-guzzling monsters.

The Upward Bound program included Judo lessons. I loved Judo. Someone who came up behind me with intention to mug would be surprised. I learned how to do the Japanese bow. My Freshman year I took Karate lessons. After I got my Fiat Accompli title and tags, insurance etc. I could take the kids to weekly lessons and local tournaments. Fiat wouldn't go all the way to Buffalo but the instructor always found transportation for us to the major events. Honey and David and Bruce loved Karate, loved to learn Katas. We even liked to Kumite until David hurt someone with a hard kick and decided not to go back. David was hurt more than his opponent by the event. Bruce took the opportunity to chicken out. Honey and I earned purple and brown belts respectively. Our instructor told me I could never earn a black belt because "There isn't a mean bone in your body." I switched to Aikido with Honey. Then, I ran out of money.

Fiat started out a radiant scarlet, non-shiny but definitely visible. It was never polished but it was painted. When inspection time rolled around, it passed. But the shop owner suggested I look for a replacement for, "that lemon." We painted it bright yellow and added bathtub appliques of flowers. It looked like a lemon with daisies all over it. With, or without, four of us in it, it felt great to have my own car.

Norman had a problem with his car one day. He asked me, "Where are your keys? I'm taking the second car today."

"Over my dead body," I assured him. He somehow managed to make his car work. The requests for me to pick up this or that became more frequent. Each time, I used the bike or the wagon or an excuse like, "Can't. Sorry. Working today."

I did work, as a substitute, usually in Special Education. There I found a child, who spent time in jail, incredibly considerate and meek. I found other kids being warehoused in their parts of the schools. I often wondered what the Special Ed kids would do if I told them about the spit wads. What if I mentioned the fleets of paper airplanes the "normal kids" threw around their classrooms? What if I told them about the loud noises the "normal kids" used to harass substitute teachers? What if I showed them the essay tests returned with 1) pig 2) pig 3) pig 4) pig as answers?

Someone from Upward Bound called to offer me a special job. He was acting for a church trying to enter the Head Start program. I was told I was the Director and given catalogs from which to select desks and playground equipment etc.. While I was there nothing I selected ever arrived. I enlisted the aid of Honey and Bruce to make lists of prices and catalog numbers. There was a staff. One "teacher" was still attending college. One "teacher" graduated from college but attended only a few meetings before she got a real job. One "social worker" actually worked full time for the church. One secretary also worked for the church but would be paid by the program. When I asked the secretary to send a letter for the program I learned she did not know how to spell. I bought a dictionary for her to call her own. Then I learned she could not read. She was attractive in a dyed, made-up, manicured, short-skirted way. She was also the right color. There were a "cook" and a "cook's helper" We were in a small one story house next to the church. The students were among the first to arrive. I worked almost around the clock for three months. Equipment and supplies were still "on order." Every time I developed a plan, the "social worker" developed a way to delay or divert it. One day I came to work and found a different person in my "office."

"Didn't you know, you're supposed to be a teacher now. You get to help (the non-college graduate)" she announced.

My first reaction was the most complete relief I felt for three months. I was one of the "token whites." Since the real "Director" earned her brand new Bachelor's degree, the remaining "teacher" could be the "token white." Proud of living with her parents, this individual never cashed any of her checks. She told everyone this, frequently. My first day at work the "social worker" asked me not to rush to the bank with my paycheck. I looked at the large diamond ring on the finger of the Minister whose church

sponsored this activity. I looked at his new Cadillac in the driveway. I looked at his shiny shoes and well-pressed suit. Right after work, on payday, I took my check straight to the bank. I did this every payday. The Director's salary was supposed to look impressive. I was properly grateful for mine and for the graduation "Cum Laude" which got me the position in the first place. I thanked everyone and departed.

David didn't write letters. He telephoned. He didn't say much. I usually got the calls and relayed his "Hi to everyone." We got an invitation to his graduation. I looked through the local department stores for something suitable to wear. There was nothing to express my feelings. When I graduated from Great Lakes Naval Training Center I wore a Navy blue suit with a bucket hat. I wanted David to be able to find Honey and me in a very large crowd. I made red, white and blue Chinese style pantsuits for Honey and me. The sewing machine work was terrible. Probably anyone could have done a better job. Norman gassed up the new used car, another station wagon, and we set out for Chicago. Red, white and blue stars and stripes adorned us when we arrived. We sat somewhere in the middle of a row of bleachers. I looked for David. I thought I saw him. Honey thought she saw him. We watched the entire review and waited while the graduates joined their families.

The parade ground was almost bare when someone directed us to a nearby building. There, someone from the graduating group came to the desk where we waited for attention. He and the counterman chatted, behind their hands, for a few minutes. After he left, the counterman walked over to us. "You're probably looking for someone named David. You can probably catch him at O'Hare. He was discharged this morning," he said.

As we turned to leave, a well-dressed mother of one of the graduates said, "Oh, I love those pant-suits. Did you make them?"

"Yes, Thank You," I said through a kind of numbness, the same numbness I felt when Keith died.

Fiat Accompli

Chapter 25

Norman got the station wagon off the base ahead of most of the traffic and went straight to O'Hare. We walked a lot around the lobbies before it occurred to him to ask to have David paged. The clerk directed David to a central point-where we met him shortly thereafter. He was taller and leaner and he looked good with a crew cut. He was wearing tight khaki pants I never saw before with a short-sleeved shirt and sneakers. He carried a blue duffle bag plus a large envelope with his discharge papers. When he saw us, he said, "Did you get to see the graduation? I was hoping you would get to see the graduation." We all said, "Yes," at once. Then, Norman said, "Well, as long as we're here, let's go see the museum." So we did. We exchanged the ticket David just bought for money and went out to lunch at a fast food place. Then we spent the afternoon looking at dinosaurs and buying souvenirs. We slept in a motel in Indiana because it was cheaper than a room in the city. We went to the Shedd Aquarium and bought a Chinese doll for Honey and earrings for me. We looked around the Loop and the business section and some shopping centers. Still without comment, without a word to David, Norman drove home.

Nobody discussed the graduation. While Norman was buying gas I asked David what happened. David said, "I knew I was in trouble when someone said to bring my rifle to the grinder and I forgot. Then, I was supposed to get it and bring it to the D.I. and I didn't. It was late by then and I just went to bed. After that, I was just discharged. I'm really sorry but I did not want to go to Viet Nam. There's some books I heard about. I wish we could get them. They'll tell you how I felt better than I can." Norman came back, pocketing his credit card slip. Later, I bought the books for David to read in his room. A few days after our return home, I came singing up the basement stairs to the kitchen, "Hello, Sunshine. Good-bye, Rain. Got My Baby Back Again." Norman was standing in the kitchen looking like he really would have loved to kill me just then.

David had an Honorable Discharge, discharge money, a purple heart I never understood, and nothing to do. He found a sailboat in the want ads, "Flying Juniors being replaced by the Yacht Club." I went with him to buy one plus a trailer to convey it to our garage. The gentleman in charge of the boats arranged sailing safety lessons for Norman, David, and me. As part of the course, we were required to, "sink the boat," by overturning it. Then we hung onto the hull till we were rescued. When our turn came, I insisted Norman be rescued first, "because he can't swim." Our teachers rescued David next while I clung to the boat. I was enjoying the pleasantly cool water. We passed the course. For several weeks Norman and the boys, or the whole family, went out on David's sailboat. We sailed about Presque Isle inlet where several houseboats were moored. Bruce enjoyed cruising with Norman or sailing with David. He enjoyed being one of the Indian Dancers with the Boy Scouts. He loved Driver's Ed in high school. Bruce always wanted to be a millionaire. Now it seemed he was pretty close. After Bruce got his driver's license, he towed the sailboat to the peninsula twice. Honey and I went along the last time. Fall was there in living color. David wanted to sail alone. He glided to the end of the inlet and back. David was so sad when they slid the boat onto the trailer. Bruce was angry. He had to take Norman's car back to pick up Norman at work. He was determined not to be late. Norman tried to teach David to drive. Norman scowled and swore. Clenching the wheel, David stepped on the gas and the car bucked in the driveway. Norman decided he was too busy to teach David how to drive a car.

We went to Quebec and Ottawa, Canada by way of Boston and Cape Cod. I bought some silver flying sea gull earrings in Mystic, Connecticut. I managed to lose them by wrapping them up with some garbage. With five people living in a station wagon for ten days, garbage accumulated. It seemed like forever unwrapping sandwiches and little cakes and trying to keep the car litter-free. We dropped off the garbage wherever we could. Only after I pulled my hand back from a litter basket on a Boston garage door did I realize the earrings were gone. I felt hurt! It was stupid! There was no excuse! The trip was like that-beautiful Mystic Seaport, majestic Boston, the North Street Church, walking where Paul Revere walked. Always, always we were waiting for what Norman was going to say. I cooked and washed dishes at every campsite. On the St. Lawrence River bank we camped. In a truly horrendous downpour Bruce got the fire going. I saw a miniature waterfall, just briefly, near Montreal, not long enough to point it out.

We drove parallel to the international headquarters of Mama's church. I was not brave enough to ask Norman to take us there so we could see it. Neither was anyone else. In Quebec City, I bought a French-English Dictionary and we took the prescribed walking tour together. In Ottawa we walked through Parliament. It was the best vacation we ever had—and the worst. When we came home we played some badminton in the side yard and a few rounds of croquet. Otherwise, the side yard was for mowing. I harvested the pears from our two trees and made pear pies from a bake-off recipe.

On the day David became twenty-one years old, Norman drove him to the Insane Asylum. He got a court order to put him there and to give him shock treatment. There was no warning—just that nameless dread of what Norman might do. This hung over all of us from the time we left Chicago. I gave Norman the money to buy a puppy for Honey's birthday. He and Bruce went to choose it at the pound. When she saw it, she squealed with joy. "Let's call him Charlie," she suggested. We did. Everyone loved the dear little mixed Beagle. He used to sun himself, like a polar bear, on a cake of ice beside his dog house. Never did Norman let the dear dog come into the house. He could not even use the enclosed part of the porch in the howling winds of winter. Norman was the same way about David. He took the family to visit David at Christmas time. Honey was devastated when she saw the human derelicts on the ward and the tiny cot with a grey blanket. This was David's "room." Bruce appeared to take everything in stride. David was concerned about how we would feel-seeing him so hollow-eyed and gaunt. I wrote a letter to the local branch of Mama's church asking for someone to visit him. I threw away the only answer I received, "Too busy. Christmas, you understand." He showed us the comb he received from another church. I didn't dare to hug him. I just hung onto Honey's hand and watched Norman show us what happened if you didn't live Norman's way. By then Norman's way was one only he could live.

I drove Fiat to the garage for a required inspection. "For $400 we can fix her and give you the state sticker," said a very kind, very dirty, very dishevelled garage owner. I said, "Thank You," and drove her away. After dinner, I told Norman I would need to borrow money to restore my car. He said, "Absolutely not." The next evening, the same plea brought the same reply. At three o'clock in the morning, I remembered George built a Model A in Ellen's yard. He might know how to fix my Fiat. In the afternoon while everyone was gone, I telephoned Ellen. George answered the phone. I asked for Ellen. He said, "She's in a home. One day she took a taxi to the head of the valley. Said she wanted to see how it changed since last time Cap took her there. I brought that to a screeching halt. She's never going to do it again." I said, "George, I need some help with my car." George didn't hesitate. "Could I help out with your car? Does that make any sense to you?" I said, "No, George. Good-bye, George." The following morning, I assured myself the battery cables and whatever else I bought for Fiat were in her trunk. I drove to the junkyard. Once there, I signed and surrendered her title—which was still in the glove compartment. For $10, "to make it legal", the junk dealer bought my Fiat. I walked the few blocks home and extracted my driver's license from my wallet. I mailed it to the Department of Motor Vehicles. I thought I would not cry about my car just like I did not cry about David. But Bruce came home from school in a rage as black as one of Norman's. "What did you do to the car? I saw the junk man driving it right by the school," he said. Bruce protested to Norman who expected Fiat to be in her usual spot in the driveway. I waited to hear what Norman would say. "That junk heap cost $400 to start with. Another $400 to make it run would double the cost," he explained. "How many cars have you driven for two years which cost $400 base price? How many cost only $400 to repair? How many $800 cars are there, Norman?" I wanted to shout. I went out to the yard to pet Charlie—and cry.

It took Norman two days to miss the battery starting cables. He came into the kitchen and asked me where they were. "Were they your property, Norman? When did you buy them?" I wondered aloud. "Do you know where they are?" He wanted to know. "At the junkyard with the junk heap they belong to," I explained. Shaking his head, he stormed outside.

I cleaned the house thoroughly after I cleaned the garage. The garage was literally full of junk which needed to be conveyed to the dump. I asked

Norman if he would do so. "Not now. Some other time. When I get around to it," he replied. Two weeks later, the rarely used garage was still full of garbage. On a Monday morning I loaded Bruce's red coaster wagon with junk and delivered it to the dump. From our neighborhood this was a journey of about two miles. In just two days, in four trips with a heavily laden wagon, I cleaned out the garage. Then, I washed the wagon and replaced it in its usual parking spot inside the garage. Saturday afternoon, Norman finished watching the TV ball games. He changed into a really old pair of suit trousers, old wingtipped shoes and a threadbare old workshirt. I was baking something in the kitchen when he strolled out to the garage and lifted the door. When he turned to face the kitchen I ducked and scrambled out of sight. His face was so funny! He was shocked. Then, he came into the house. By then, I was doing something in the basement with the laundry. The something was noisy enough to cover the laughter which just kept bubbling up.

David was released from the Insane Asylum and put in a group residence. Here a young lady set out to teach him how to fend for himself. Norman told Bruce loudly enough so I could hear him, "David is hopeless. He buys books instead of bread, marshmallows instead of turnips. He's hopeless." Since David hated turnips, didn't care much for bread, loved marshmallows and books, I was delighted. It meant his spirit had not been stifled, yet.

The living room couch was used and cheap when we acquired it. Now, its springs were springing through the upholstery. Norman read about a place where one could "learn how to do your own upholstering." Setting aside the want ads, he addressed Bruce. "Would you mind watching your sister while your mother and I do something about the couch, Bruce?" Without ever having been asked, I soon found myself running a commercial sewing machine. I made tight seams on arm covers and the cases for sofa cushions. For several weeks, we worked on the couch. We were the only ones at the small workroom except for the teacher/owner and an assistant. I hope we were not the only ones who answered the ad. The couch came home at last, red, white, and blue striped on a beige background. The stripes lined up. It looked all right.

Then, Norman painted everything again. His first painting on this first house we ever bought was strange, to say the least. I chose bright colors, sailor's blue for the trim of David's room, yellow for Honey's (their favorite colors). Red was for Bruce with sunlight yellow walls to reflect maximum light. The dining room was supposed to be lavender but after Norman mixed the paint it became a deep purple. The living room was as sailor blue as the wood trim in David's room instead of the mild blue I selected. The master bedroom was really bright orange—several shades darker than my original choice. How could I tell Norman the colors were too colorful? He was saving money by mixing his own paint. The newly covered couch would have looked great in a bright blue living room. It looked ghastly against white walls. The beige background looked like permanently dirty white. Once again, I didn't say a word.

While David was trying to master grocery shopping, Honey was swimming on her High School swim team. Bruce and Honey were in the marching band and taking music lessons. Bruce was really involved with the Indian Dancers. I was working for Man Power when Norman decided he wanted to talk to a divorce lawyer. I recommended one I already knew from the Bridge Club. Norman drove us to our appointment at the lawyer's office. On the way, I asked him, "Why do you think I went to the Insane Asylum when we lived in State College?"

Norman's reply stunned me, "You were having a tantrum."

I continued, "We drove all the way from State College with the windows open. How did I look when we reached the hospital?"

"Dishevelled, I know. I looked it up" he said.

"Did you try to help me look more presentable? Did you give me a comb or ask me if I wanted to comb my hair?"

He laughed. He told the lawyer I was 'vicious.' "She only got married because she wanted to play house," he said. Norman and I chatted with the lawyer for at least fifteen minutes. Norman announced I could have David and Honey. He would keep Bruce and the house and the car. I could leave anytime unless, of course, I wanted to start contributing to the family.

"I'll do better," I promised. The lawyer's bill was $300. I quit the Bridge Club very quietly. I just didn't reappear.

The kids were getting used to our verbal battles. Once, I asked Norman for the checkbook so I could go grocery shopping. This was not an unusual event. I could see the shock in their eyes when he extended the checkbook, then pulled it back toward him. I grabbed for it, in a kind of keep away game. He hit me across my cheek with the back of his hand. I backed away as he kept hitting me, right into the cul de sac of the bathroom. Under his onslaught, I sought safety, trying to get behind the toilet, then below it. There wasn't enough space. Honey and Bruce were suddenly behind Norman yelling, "Stop." He did stop. He threw the checkbook at me and drove away for a while. I soothed Honey and Bruce, childishly repeating, "I talked him into getting an education and this is what I get!" The kids were angry with both of us. We reached the point where we didn't talk to each other. We yelled at each other—when the long silences were broken. I said something like, "You said yourself, without me, you'd be a used car salesman," for the tenth time in a week. Any one of the kids snapped, "I don't want to hear it." They could stop me with that. To stop Norman, one left the room, quietly, of course.

Then, Pansy, my half-sister, wrote to me. She was going to be, "in the neighborhood," at a specific time. She was willing to go a couple of hundred miles out of her way to visit me. I sat down at the typewriter with no idea how to reply. My family was going to break up. I was terribly short of money. Most of all, I didn't believe there was any kind of a relationship between me and Pansy. There were several children by her second husband. Theirs was an entirely different lifestyle. I was typing along when my fingers struck the letter T. I couldn't find my typewriter eraser. "What goes with T?" I asked myself. "Trash, came the answer. That's it!" I knew how to answer Pansy's letter. I wrote, "Dear Trash, Please don't go so far out of your way because we won't be home when you get here." Then, I cut the paper down somewhat, put it in an envelope and mailed it. I was sorry about the wording but I could not face Pansy by herself, certainly not with several children.

Shortly thereafter, Norman announced at the dinner table, "For your convenience I'm going to bring a psychiatrist home tomorrow evening." I did my usual evening work, the dishes, tucking in Bruce and Honey, a brief rite by now. I gave Charlie a little extra food and some fresh water, gave myself a bath and went to bed. It wasn't one of the nights for sex so Norman was already sleeping. The next morning everything was normal. I made breakfast. We ate it. I washed the dishes while Norman left for work. Bruce yelled, "Good-bye" as he left the house. I walked with Honey to the door. In other years, I closed the door between us and held it closed, requiring her to go to school. She smiled up at me, "See you later, alligator." I smiled back and closed the door and found my suitcase. A few minutes later, I was at the bus stop. A little while after that, I was at the bus terminal buying my ticket. I couldn't go far with money I saved from the groceries to buy cigarettes. I didn't want to go far. I didn't want to get caught.

After a short bus ride, relatively speaking, I found a hotel room. In the telephone book I found Man Power's address. I took a bus to get there, signed up and went out for an interview. Tonight, I would sleep in the worst room I have ever even seen. The walls were scabrous with peeling paint, the tub was flaking apart. It was Tuesday night. My job as a temporary would start Thursday night when I replaced someone who was quitting. Meanwhile, Wednesday night was almost upon me. I changed from travel clothes into something less casual and went to church. This address, too, came from the telephone book. I prayed hard for a long time for a bad situation to improve. Now I was a fugitive. I would probably spend the rest of my life in an asylum. I went to church and I prayed and I sang hymns and I prayed. I gave a testimony. Then, people near me gave testimonies—one of which I never forgot. After church, a lady came up and introduced herself. She drove me to meet a young lady with a spare room and a chronic fear of being alone. We moved me out of the hotel immediately afterward.

College Four

Chapter 26

I was back in a bank and it was awesome! A connecting bridge between two departments was suspended over a major downtown street. It was a night job. I started in the afternoon and left the building at sunrise. As I walked homeward through a long hall, a rising sun would gild the bridge girders. The solo walk, with the sun making a shining carpet before me, took my breath away every morning. It was so quiet and so special. Down on the street there was never a long wait for a bus. I used a key to the oldest house in Buffalo where my hostess lived as a recluse. After her husband died, she ordered carpenters to construct a completely enclosed room.

They tore apart three rooms to create a box inside her house with its own heavy door. This was her bedroom where she retired every night. Both the house doors and her bedroom door were locked and bolted. One winter, she walked her dog on the ice. He pulled on the leash. She slipped and fell and broke her hip. Hobbling with a cane and rarely leaving home, this childlike person became prey to countless fears.

My first payday I recruited two friends of my hostess, and their red wagon, to go Safeway shopping with me. We brought home a reasonable supply of staples. I tossed the rotting potatoes from a kitchen drawer and the even more rotten onions into the garbage. I began to make real meals. It turned out the frail woman whose house it was preferred cheezits and cherry pop to a regular dinner. The neighborhood children played cards with her after school. Their parents appreciated this free baby-sitting. At least they knew where their children were. These people were not happy with my interruption of their lifestyle. When my friend from church came to check up on us, my hostess surprised me. She complained I "threw out her perfectly good vegetables." Besides, I "wasted gas cooking frivolous meals."

An older lady, who was a private investigator, befriended me. The first night I attended her church, she said there was a spare bed in her house whenever I needed it. Now I pulled her card from my wallet and telephoned her. My first rescuer moved me, again, much closer to the bank. The spare bed was in a room with more space than I enjoyed with the young lady. This friend didn't smile and fondle the rent money like my most recent hostess. The money I paid her for rent was always spent on something for me, or us, before the next payment was due. Despite different schedules, we had fun together. She was glad I loved to cook. Before his death, her husband did the cooking. We ate well. I shopped at the store on the bottom floor of our apartment building and took over the meals. She taught me how to clean a bathroom so it sparkled—with rubbing alcohol. The things she couldn't do, the places she couldn't reach, I could. We talked and read. I accumulated money, went to church and learned new skills. I did a lot of busy work no one else found time to do. I did useful work when someone called in sick and there was a deadline. Other temporary employees came, got bored and left. Others kept calling in sick and weren't invited back. I prayed a lot. Gradually, I began to feel like a person. I bought clothes suitable for a real job. I even bought a scarlet tailored coat with a shako and gloves to match.

While I was in Buffalo, my church friend took me to spend the day in Niagara Falls. While she did her visiting, I walked about the Falls themselves. I admired the big black squirrels I never really appreciated when we were here as a family. Another day, I provided company to and from Binghamton, where I walked about and enjoyed and felt free. My private investigator friend, "asked around," as she put it, to see if I was on any police blotters. She said no one was looking for me, at least, officially. I thought this was kind of odd. I was also grateful not to have to worry about being involved with the police.

My twenty-fifth wedding anniversary came and went. I didn't mention it to anyone, of course. I was so glad to be able to live my own life every day for a while. Whenever I thought of David in the asylum, I quietly prayed. Whenever I recalled the fear on Honey's face when she saw the grey blanket on his cot, I prayed some more. Bruce and Norman were in their own world. I needed strength to face their world again. Of course, the strength came. The worst weather of the winter was over when I telephoned Norman. I asked him if it was all right to come home. On the telephone he said, "If you agree to marriage counseling." I said, "O.K." I told everyone at work and, in due time, they gave me a farewell party. I heard there was going to be a potluck. So I bought a small chocolate fudge cake at the store in our building. It was on the table, at one side, all night as we worked and ate. When I went to get it afterward, it was gone. One of the temporaries threw it away. I couldn't find it immediately so I left without it—marvelling it was tossed without even being tasted. The potluck surprised me. These quiet and very efficient housewives created a party for me! There were hugs at parting. My eyes were full of tears when I walked the shining path out of the bank.

I took the bus home after I packed and handed my dear friend, the P.I., my key to her home. We gave each other a brief hug and then we shook hands and I hurried to the bus stop. She "was going to visit some relatives in Florida," she said. I didn't worry on my way home. I tried to see as much of the steel mills and New York scenery as I could. I didn't expect to see them again soon. When I reached the back porch, I saw Charlie lying on his cake of ice. He wiggled all over his body while I took his frozen water dish in, and his food dish. I thawed and scrubbed and replenished them. The parrot who always tried to bite and, therefore, never got out of his cage, dear Sam, needed attention. My first hours in the empty house were spent cleaning up and feeding the pets and caring for the plants. I was beginning to clean the house when Honey came home. We just glowed when we saw each other. Bruce smiled warily, but somewhat more respectfully, than he usually did. Norman didn't smile at all. He was almost tender when everyone else was finally asleep. David was no longer in the asylum, living in a group home, and evidently not to be discussed. Erie was monumentally unchanged.

There were weeks to do a thorough housecleaning and cart away junk in the wagon. I raked the winter debris from the yard and made things look people-friendly again. I found pills in Honey's room, in corners and nooks behind toys. When I asked her she explained. She finally began to swallow the pills when Norman cried real tears of frustration. The marriage counselor sessions were now a family event. Even David was included. We did role playing. When it was my turn, I tried to include the group as a whole. Everyone allowed me to pull him or her toward the center of the room. Norman was farthest away. When I reached him, he folded his arms across his chest and planted his feet solidly on the floor. He was determined not to let me take him anywhere—not even to become part of his own family group. There were several moments of complete silence. Then, the psychiatrist in charge suggested another appointment.

It was for two, Norman and me. Again, Norman folded his arms. Again, Norman told the psychiatrist, "she doesn't get involved. She just will not get involved in anything." The psychiatrist in the asylum where David was promised to "teach you how to fight each other without getting hurt." What he actually did was ask me a question. While I took a deep breath, he turned to Norman with another question. This psychiatrist didn't promise anything. I think we were scheduled to go back in six months. Norman solidified.

Meanwhile, Norman took Honey to a psychiatrist whom she now saw, occasionally, by appointment. Gradually, the pills he assigned for her were reduced until they became one each day. Bruce still took his daily rheumatic fever pill.

David was a failure at grocery shopping, shining shoes, (he always wore sneakers) and keeping his belongings in order. The young lady in charge of his residence sent him home. It was just as well. He came home for lunch for some time. His memory was coming back. He told me about "Pops" in our second Erie neighborhood. The man with the wonderful garden lost a thumb in a foundry. For the first time I discovered it was he who taught David how to throw a softball the right way. Norman was at work. Bruce and Honey were in school. No one wanted me to work for them. The house was organized. I was always glad to see David stop to pet Charlie before coming onto the porch. One day, he brought me an Amaryllis. Years before, I admired a blooming Amaryllis in the Boston Store. It cost $19 then—way out of sight. Now, the wonderful plant was much less expensive. It was even available in the grocery store where David bought it—probably instead of turnips. I loved the tall, slender, beautiful plant.

How easily David slipped back into the family. I remembered my uncles in Canada, the ones Mama talked about. These were brothers Ellen settled there by paying their passage money over the years. There was no way to contact them. I lacked the nerve to try such a thing. But Canada itself? Maybe, David could find a niche there. He was getting money from the state, Norman said. After a prescribed interval, he would have to go back to the asylum because the residence program did not work. I asked David if he would bike to Niagara Falls, try to get into Canada and get some kind of job. He was eager to try just about anything. He already owned a tent, bedroll, Scouting gear. One morning he rode away. Three or four days later, just in time for dinner, he eased the bike back into the driveway. He was exhausted but happy, so tired his legs wouldn't work for a while. I sent Bruce to get the stove and pack which fell from his bike at the top of our hill. Bruce was not happy to have to walk two blocks to "pick up after David." I remembered the second son in Jesus's parable of the Prodigal. Honey's face glowed when she saw him. Norman just scowled.

So David was at home and Bruce and Honey were relaxed. Norman was cooking up something and I couldn't trust him out of my sight. I wrote to my father explaining David needed a place to live for a while. Would he, please, let him live in Alaska with him? I walked to the bank and withdrew all the money in David's account before he became a ward of the state. When Norman told me David was a ward, he also said such beings were not allowed to possess more than $50. Immediately, I informed Norman the money was actually mine and, surprisingly, he didn't object. Therefore, from my account I could now take enough money to buy an airline ticket for David. I wrote another letter to his grandfather and mailed it. I put some cash in his wallet along with the ticket. I told Norman David was going to Alaska to visit his grandfather. Two days later, Norman drove us all to the airport where we said, "Good-bye," to David. We spent several hours renewing Norman's love for airplanes as they took off and landed, were parked and gassed and loaded. My father's reply was in my purse, "Tell him to come ahead. We'll be kind of crowded but, if it's what you both need, it's what I am here for. I love you. Dad."

With David satisfactorily gone, Norman discovered Florida. We went to Orlando with a travel trailer behind us and without the side trip to Grandma's house, either going or coming. There were no diapers to wash and the parks were lovely. Bruce showed off his grilling skills and we saw Busch Gardens and Disney World, Tampa and points between. Herded like sheep from dazzling adventure to dazzling adventure we took a "real vacation" at last! Bruce did one unorthodox thing. After everyone else fell asleep one night, he went for a run on the beach at Daytona. We almost got lost in St. Augustine.

No one called me from the School District. It was just as well. Dodging spitwads no longer appealed to me—not that it ever had. I did need money so I went to work for Manpower at an insurance company. I did meaningful things like collating huge reports. I learned from my co-workers juicy tidbits like "if a man has a reputation for being an early riser, he can sleep all day." I wrote a letter to Manpower suggesting they push temporaries in the local banking industry. Weeks later, I finally got to work in a local bank as a temporary. Here I noticed one of two people, working together, dropped a paper clip. They both dove for the floor to retrieve it. He said, "We've got to stop meeting like this." She was laughing so hard she couldn't pick up the clip so he did. Unfortunately, the special project, for which I was hired, didn't last long. I enjoyed working in a bank. Every day on the job, Honey came to meet me when I got off the bus. "Can we go yet? Do we have enough money yet?" she asked.

Bruce and Norman did all the paper work. Now Bruce needed to present the family at Penn State University. So Norman drove his ninth or tenth used car, a station wagon, to State College. I remembered how drab our years there were. I wore a new chartreuse pant-suit with matching floppy hat, stockings and sandals, good underwear, nothing see-through. It was very warm but the drive down was comfortable. Honey wore clean, neat school clothes as did Bruce. Norman was in his usual suit and shiny wingtip shoes. We went to the School of Architecture. For years a question, "What do you want to be?" brought from Bruce only one answer, "A millionaire." He never showed any interest in buildings, drafting, even drawing. Now here we were with several other families. We heard a distinguished looking professor explain how many years it takes to become an architect. He told us how extremely difficult the courses are. He was an honest man. We looked at each other and both of us knew Bruce would never qualify. Honey was restless. I eased us both away with a slight bow to him. We passed other parents in our group. I heard a woman in a sheer summer dress inquire loudly, "What boat did she come in?" I didn't bother to look back.

We went to see the cows at Penn State. On our way Norman asked, "Why didn't David stay in Canada?"

"He needed $300 to get in and a place to stay while he was there," I said.

"I could have told you that," Norman explained.

I saved enough money from Manpower jobs to pay for round-trip tickets to Anchorage, Alaska. These plus $200 cash were for Honey and me. I told Norman and Bruce we were going to visit David and his grandfather. I wrote David and my father we were coming.

"Don't plan on getting a job here," came the reply. "It takes a year to get a job in Alaska."

While Bruce was selling shoes at a megastore and then selling used cars for a dealer, I worked and prayed. While Bruce was buying two used sedans which he parked in our driveway, I kept working. I ran out of work just after we met our goal—the tickets plus two hundred. One perfectly beautiful day I walked to the airport to start things moving. I sang all the airplane songs I could remember. On departure day, I telephoned Norman at work to remind him he offered to take us to the airport.

He said, "Good thing you called. I forgot all about it!" Norman drove us to the airport, unloaded our luggage from the car, explained he had to go back to work, and departed. Honey remembered Norman took us to Dairy Queen for two scoops the night before. Then we were airborne on our way home.

North To The Future

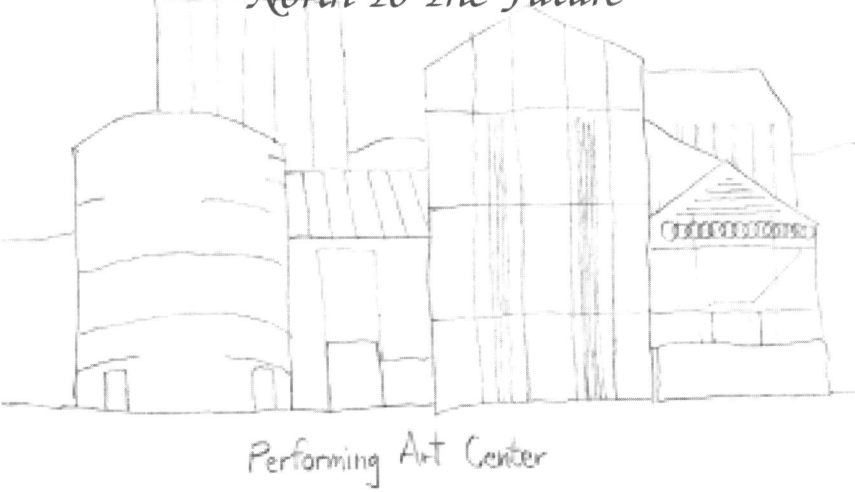

The Boeing 747 circled Anchorage International Airport for three hours while Honey got sicker and sicker. There was an "obstruction on the runway" announced our pilot. When we finally landed, an observant steward made sure Honey found a bathroom. He sent someone to stay with her till she felt better. Juggling our coats and carryon luggage, I searched the crowd for David. Then someone came forward. A tall, lean and very dirty young man metamorphosed into my son. He and his friend got our footlocker and suitcases from the conveyor belts in the basement.

Four of us squeezed into the cab of his friend's truck for the ride to Hope. I said afterward, "I fell in love with Alaska the minute I stepped off the plane." My son always clarified, "You couldn't see anything when you got off the plane. It was the middle of the night."

Cal believed his cabin was too small for bath or shower. In his letters he explained it was a one man cabin built after the '64 earthquake. That's when he lost his home and got his picture in the Seattle paper. Cal and David lived there together for more than a year. When the truck rolled along beside Turnagain Arm Beluga whales were playing in the moonlight. Our heavy old luggage and my Navy footlocker were off-loaded beside the smallest cabin one could imagine. It was some time in early morning. Honey and I finally crawled into our sleeping bags on the two cots lining the walls. We laid there for a minute and held each other's hand across the aisle. The room was so small and we were so weary. It was cold and our hands were much warmer inside the sleeping bags.

In the morning Honey was still asleep when I sneaked onto the front step. I looked out at other mini-cabins and a barbed wire fence. There sat a swallow, shiny green and not at all afraid, singing in the shower which lasted all day. We were alone in a small town crowded with mountains. We walked up and down the highway trying to find Cal or David or the truck we came in. After awhile my son found us and took us to Cal's cabin.

He was standing in the middle of the biggest mess I ever saw. Ancient *Life* magazines once tumbled over towers of *Popular Mechanics*. These became layered with dust and cobwebs and mounds of *Time* magazines and *Seattle Post Intelligencers*. In the background a bookshelf held grimy camera equipment and tools. On the ancient stove were a kettle and a blackened skillet. The wood for heating and cooking was on the porch by the chopping block and axe. Dirty clothes were in piles and I couldn't see any food at first.

He was standing there and my knees were jelly. I wanted to sit down but the two cots which lined the rear wall were so dirty I couldn't. He said, "I guess you didn't get my letter telling you not to come to Alaska. There aren't any jobs and you can't stay here." I said, "I guess you didn't get my letter telling you I just wanted to see you guys."

I made Honey and David carry old magazines to the dump. About ten per cent of them were rescued for the local museum. For three days we cleaned Cal's cabin, and there was still no place to sit. When David's friend had an errand in Anchorage we rode in the windswept back of his truck. We froze, and found a mini-apartment "in town." A day later, we three moved to Anchorage. Cal left us alone for five months just to prove he was right. I brought along his letter warning I would not be able to get a job for a year. It was in my purse when I went to work for a local tycoon. It was still there when I found Cal walking on a downtown street. Forty five years before, in a San Francisco courtroom, I swore I would find my father. Now, there he was, clean and wearing a shirt I got him for Christmas. He looked strong and proud and when he saw me his face lit up like a Christmas tree. I was glad I kept my word.

Wild roses and lupine were ablaze along the roads. Those first days after we moved into the tiny apartment we walked many miles looking for work. Now and then, a bus would stop and pick us up. Usually, a bus would roar by after we tired of waiting at a bus stop sign and took a few steps away. We looked for summer jobs for Honey and David. There were none so they went to school after school finally started.

I walked into one of the tall buildings built after the earthquake and filled out an application. After two interviews I was hired. I was to start on a Friday so as to be eligible for pay two weeks sooner than if I started the following Monday. This was a blessing because all we had was $200 for rent, food, start-up gas and lights. We made it because our landlord took the rent in two installments. He gave us knives, forks, spoons and plates. I expected to cash the second half of our round-trip airline tickets. The airline went on strike while we were cleaning Cal's cabin. It was months before we got our ticket refund.

We lived just a short walk from a mini-mall with Safeway and Payless. The young manager at Safeway approved my check with just my social security card as identification. Then we walked more miles to the Department of Motor Vehicles for state IDs. Honey was required to get a social security card to work a few hours a week at a coffee shop. Cal appeared on the tenth of November. We bought a turkey at Safeway and a black enamel roasting pan at Payless. I made a real Thanksgiving Dinner with turkey, dried corn, yams, mashed potatoes, gravy, cranberry sauce and pumpkin pies. It must have smelled good because suddenly our front entry door opened. Three large Indians, one female, stood in our kitchen. They were quite drunk. Cal stood up silently. When they saw how big he was, all three smiled and backed out. The girl who lived in the other half of our duplex came to chat. She was going back to the Lower-48 because her husband could not afford the birthdays. Every time someone at work celebrated a birthday a big expensive party erupted. She regretted her young family couldn't afford to compete. We celebrated a second Thanksgiving on the legal holiday because there was so much for which to be grateful. I got a ride to and from work until the week before Christmas. Then my fellow worker decided I worked there long enough to buy my own car. So I walked and saved the $5 every week I used to pay her. The first night I walked the two miles home from work a snow plow driver almost scraped me from the roadside. Another time a car driver passed me with dazzling headlights in my face. He stopped the car and ran up behind me, tore my purse from my shoulder and ran back to his car. I put a Stop Pay on my checking account and filled out a police report. I heard no more about it.

Honey hated school because she wasn't on the swim team and there was no marching band. David loved the library and the librarians sent him a Christmas card. Meanwhile, Honey missed her friends and practiced her clarinet. Her years in a high school marching band made her the only person in her school who knew how to march. When the army drill sergeant came to teach the band members how to move their feet he was impressed. When uniforms were being fitted for the annual Fur Rondy Parade she was handed a huge uniform. She hiked to the variety store, bought lots of safety pins and pinned up the cuffs and sleeves. Then she took the bus to the stadium. Honey was the only one at the football game "in uniform." She played for what was left of the game and got lost walking home in the dark. On Monday, all the new band members wore their uniforms because there was to be an initiation. Honey forgot to wear hers. After class she walked up to the Band President to explain. This young lady said, "Don't worry, You've already been initiated." Cal was visiting us at the time so he loaned her the "pin money." Two cars stood like bookends for his two snow machines on the ridge above his cabin. Cal did not drive because of his health. When he came to see us someone brought him in a car or truck. Otherwise he took an airplane which regularly delivered mail to his area.

We went to church every Sunday with wonderful ladies who drove their family cars. It was three years before we had our own telephone so they made the arrangements. One of the church ladies was a history buff briefly interested in us because we were related to Cal. She took us cranberry picking and to lunch in her home. The walls were adorned with the mounted heads of Dall Sheep and Wolf and Bear. She brought us clippings from the newspaper when the Times ran a feature on Cal and his chosen home town. There he was—looking venerable on his front porch. Once his porch held all the local rifles and shotguns. These were leaning against his outside wall when a Colonel from the Army came to mobilize them. It was early in World War II. As the only one with wartime experience, Cal should have known better. How easily an enemy could have removed their artillery from the porch without anyone inside knowing it. Cal took his scolding like a man.

Whenever I thanked Cal for anything he would smile radiantly and say, "It's my duty." He lived on a small veteran's pension and a state longevity bonus. He ate boiled beef, drank coffee, and visited his friends near the cabin. When he was with us he was restless, walked about the neighborhood, and slept a lot. He told us there were 13 kinds of bananas in the Phillipines when he was there. One day I brought home some mushrooms from Safeway. "What's this stuff?" he inquired. "Oh, Cal, you must know what mushrooms are," I said, slicing them for a sauce. With a straight face he assured me he did not. A new girl came to the office from the same part of Alaska. She heard my name and asked if I was related to Cal, "the mushroom man who taught me how to recognize mushrooms."

As a young man, Cal contracted with the Alaska Railroad to deliver railroad ties for several years. He kept one dog from his team, named Knik, who survived the '64 earthquake. Knik's picture was in the *Seattle Post Intelligencer* beside the wreckage of Cal's first home. One morning in early spring a mixed poodle followed me almost all the way to work. I tried various ways to discourage this creature but I dared not be late. I hoped the dog would attach itself to someone else. He did not. By noon this adorable beast attracted lots of attention. One of my co-workers came up to ask if she could adopt it. She put a notice in the *Times* and took Bubbles home to keep forever. Cal said he used to catch and dry salmon to feed his dog team.

The next dog who followed me came from the opposite direction at night. I took him in temporarily. Nobody minded when he adopted us. Cal would say, "Mush" when he pushed him off a chair. He was the best-trained dog I ever knew. Ads in the *Times* brought one reply. A man said the dog jumped out of the back of his pickup. Since he couldn't afford the freight to send him to Fairbanks would I please accept him as a gift? I was walking King one night after work when I saw the Northern Lights for the first time. I just stood there holding the leash with the big German Shepherd beside me. We were watching blue-green lights dance across the sky. It was awesome!

Some of our Neighbors

Chapter 28

Clusters of ravens congregated around the dumpster, in our front yard, scrapping for garbage. One night I detoured two blocks on my hike home to avoid a moose with her calf. It was years before I saw anyone who actually was mauled by a moose. She came to class with two black eyes and a gashed chin. What initially prevented me from trying to pet a moose was the sheer size of the beast. Male moose support natural headgear. The enormity of those racks on their heads is impressive. Frequently, a calf can be seen alone awkwardly striding between the snowbanks lining a plowed street. Almost always, a mother moose will soon appear from behind a building. A mother moose trying to protect her calf is dangerous. Mother moose are remarkably protective. In the Spring the ravens moved north to Fairbanks. At least two kinds of gulls, arctic terns, Canada Geese and many species of shorebirds glided into the city. They came to have their families in the swamps which dotted Anchorage. We rode bikes from the time the ice melted until the first snowfall.

Eavesdropping at work, I heard someone needed a "hand for a week in Homer." I stepped up to the speaker and volunteered David. To my utter amazement, the young man arranged to meet my son. They spent a week together fishing for halibut. David came home, tan and happy, with a fish so big it filled our American Standard bathtub. Grateful for the many times she drove us to church, I offered each ride provider some fish. One of the church ladies accepted a lot of it. King would have loved some of the fish. Alone in the tiny apartment while we were at work or school, King bit an electric cord. He became so unlike himself we called Animal Control to remove him.

Sunday morning, the church lady asked how we were getting along, heard about King and took us to the Animal Shelter. King was there in a cage—changed. We walked by him, pretending not to know him, and chose a dear little dachshund. Our friend from church took us to the vet for Ginger's shots before she took us home. Mourning for King led to an inordinate love for the little sausage hound. Cal offered us one or more of his guns to protect ourselves in what was definitely not a high rent district. I didn't want a gun anywhere near me but I did feel better with a dog. Diagonally across from the mini-mall was a dry goods store where we bought many useful items for Cal and ourselves. Next door was the laundromat where I adopted a towel which appeared to belong to no one. It was lying on a bench when the laundromat was empty of other washing and devoid of people. The next week someone came up to my laundry, seized the towel and departed in a huff. In my consternation, I forgot to take home the National Geographic I brought there to read during the wash cycles. On another Saturday, I slipped a $5 bill into David's back pocket with a murmured "This is for the dryer." Someone sneaked the bill from his pocket. We missed the money. However, the next week David bent down to pick up a bill on the street outside the laundromat. It was a $5 bill. Now we were even, we thought.

I always felt a need to repay the church ladies for those long rides to church. When one of them became active in Amway I was very glad to become one of her customers. The people at work gave me a large order the first time I asked. I didn't know their first order was also the last. Fortunately, my stock of Amway was no more than a two year supply of everything you could possibly think of. David delivered a daily newspaper in competition with the *Times*. He came to know the city thoroughly. A feature photographer captured Honey on her bike. There she was, one hand on the handlebars, one carrying an umbrella. Another photographer stopped me near Merrill Field for almost the same shot. My rainwear hood shaded my face like an arabic veil so the picture was never printed. We were learning how to live in Anchorage.

Saturdays were normally busy for all of us. We shopped for groceries or clothes between washer/dryer loads or took turns. One of us watched the wash while the others shopped or carried things home. Living here was convenient compared to living in the overpopulated East. I rarely missed a car. There were surprising events. Once we walked five miles to the center of the city to spend Christmas money. We bought a brown earthenware teapot and carefully carried it home through what looked exactly like a Christmas card. Ice crystals in the snow sparkled on dark green spruce along a winding road over a hill. There was even a cross on a distant steeple. Our decorated Christmas tree was in a six inch flower pot. We bought a camera to take pictures of each other and our home. Honey's friends took her skating.

During Fur Rondy we rode the Ferris wheel. On our way home we bought a Beta. We carried the tiny blue fish in a few cups of water inside a plastic bag. The bag was carefully packed inside a layer of crumpled newspapers. This was inside a cardboard box for more than two hours at well below freezing temperatures. Peppy as ever when we released it in a bowl, Anemone lived more than two years. A cardboard and plastic wrapped Cyclamen plant died on its way home from Safeway. In the spring Honey went to a dance at someone's house. In the summer she and David went with a group to Resurrection Pass. They enjoyed a long hike, camping and their first sight of a real porcupine. Once we took a bus to the zoo. A church lady picked me up at work to go hiking. On two Saturdays, we two hiked to the top of Flat Top. Other Saturdays we hiked the Powerline Trail, parts of the Iditarod Trail, around Point Woronzof, and The Two Sisters.

One evening David came home from a long talk with a local university admissions clerk. He brought a list of subjects, their sequence, and the price. I had to say no. Still smarting from the hurt of this, I turned on the TV.

"You too can learn to cook in Chinese" cooed the announcer.

"I'll make you a deal, son," I declared. "You prove you can go to every class, do all the homework and never be late for any session the entire two weeks of this cooking class and I'll think about sending you back to college." There was enough money for the cooking class—just barely. I hoped, but I didn't expect, David would meet my conditions. He did.

When our neighbor in the duplex moved, she left some cacti on her porch in the sun. Then, Ginger began to scratch inordinately. I stepped on a cockroach when I got up the next morning. Suddenly, we were finding large cockroaches under the rug, in the corners, everywhere. I tied Ginger to a tree in the yard, washed and dusted her with a powder from Payless. She began to lose her hair. I called the new landlords who called the vermin exterminator who left a note on our entry door. We would have to leave while the duplex was being sprayed.

This presented a problem. It was late May. Honey's big elaborate birthday cake was already on order. One of my co-workers made special cakes as a hobby. Honey's cap and gown were ready to be picked up at the high school for graduation in two days. I was going to have the day off from work. Although we didn't know it, Floral Telegraph Delivery was en route with one dozen fresh cut American Beauty roses. Bruce sent them. One of the church ladies came to drop off my Amway order. I didn't have to say anything. She took us to her house immediately.

Honey graduated on her birthday with an immense cake and a family to share it with us. When we went back to untie Ginger to take her with us, we found the flowers. They looked great beside the cake. We all went to Graduation together. The exterminator delivered the duplex from several hundred multiplying cockroaches. Ginger looked like a moth-eaten rug; Honey's roses almost glittered.

Hunter Home From the Hill

Chapter 29

Honey's birthday roses came from Bruce. For my fiftieth birthday, he sent me a colorful cup of cut flowers. For several years, he sent humorous cards for the various holidays. One Christmas he sent a Christmas pickle card. The day after Honey's graduation we returned to the duplex. I bought a newspaper where I bought one two years before when we came to Alaska. With nickels collected from Honey and David, I marched to the pay phone and made several calls. One person I called twice. Later, he said he felt sorry for me, so he made an exception to his No Pets rule. Since most of his apartments were without tenants, I didn't believe this was the only reason. He let us rent considerably less space for more money than we were paying. There really was no choice. The duplex was a disaster of dead insects with a smell you would not believe. Our dear friend appeared with a borrowed van and began to carry things out of our kitchen. Honey wanted to be responsible for moving what belonged to her and she said so loudly. The church lady departed. David borrowed two shopping carts from Safeway. Honey packed. David and I unpacked three blocks away. It didn't take very long.

Six months flew by. Honey took a class in flower arranging. She brought home wonderful creations of Holly and Pine boughs aglow with Christmas ornaments. These special things filled half our dining table. Honey made a pair of Mexican bird candlesticks, a Flicker for me, an elephant for our Amway friend. All these creations came from newspapers mashed and soaked with chemicals and colorfully painted. The bikes lined a wall near the closet in an alcove facing the "living room." David wanted to become a docent at the Museum but the paper route brought us money. When Cal visited, David slept in a sleeping bag on the floor. We talked about biking to Valdez with a group in the spring. One spring day, I asked the church lady why someone would be holding a drinking glass to his ear. I noticed this several times in the normally vacant apartment on our left.

"Like this ?" she asked—demonstrating.

I nodded and understood. We were being eavesdropped upon through the thin walls. My accidental glimpse of this practice sent me back to the newspaper to look for more space for less money. Our one year lease was up.

Someone at the church knew someone who was in the real estate business. She came to our abode, chatted for a few minutes and left. She was young and attractive and professional. The next day she telephoned me at work suggesting she pick me up after my eight hours. We were changing neighborhoods, she explained. "I felt so bad about the way you were living. I drove around this park last night, all around, looking for For Sale signs. Something made me stop at the end of a road. I asked a young man if he knew anyone who wanted to sell. He said he did. He has a new wife and child and there isn't enough room. So here we are. I know you aren't even thinking about buying. Just come and see and then we'll talk."

So we bought a mobile home, six real rooms, and a real bathroom, even a porch. We paid our dog damage deposit, the first month's rent, the fees. We signed the papers for the bank loan. There was nothing left for the real estate agent who made everything happen. Her countless trips to make deals and get signatures brought her no reward. I tried to repay her by mentioning her name loudly and clearly. I did this whenever I heard anyone talk about wanting to change residences. For years I pointed out the signs with her name throughout the city. She was a real lady.

This time when we moved, a friend of David's brought a van. Honey packed everything in boxes and set them by the door. David and I picked them up, took them to the van, emptied the cartons, brought them back, and started over. Honey kept the door locked while she packed, letting no one in till she finished. It worked very well, no arguments, no breakage, no waiting.

A church lady vacuumed every inch of carpet with her powerful sweeper. I scrubbed and washed the newly emptied apartment and polished the fixtures. Then, grateful for the loving help, I turned in the key. I frequently believe I can afford to buy a luxury, buy it and then get an unexpected bill. This time was no exception. As we began to unpack in our new home, a process server appeared at work. With one day's notice, I was being sued. It was for failing to pay a cleaning deposit the previous year, the deposit verbally waived at the time. I rushed to pay our former landlord, but was still required to present myself in court. I took the day off from work and prayed a lot as I bicycled downtown. The church lady met me outside the massive court building. I tried to counter sue to get my deposit back since the apartment was squeaky clean. The Judge questioned each contestant and my friend at length. Finally, the Judge solemnly assured us we were "all liars. Case dismissed."

The first year in Alaska I computed my own income taxes. I was horrified to get a bill for $900 which I promptly paid from our savings. Since then I have never tried to comprehend the W-2 or 1040. Cal contributed to the down payment for our home and gave us what he could spare when he visited. Honey worked at various fast food places. David delivered newspapers for almost 15 years. I never missed more than two work days per year and we all went to college. Honey was a full time student until she carried too many classes and flunked out. She waited a year, working, then took two or three classes per semester till she got her B.A.. David took Art Classes, drawing, painting, illustrating, art history, lithography, photography. I took Bird classes with Honey at first, then, ten years of Japanese interrupted by two semesters of Chinese.

We never did ride our bikes to Valdez but we did go there on a midsummer trip. Someone canceled reservations so we got their seats for less than tourist rates. Honey worked for the state for two weeks one summer painting picnic benches in Kodiak. She flew there and back on a small plane. I was so grateful she forgot her sincere, "I'll never get on another airplane as long as I live," when we landed in Anchorage. With our bird classes Honey and I went to Homer and to Denali. With our musical association membership we three went to Sitka for a weekend of classical music and shopping. Another weekend we flew to Fairbanks to the Tanana County Fair and a cruise on a riverboat.

All this time my mother and her second family (after Cal and me) lived in California. We were out of touch for years, having long ago reached the stage where whatever we said was too much. Some years there would be a Christmas card from one of her children. I usually sent Christmas cards. When Florence Ryder died, Pansy sent me a newspaper clipping.

I knew I was in Mama's will but I refused to be her executrix. When she died the will was broken. Each member of her second family, their heirs, and assigns received an equal share. So did my children and I. First came the legal notice. Mama was dead. Then came a request we not spend any resulting money for a full year to comply with some kind of law. Mama was cremated. Her home and property were sold. In due course, each of us received a share of the proceeds from her estate. For a year we kept this money in savings.

In the summer, Honey tried to sign up for golf lessons at the University. She came home in tears. Her grades in music were too low. She was dropped from the rolls. One of the things which broke my heart was the piano she didn't have for a required keyboard class. There was no space to keep one, no money to rent one. So she made a paper keyboard and, of course, it didn't work. Honey yearned for a piano of her own. When her inheritance from Mama came she thought it would help her pay for one. During the waiting year, I got her a new clarinet and David got her a piano. He regularly delivered a newspaper to a piano dealer. One day the store featured a large sign, "This piano goes to the highest bidder." David wrote a dollar amount on a scrap of paper which he dropped into the designated bowl. Then he waited, walking nervously, each day for a week, right past our prize in the showroom. When he strolled into the building on Friday one of the salesmen said, "Congratulations! The piano is yours. Someone else bid higher but we decided you should have it. For $90 you can have the piano and we'll throw in the bench free. When can we deliver it?"

The next week David saw the delivery truck approaching. He told Honey, "Umm. Must be the men delivering our piano." Honey believed he was joking. Only after I held the door for the delivery men and David gave them the check would she believe it was ours.

It was a massive upright, several shades of brown. Some of the keys were minus their original ivory. A medallion of some sort was scraped off, leaving a glaring glue spot on the front. The spot reminded me of Mama's liquor cabinet. Honey was so disappointed when she saw it. Then, she sat down to play. Her rinky-dink piano sounded like something from the Gold Rush in the Yukon—deep and throaty and alive. I loved it instantly and so did David. So did Honey as the notes sprang from her fingers to every corner of our home.

Each one of us always voted in every election. I served on a Grand Jury which tried a man who attempted to shoot everyone in McCarthy one day. He almost succeeded. When the state dividends arrived we first banked them and then spent them. Cal never received a state dividend because he died the year they went into effect. He spent a few days with us. He watched the moose trim the trees in our yard, and commented, "I had a big bull moose in my sights a couple of years ago and I just had to put my gun down, couldn't pull the trigger. That's the last time I tried to kill a moose." While waiting for an early flight back to his cabin, he stayed overnight in a hotel. His room was broken into. He was robbed and, probably, injured. Without notifying anyone, he went home. He died in his sleep. It was two days before his neighbor found him.

I got the news at work. It was just after a promotion to a different department. I didn't dare take the chance of not being able to get back to work on time. I did not try to fly with the mail like Cal. I did not know who to call (long distance) for a ride. There were no buses or trains going that way. I missed, we all missed, Cal's funeral. But we heard about it. With our new home came a telephone. For several days people who knew Cal telephoned me. They were trying to buy his cabin. Some of them were insistent, persistent, and downright disturbing. It never occurred to anyone to arrange for us to go to the funeral. Many did want to own his home. Then the young man who gave him rides bought Cal's guns and cleaned his cabin. He brought us Cal's personal things. He even arranged the paperwork for the sale of Cal's cabin and the vehicles on a ten year lease. He said the funeral was impressive. There was a flag over the coffin because Cal was an infantry veteran of World War I. The Veteran's Administration sent us $50 burial money We missed him.

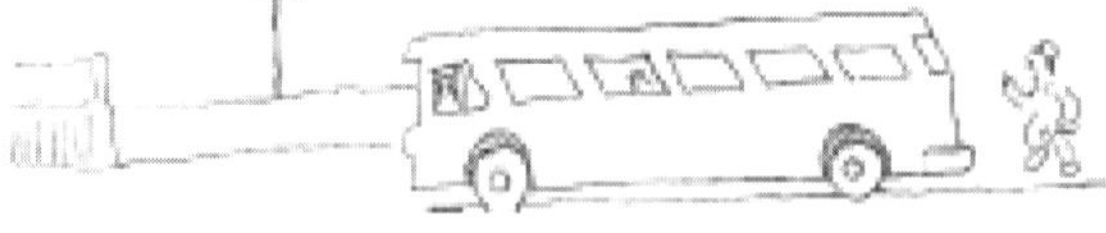

Chapter 30

Honey was removed from the roster of the school she attended after high school. However, there was another school, a junior college next door to the University. This could and did accept her. David and I paid our fees and took classes there, too. We rarely met on campus except when we took Elementary Japanese as a trio. In the summers I helped David deliver the newspapers for which we held ourselves responsible. After work, I would bike an additional ten miles per day. I was usually late for my classes, never having the opportunity to chat with anyone except during breaks. In the winters I took a bus straight from work and didn't come home until the last bus from the college. I reached home at around 10:30 P.M. in time to make dinner. Work started at 7 A.M. so it was a long day twice each week but I loved it.

Then, this lovely school employed a great teacher who took our classes on field trips to Homer and Denali. In Denali Park itself, we first encountered the "Alaska State Bird." This was the herd, flock, army torpedo battalion, mosquito headquartered at Wonder Lake. True, we saw grizzly bears romping along the roadside. They were being photographed by tourists in massive tour buses and by us in our van. True, we saw a single wolf resting beside a stream, eagles soaring overhead, and Dall Sheep. Our teacher taught us how to stalk a sheep. Our group patiently, silently, stalked Dall Sheep diagonally across a mountain. Finally, as we hunched just out of sight of those sheep, we also saw a commercial photographer. He came climbing, picture shooting, straight at those same sheep. They couldn't have been less impressed by him, his equipment, or his noisy approach. We enjoyed a good laugh.

The church lady who sold Amway moved. Quite another church lady's husband tired of working for the state, as so many people eventually did. He went into business for himself. This business lasted long enough for her to explain why she couldn't give us a ride to church. Theirs was now a company car. Insurance rules prohibited non-family members from riding in the company car. Another church lady graciously and generously read a book in her van. Meanwhile, we three raced around the grocery store trying to do a week's shopping after church. At least twice I bought a $5 bread basket for her. The arrangement didn't last. I thanked her for having cared so much for the environment for so long. Winters in Anchorage became grey from exhaust fumes as more vehicles clogged the roads.

The assembly decided for the hundredth time one year "the oil money isn't going to last forever." Their solution was to cut down the number of buses and try to eliminate "park and ride." They shortened the most heavily used routes and laid off some drivers. The last night run from the college was eliminated so entire classes ceased to be practical. I heard about this and tried to do something about it. I wrote twelve long letters to the editors of the two local papers. The computer age sneaked in while I was trying to learn about birds. Now, I needed to communicate so we purchased a computer. I dashed off diatribes and mailed them. I pointed out Anchorage is a bowl which collects noxious fumes in the winter because it is a bowl. I noted those noxious fumes make people sick. I mentioned sick people are not attractive to tourists. I added whereas oil can be sucked up and disappear, tourists may attract other tourists. I concluded tourists are innocent people who bring dollars for assemblies to spend for libraries and schools. I remarked how efficient a bus is, how convenient to not have to park at work, how simple to carry home purchases from stores along a bus line. Six of the letters were dissected and published. People hated me. It was, all things considered, great fun.

We were still getting settled when I opened the cupboard door one morning. There were mouse droppings under the sink. I mentioned this at church and at the park office. The park people put a container of something toxic under our front step, grumbled, and departed. On Saturday, a visitor drove right past the No Pets Allowed sign to our door. Clutching a purse under one arm, she called when she reached the door. Her hands were full. We gratefully accepted two coal black kittens.

After the lady left, Ginger discovered the kittens. She thought they came for lunch—her lunch. Now Honey's hands were full. The only doors which worked were those leading outside, to the bathroom, and to her bedroom. Her room was the only safe place where the infant cats could reach some kind of maturity. Honey loved them, cuddled them, fed them, cleaned up after them, and regularly saved their lives. Gradually, Ginger was able to see them as something other than food. Meanwhile, the mice took advantage of a change in the weather to head for the fields. Ginger loved us with her whole brown sausage body and all of her heart. She loved us so much. She would never allow any one of us to make what she obviously considered a terrible mistake. Just let one of us pet a kitten. There would be Ginger, easing her head under the petting hand; separating the hand from the kitten. Tirelessly, she prevented those kittens from being petted as long as she was anywhere near. When the gentlest of the two kittens ate a staple and died, Ginger's job was easier for a time.

Neighbors would give us rides. Coming up the hill from the bus stop, I would hear a horn or see a car stop ahead of me. I could chat with the neighbor who stopped—until we reached my door. Next door was Henry, a tall man who frequently gave me a ride, as did his wife. I bought wicker baskets from her. David gave her children rides in the bicycle cart in which we carried summer groceries. He pulled them in the sleds we used to bring home winter supplies. When our dividends came we bought a microwave and a real working aquarium from Henry. He was a cheerful man with great patience. Henry had problems with cars and many friends who stayed at his house for varying periods of time. One of these friends set out to repair a large car which seemed permanently settled in the Henry parking pad. Every week, or so, this gentleman replaced a part under the hood of the vehicle, a carburetor, generator, battery, etc., etc., He tinkered and fretted and discussed every detail with Henry for several months. He lived in Henry's house, frequently baby-sitting Henry's kids. Then, one day there was an argument. Management was going to enforce the "no junkers rule." Henry got into the driver's seat, turned the key, heard the engine cough, looked at the gas gauge and sputtered. Henry's friend began to run. The car was, all these months, almost, not quite, out of gas.

Honey got a job in the school laundry. She was responsible for washing and drying hockey uniforms. She got a painful crush on a team captain. Honey was much too shy to know how to chat with him. For several months she would see him coming. Then she would walk by him like a young lady in a Spanish paseo of centuries before her time. After they passed each other, she found another way back to the laundry so he wouldn't notice she was just looking at him. At last, she began to ask him, "Hi, where's Lenny ?" or "Do you know where Lenny is ?" She didn't care about Lenny, just needed to say something. Finally, hockey season ended and so did Honey's misery from this source.

Many people who live in Seattle earn a living from Alaska. They are well acquainted with the business cycle. We went through mild booms and busts. I didn't worry about property laws until I bought our home. Then I found myself fortunate to be able to buy a home. Most women needed a man to buy it for them, or with them, until women became more "legally responsible." I discovered our loan was, therefore, grouped with "poor risks." I ascertained the payoff figure and made double payments. A law permitting early payments was passed by the Alaska legislature just before another business cycle kicked in.

The city was building a new library. There was a massive husk on an enormous bare spot to prove it but not much building was actually happening. Meanwhile, several small libraries existed for years. In them lonely old men, and a few lonely old women, sat for hours leafing through magazines and books. Now and then, they quietly chatted in a corner, staying warm and out of the weather. Local art students brought their works to decorate the walls. The librarians were friendly and knowledgeable. I would see the old people and be grateful. Here was a shelter. Here was a place of dignity where they could even learn something, a haven from the bars of 4th Avenue. David brought one of his huge fish tank paintings, all color and shape, dazzling on Masonite. Astonishingly heavy, it hung in a branch library for a couple of years. In the area, waiting for a bus, I loved to slip into the library to enjoy the painting.

Then, the city fathers decided there wasn't enough oil revenue to keep the libraries open. They were closed, gradually, one or two at a time. Some shortened hours, at first. An editorial drive began to "throw the bums out." The "bums" went back to the bars where a drive began to "clean up 4th Avenue." A lonely old man froze to death in front of an abandoned store. David was notified his painting must be moved since the library was going out of business. A church lady and David moved it in her van. We found room for the wonderful "Fish Tank" in our hall.

Our neighbors on the other side were a large family with a big dog. The boys did not like us at first sight, probably before. Their Scout Master used to own our home. Under his careful tutelage the boys planted rhubarb and potatoes in his, now our, yard. The potatoes rotted but the rhubarb thrived. I would cruise home from work on my bike. Henry said once, "You look so happy on the bike. I ought to take a picture. Bet you're the happiest person around." I would check the yard and, for part of the first spring, my grin would vanish. Some nameless miscreants scattered broken rhubarb stalks all over "my lawn." I retaliated. Boy, did I ever get back at those guys! I made rhubarb jam, rhubarb jelly, and rhubarb pie. I gave their mother jars of jam or jelly whenever we chanced to meet or even be at home at the same time. Once I worked in a candy factory. My boss encouraged us to eat all the candy we wanted. I used the candy factory principle on those boys. The rhubarb was no longer snapped off and thrown around. Their mother became the friend we needed to watch our house when we went on vacation.

The waiting year was almost up. First, we needed passports. I felt trepidation as we waited for ours. What if the State Department knew my stepfather was a German pilot in World War I? What if they knew about the scar where a Frenchman winged him with a revolver? What if someone was watching as they blundered past each other in the air? What if the State Department knew my mother didn't like President Roosevelt? What if I really should have decided to stay in the WAVES when the Korean War began? What if I should not have let myself be talked into leaving because I was married? The passports came. Some of my naivete began to be whittled away gradually but decisively.

We went to London. David delivered papers at the airport. He knew people there well enough to chat with some of them. He loved the bustle and the big planes. He saw our inheritance from Mama as a way to actually become part of such excitement. Honey's textbooks were full of Eleanor of Aquitaine and the wives of Henry VIII. I wanted to see the buildings I read about while California rain sloshed through my sox in grammar school. David wanted to see Hendon and Honey wanted to see the Tower and I wanted a kilt. David wanted to see the works of Seurat at the Tate Gallery. Honey wanted to go to Madame Tussaud's. I wanted to shop on the day after Boxing Day. We did all these things. We used American Express Traveller's Checks. We bought duty free Bulova watches while the 747 soared over Greenland.

Our hotel faced Picadilly Circus at a time when Eros was missing from the traffic circle. Graffiti on a building queried, "Where is Eros ?" We arrived on Boxing Day. I took some coupons from the newspaper David always delivered to Harrod's. There no one ever heard of his paper, or would admit it. Honey and I got kilts, vests, blouses, hats, and underwear from a shop in our hotel. David joined us for a continental breakfast in the dining room. At night we bathed in a huge tub on legs down the hall from our rooms. David's room contained a high bed just like the two in our room. In each room a kettle plugged into an electric outlet so we could always have a cup of tea. Excellent English tea was in the basket nearby.

Honey found a patisserie named Savoy where we shopped as often as possible. Usually the seats were all taken so we would eat in our room.

We unwrapped the pastries and sandwiches and made our tea. We ate and drank tea, watching the telly, before sending David to his room for the night. We lunched at the Tate and bought books, and got more books at the National Portrait Gallery. We saw the Changing of the Guard at Downing Street, walked through Hyde Park, bought from the fence at

Buckingham Palace. This was a real fence draped with miniature paintings, postcards, dolls etc.. We chatted with a tall London Bobby as we walked under the enormous oak trees near the magnificent Victoria. We rode the subway to Hendon and back. I found a wonderful wool scarf on the ground where we caught a doubledecker bus. We lost David at the Tower as dusk fell one night. He went one way. Inadvertently, we went another way. We met later at the hotel. According to the telly, the Queen was at Sandringham for the holidays.

For one week, we explored. We lunched opposite the Parliament buildings and walked over the gravestones in Westminster Abbey. We read the familiar names aloud to each other. We walked Fleet Street, crossed London Bridge, got lost at the Tower and recrossed London Bridge. We saw where Roman soldiers stood. We watched boats in the Thames. We marvelled at London cabbies always hiding behind the Times while the world rushed by them. We even bought rings "just like Diana's engagement ring" at the wax museum. It was just wonderful, all of it! Once Mama was a happy young lady in San Francisco. This is how she would have wanted her money to go—joyfully!

College Vacation

Chapter 31

I remembered helpful things from my student days. For example, colleges sometimes show excellent movies for not much money. This was true at the Junior College, which was not more than two miles away, an easy bike ride. We watched classics for nothing once a week until we could afford to join the Concert Association. Then we biked or took the bus to hear Peter Nero, Dave Brubeck, and several dance troupes. When Honey became a volunteer at a little theatre we went to every play. Her specialty, at first, was hammering and painting and screwing the sets together. Her Christmas present from me was a set of hand tools. For her birthday she got an electric drill, for Easter a power screw driver. Her stage debut was in *The Music Man* as part of the River City crowd. We three were invited to a family Christmas Party. Honey's friend from the theatre came from a big family. Theirs were huge houses and even bigger hearts. We sang carols. I sailed through three verses of Good King Wenceslas before I forgot my lines. Total silence in a large room can be unbearable.

Only once did I have to excuse Honey from her swimming class. My written explanation, "she is keeping the Kleenex people in business" was sufficient. As a family we went to the high school pool after church several times. As more people availed themselves of this privilege the fees increased and the open swim hours decreased. When the first snow fell we got skis and skates. Again a school was the site of our weekend skating. With a church group we skied. One of the leaders said, "David plays suicidal soccer" when we went to a church picnic.

Honey decided to become a chef. I telephoned the school because I could not believe the fees. Then I learned equipment was included. Equipment included ladles, knives, rolling pin, cutlery-sharpener, apron, even a chef's hat. I paid the tuition and admired the equipment. David and I listened to horror stories reminiscent of Army K.P. tales. One morning at work I was informed there was a visitor in the lounge waiting for me. It was the cooking instructor from the college. After two expensive semesters, this gentleman assured me Honey could never become a chef. He insisted she was not physically strong enough to lift the huge pans of food for the cafeteria lines. Here the students worked as part of their training. I believed him. Only later did I see someone smaller than Honey in a chef's hat assisting someone else—lifting the pans. It was too late to protest. Honey transferred to computer classes.

Then, the cooking instructor resigned and so did several others. Meetings were held. The junior college was going out of business. I was really unhappy about this. I telephoned a talk-show host. I suggested there be some kind of a vote. Somehow the students should be represented since their futures were involved. The talk show host didn't like my attitude so he told me to "go to Hell" on the air. I hung up rapidly, determined never to go near a talk show again. The college was adopted, legally, by the university which showed Honey its door. The dear little college with its excellent audio/video learning lab, lively art department, and excellent biology section, ceased to exist. An enormous building was planted where a bike path used to be. Unnecessary roads were constructed, a real sit-down restaurant was created, fees went skyward. The students from the junior college were absorbed with the rest of the scenery.

Honey took dancing classes. David and I biked to a dance recital through a pouring, steady, rain. It wasn't great. On the way home I didn't stop in time at a stop sign. I found my bike going one way, myself vaulting over the hood of a car. I held my glasses to my head with one hand, landing on my shoulder. We were on our way back and I was trailing, as usual, so no one noticed. I picked myself up and located my bike. The driver and a witness stopped. I assured them I was fine and biked home. The next day the driver brought me flowers. She was so concerned and very sweet.

The air was getting dirtier, the snow blackened by automobile exhaust.

The neighbor whose sons planted our rhubarb combined their dividends to buy a three-wheeler. She hired someone to build a shed beside her house for the new machine. It was a fine shed. I thought of hiring the same person to build one for us. One day I looked out my window to see what was causing a loud noise. There, next door, scant yards from my kitchen, was the shed builder in his four wheel drive vehicle-ramming her front room. He backed away, stepped on the gas, rammed again, and I called the police. Four more vicious rammings later, with slight pauses between, the police arrived. They removed the man and his vehicle. Then, I learned the neighbor was in the house, with her family, too frightened to move. Someone else built our shed two years later.

The next time I saw police in our neighborhood they were parked in front of Henry's house. Henry was seated in the back seat of one of the two patrol cars. A cop was helping him smoke a cigarette because he was handcuffed. I heard later he was wanted in another state. His house was empty, unsold, for a long time. Then, it was rented to a lady who used to work for a moving company. She offered to carry a book case I bought which was delivered to the front of my house. With one hand she carried the book case up onto the porch, through two doors, and into Honey's room. I could not have lifted the bookcase. She wasn't even my size, physically.

The Little Theatre set-designers went into business for themselves. The Arena was built. Suddenly, major companies were available for the huge auditorium, union labor was required. Honey was learning computers. I was reading *Silent Spring*, *Sand County Almanac* and Audubon. David was doing portraits of models in oils and acrylics. Honey volunteered to work on computers, mailing lists and whatever else was necessary. Her goal was to keep first one, then several, environmental protection groups alive.

Our beautiful loving dachshund, Ginger, died, leaving Sage, the surviving cat, alone. I was buying filter floss for our aquarium at a neighborhood pet store. I felt something underfoot, looked down and saw another black kitten. She was holding her paw like, "Look what you did!" She was not whining, not in the least apologetic for having been in my way. I bought her immediately. There was just one hitch. David saw her litter mate, a tan striped kitten, which he liked. He didn't see the contents of the box we brought home until I opened it at home.

"What happened to the other one?" he asked.

Of course, it was too late to change cats. The new kitten was named Abbey after Westminster Abbey and Colette because Honey liked the name. We called her Little Cat. Sage became Big Cat. When Little Cat misbehaved, which was often, David unfailingly reminded me, "You could have bought the striped cat."

Honey spent many weekends volunteering for the environment. She did the data base for an all-Alaska survey on a contract labor arrangement. One weekend she did not volunteer. It was her birthday. She arranged to go skydiving. David went, too, but the plane didn't have enough fuel, when his turn came—which he didn't really mind. He watched Honey descend and was glad it wasn't he. I missed the entire event. I was spending $500 for a new toilet (with labor). It was a weekend, the toilet was broken, a victim of age or overweight or whatever. I was required to be present while it was replaced. David showed me the pictures he took of Honey coming down in a parachute. The sky was never so big, the mountains so near, or Honey so brave. She enjoyed it.

Her mentor, a paid environmentalist who kept in touch with the powerful, mentioned Honey's skydiving in a letter. Pictures of her carrying posters protesting a wolf massacre were in a national magazine. All the publicity didn't help her land the environmental expert for whom she carried an agonizing crush. He moved to Seattle. She got an Associate of Arts degree. Her mentor delivered a briefcase to my workplace as a surprise for Honey.

The environmentalists we knew made a lasting effect on us. David substituted for Honey at least once when a U.S. Senator held a hearing. It was packed with people who supported his view. Those who were not of the Senator's opinion were not allowed to speak. David came away disgusted. Honey's friends among the people who really cared about wilderness bought tickets to the semiannual band concerts. Honey played clarinet or piccolo or flute or banjo or, once, piano.

I made a terrible mistake when she was a fourth grader. Instead of piano lessons requiring two hands, I provided guitar lessons for her. With her teacher, she concentrated on playing the chords with her small hands. She never acquired finger dexterity or the memory techniques required for piano. In grammar school, Honey studied and played the clarinet. She took clarinet lessons from the fifth grade into high school. In Anchorage she played in the high school band, took flute lessons for college credit and joined two bands. She tried to play the piano in college one summer. No one encouraged her. I was horrified when I realized starting with the guitar was a disaster. Honey played our piano with one hand carrying the melody so well. I could only rejoice and sing along with David.

David and I went to listen to the concerts. Two environmentalists took us home after each of four concerts. We drank tea from the cups I bought at the college pottery show. David asked intelligent questions about wolves. "Why would anyone want to kill a wolf? Don't people know caribou would multiply like rabbits without natural predators?"

Watching outsiders being hired for jobs she applied for, Honey realized she was never going to be hired. None of the jobs in any of the offices of any environmental group would become hers. Painfully, she stopped volunteering at all. Days and nights and weekends of doing mailouts were suddenly available for other things. Having failed to memorize classical music assured her failure in the performance category at the college. The powers would not let her continue. She could be neither a music arranger, her first ever career choice, or a performer. One band played at baseball games. We biked to Mulcahy to watch the Pilots and listen to the band perform. Someone stole the light from her bicycle. Someone from the band bought her a hot dog. David and I watched baseball games for at least three years. We saw Mark MacGuire and Mark Grace work on their batting averages in the cool Alaska summers. It was fun.

Our Alaska dividends were useful. David was the one who answered surveys in our house. One survey questioned, "How do you usually spend your dividend?" He replied, "We spend part of it for food. We spend a lot of it for things we need like a vacation." This was true. Once I carried a payment to the bank for a friend in our office. I learned her electricity cost notably less than mine so I asked her about it. Hers was a gas hot water heater. Mine was not. It made a big difference. I requested an energy survey. The surveyor's first suggestion was, "Change your hot water heater." So we did. The people who came to change the hot water heater made other suggestions. We became real environmentalists when we bought efficient light bulbs, then insulated our windows and doors. We got a kitchen range without a pilot light. This was all in good time, gradually, over a few years. We also travelled. David delivered newspapers to a travel agent whom we came to regard as a friend.

David met someone at the college who needed money to go home to study medicine. He volunteered to teach David how to fly a small airplane. Remembering Cal's tale of his first and last flight, when he wrecked the plane, David was cautious. He brought the young man home. Honey was in class. We brought Henry, thereby making a cost-effective foursome. We took off from Merrill Field. It was bumpy from slight winds but exhilarating. Henry was pleased. David was ecstatic. I agreed to the young man's schedule for David's flight training.

Everything went according to his plan. Everyone was happy until David's solo flight when he landed too fast and damaged the aircraft. He got a T-shirt (his own) inscribed with his name and the date plus a certificate saying he soloed. Then, his instructor announced he was leaving for medical school. David's membership in a flying group was transferred from Merrill Field to Lake Hood. He was sorry to say good-bye to his teacher, even sorrier when he was not welcomed by the new group. They kept his log. His dividends were no longer unspent and his flying career appeared to be over. We were very sorry, all of us.

Honey's second of three graduations in Anchorage gave her an Associates degree. It did not include the man who taught us all we knew about birds. He retired and moved, with his wife, to a less harassing position. From our field trip to Denali I brought home a rock. All gold and white like Mt. McKinley in one of its special kinds of light, it inevitably inspires awe. We bought many bird books and a scope from London. One Christmas Eve we were the only ones in class who showed up for a get-together. I was glad we went. Their house was as full of clutter as his office where the canary, in its cage, balanced precariously amid towers of books. They were so completely honest, so interested in ornithology, so devoted to teaching. It was a very special holiday.

The graduation was special in its own way. We rode our bikes to the Arena where Honey changed and we separated. David and I climbed to the balcony where we three went to hear John Denver and Bill Cosby on other occasions. The speeches were endless and the line of degree recipients interminable. We watched Honey accept a paper from the Chancellor. He headed the same university which broke her heart by kicking her out a few years earlier. Honey started in music, toiled in cooking, labored in chemistry and biology. Having fulfilled the basic requirements, Honey was going to try for a degree in Anthropology. We were going to celebrate this birthday in Hawaii.

We went with a group from Anchorage International Airport to Honolulu. There the group leader was handed a lei for each member, a real lei of plumeria. It smelled and looked great. We were impressed. We were dropped at our hotel a block from Waikiki and, thereafter, for a week we were on our own. Every other day we bought a fresh lei, usually plumeria. White doves flew to our balcony for short rests while we watched them with pleasure. We called them "Our fly-in doves." Our room looked out on the Pacific. There was a double bed for Honey and me, a single bed for David. Across the street were restaurants, nearby were the zoo and the aquarium.

We bought swimsuits and T shirts. David took snapshots of Honey and me in a rainstorm which lasted five minutes. Our sunsuits were dry in three minutes. We bought wooden jewelry and shells and pearl rings at International Place. We lunched, Chinese-American, at Ala Moana, and took the bus to a pineapple plantation. We went to the Polynesian Village and brought back a video. I got a pineapple shaped wooden dish. We swam and sunbathed on the beach and ate dinner at a different restaurant every evening. We bought sandals and sun dresses, hibiscus hair decorations and shell beads. We flew around the island of Oahu in a small plane, snorkeled at Hanauma Bay, walked along Waikiki beach. We tanned and peeled and tanned again. We bought a bank made from a coconut and did not buy a ukulele or a grass skirt. Then, we took a taxi from Anchorage airport and brought everything home. Little Cat and Big Cat welcomed us in the wee hours of a beautiful morning.

Ups and Downs

Chapter 32

When we first came to Anchorage, David habitually stopped whatever he was doing to watch an aircraft landing. To me a 747 was just a source of loud noises until I flew to Homer in an Otter. The other passenger was a hatless teenager in a T-shirt and levis carrying nothing but a fishing rod. His smile did not provide any extra courage after I noticed the door lining strip was missing. There was absolutely nothing between the door and its frame. Daylight and fresh air freely entered the cabin. Nobody else even seemed to notice it. I wondered why David wasn't wearing his baseball cap. He sat near me, grinning, a couple of seats away. After we landed, I learned he was holding the hat in case he needed to upchuck.

Gradually, the aircraft landings and takeoffs became fewer. Very gradually, they became almost rare. I thought it might be seasonal, the end of a boom. It wasn't. Then, in one of my classes I heard a pilot's wife talking about buying an airline. Her husband worked for the famous local outfit. He and his co-workers wanted so much to keep it alive. When the deal fell through, someone else bought the airline. The first real, local freight and passenger flying system ceased to exist. Afterward, the business went under twice. Things we loved to bicycle past, from the original signs to the hangers and flight lines, changed beyond recognition. One of my coworkers brought us, loudly, the daily tragedy from the news. She didn't even notice the disappearance of "our airline."

Our office was large enough to have factions. For some time, being relatively mature kept me safely out of them. When it was our turn to have someone written up in the company paper, the boss chose me. The boss wrote the story and a picture was taken of me at my desk. I was amazed how much winter fat was there when I saw my picture in the "Tabloid." David was adding weight too, going as far in ground school as he could without actually flying. He tried welding next. After we acquired all the necessary equipment, he learned he was not destined to weld a straight bead on anything.

The concept of a Town Square came to Anchorage with someone from New England. It was neat—with a skating circle children and their parents used on weekends. Whenever the ice was right someone would skate. In summer there were bright flowers along its paths. The city's flowers were always a joy. Before we arrived a Japanese group donated a bamboo water pipe and a brass crane (green from exposure to the elements). There was a small shrine and a goldfish pond with living goldfish in the summer. These were delicately placed in a narrow rectangle beside a lovely little theatre. Progress arrived.

I was shopping in an old-fashioned downtown general store when the owner abruptly excused herself. She accompanied two rowdy citizens from the shop to the street. Patiently, she explained, "I will take you out to lunch and watch you eat but I will not give you a penny." She did exactly this, regularly. Her store somehow survived when the little theatre was replaced. I was never able to learn what happened to the copper crane. Nobody knew what happened to the bamboo pipes which brought water to the gold fish pond. I suppose the lady from New England, who was responsible for the Town Square, either died or moved away. Where flowers and people-friendly benches used to be, a set of concrete bunkers appeared. Town Square became as inviting as a bomb shelter—even with the municipal flowers.

In another part of town, an immense auditorium was built. There were special provisions for hockey games and basketball on a hitherto undreamed level. Once, then twice, a year craft fairs and Christmas exhibits were held there. People from Las Vegas came to sell wooden jewelry. Others sold Swedish sweaters, Mexican serapes, Australian boots. I loved it. I bought a faucet strainer from Italy and Genshu knives from Pennsylvania. Once Honey, David, and I met after work. We got take out food and, still munching, lined up just in time for a performance of Barry Manilow. Someone standing on the sidelines grabbed the sandwiches from our hands. While we watched, he threw them in the garbage. We were, apparently, not allowed to eat there unless we bought from the stands. We were so hungry and so angry we didn't buy anything from the stands—then or ever.

When we first came to Anchorage the downtown bus station was an open air affair. There were concrete benches and a red painted metal roof. The icy winds of March whistled about the open tent-like structure. It didn't even pretend to be a shelter. Someone explained, "the designer lived in California." In the general downtown destruction it, too, became a casualty. It was replaced by an enclosure with shops. This was replaced by an enclosure with a police station and several businesses including a gambling outlet. The remaining space held concrete benches. Police in uniform regularly cleared the benches of people who tried to sleep, or even thaw out, there. The cold from the benches seeped into one's marrow. After one summer tourist season, the wooden benches near the park were removed. A television announcer explained, "Too many people were using them too frequently." An enormous theatre and almost as huge convention center appeared. Since there was nowhere to sit and chat the area was usually deserted. If a theatre performance was being held or a convention was arranged people raced between parking lot and lobby. Other cities were rediscovering the heart of town. Anchorage taxpayer dollars were stifling downtown business again.

The library was finally completed, very modern, very accessible by bus. It was definitely not a place where old, lonely people could learn something or become a little less cold. We missed the neighborhood libraries and the Town Square. We missed the glassed in bus shelters. These sensible windbreaks were shattered, systematically, by bullets. The city insisted it could not afford shatterproof bus shelters. The city could, and did, buy two complete uniform outfits for every bus driver plus coin collectors for every bus. Gradually, we learned to love the new library. On its surrounding slopes Canada Geese browsed—providing free fertilizer for a grumbling city.

The Little Theatre downtown became a big theatre. At its formal opening Honey's dance troupe from the college performed. She brought home a blue ribbon from the event. We rode our bikes from the church to watch her group perform. Afterward, we three biked along the new trail beside Cook Inlet looking for Beluga whales. We watched an eagle, then a flock of ducks, several geese, a rabbit.

In February the annual Fur Rondy was held. We bought pins to wear on the bus for a free ride on one of the Rondy days. We traditionally rode in a dog sled, dined out, and bought books from people who autographed them. At the college was an Arab Chief cook and an Aleut Indian lady. They kept a watchful eye on the cafeteria where people munched and studied. Progress arrived. Studying while munching became uncouth. The Arab and the Indian sorrowfully departed before the new dining facility appeared. One went to Nome. Another, the native, went back to her people. We missed them.

Our heater ceased to work and could not be repaired. I got a loan to pay for a new heater. Then I repaid the loan as quickly as I could. Tufts sprang from the original carpet as we walked over it. We decided to replace the carpets and selected new ones. It was easy to carry things out to the yard where they remained a full day. Meanwhile, two professional carpet-layers attached the new rugs and carted away what they replaced.

The trailer park manager appeared just after the carpet-layers departed. "What in the Hell is going on here?" he demanded, marching into our home.

I ushered him out explaining, "we needed new rugs so we got them." This was one of the rare times I ever saw this gentleman. His policy was to maintain strict office hours. A power- outage or water shut- off better happen between nine and five Monday through Friday-or else!

Since we biked all summer, there were certain spots where I expected to find muskrats. We saw beavers, widgeons, kingfishers, mallards, Canada Geese, plovers, and eiders. In season, the red kings, the salmon, swarmed up Campbell Creek. I recorded daily temperatures and animal sightings in my diary, mourning each species' gradual decline. More swamps were drained and more massive buildings were constructed. Fluoride was added to the water supply forever, it seemed. An attempt to stop this practice was ridiculed into defeat. People knew Fluoride is an active ingredient in rat poison. In an odd juxtaposition, they assumed what was deadly to rodents was completely harmless to humans. So much for centuries of animal testing. The Assembly was noisily grateful fluoride was really great at fighting cavities. Someone visualized a survey of the cemetery to see how many people died prematurely with beautiful teeth. The dated gravestones were not studied before the idea died-prematurely.

David got a temporary job with the Post Office and an early release for not reading the bulletin board. While he was off overnight, someone changed the schedule. He did not notice this. He enjoyed what was listed as his day off. On his return, he was fired. I didn't know this was standard procedure until after I made unchangeable plans. Honey expected to work with her dance instructor, and some of the other students, entertaining tourists. After most of my second semester of Chinese one of the students lost her job. Bemoaning the fact she was signed up for a trip to China, she fled home to the Midwest. Another student came to class white-faced the first semester. She believed her retirement savings were lost in the Stock Market Crash. She was not sure she could go to China this summer.

I was only taking Chinese because the Kanji was so hard to learn in Japanese. I thought getting closer to the original characters might help me. Gradually, it became clear a trip to China, for those who really wanted to go, might not happen. I began to wonder, "What if I went, too?" So I did. I paid my share of the fare plus fees for a summer class in China. The next day Honey's summer dancing job disappeared. The good news was I didn't have to wonder about who would take care of the house and pets. David would do the shopping and cooking. Honey would do the laundry. I read *Life and Death in Shanghai*. I wondered if this would really be a round-trip. We would be gone twenty-eight days.

I bought something like a suitcase. Lots of strong straps enabled me to wear it like a backpack. During a meeting at the teacher's home, her travel agent took me aside. She informed me there were no reservations for the hotel in Shanghai. I was eating summer squash in a sea of butter. Everyone made a list just like the children's lists for scout camp; "toothbrush, toothpaste, comb." Everywhere we went in China, in each hotel, we got a free toothbrush, tiny toothpaste tube and plastic comb. I forgot about the missing reservations in Shanghai. I remembered writing a check for a college credit summer class in China. How exciting! Even more exciting was the news. No one knew exactly which cities we were going to see. China wasn't always open everywhere. I took the bus to Anchorage International Airport on the appointed day.

Someone suggested we be there two hours early. We reached the airport quite early when we went to London or Honolulu. The bus schedule left me two choices, too early or too late. My bus dropped me off extremely early. I checked in and went to the international area. There I found a group of Japanese tourists on their way home from Spain. I struck up a conversation with a lady from Nagasaki who spoke perfect English. She was born in the U.S., educated here, and married while working in Japan. She was so poised and generous. Of course, I began with a formal "Ohayo gozaimasu."

"Good morning" she answered.

So much for practicing my Japanese! She enjoyed practicing her English, and so did I, until she flew away.

When the rest of my group arrived, we checked our luggage. I met my assigned roommate, an accountant from outside Anchorage. This was her second trip to China. She was looking forward to another good massage. Basically, I just wanted to survive in a country so recently opening up to foreigners. I felt very foreign when we took off from Seattle after the usual turbulence over the Gulf of Alaska. Christy brought an air pillow, shaped to fit her neck, and a worn guide book. She seemed to have lots of common sense. I could not have chosen a better roommate if I chose her myself.

We waited for a change of planes at Narita. Everything was extremely expensive. My roommate assured me my travellers checks would go farther in China. I just looked at the dolls and Kimonos and miniature tea sets on display. It was night so there were runway and aircraft lights but no outdoor features. We knew it was raining because we got wet going from plane to waiting room. We were tired and grumpy. Our next stop, Hong Kong, was also dark when we arrived, went to our hotel in a bus, and discovered our rooms.

Our room in the Mandarin Hotel in Hong Kong was as close to heaven as I expect to be—ever. There were white orchids in small vases in the huge bathroom. Thick white terry robes matched the towels and washcloths. There were big mirrors and soft lights and gilded furniture. There were heavenly beds with incredible pillows. I took a long luxurious bath in something foamy from a package. I washed my hair and wrote in my diary and slept as one dead. The next morning a young lady tour guide met us in the lobby. She gave each of us a tiny vase before she vanished forever. Christy and I went to a coffee shop around the corner for breakfast. It was an American breakfast, coffee and doughnuts. In a square beside the hotel a large group of Chinese people performed their morning Tai Chi. We took the ferry to Kowloon to buy Pan Am pearl necklaces.

Kowloon by day was interesting, zillions of shops side by side, murderous traffic. Kowloon by night was fascinating, miles of neon signs as far as the eye could see. They made Times Square look insignificant. The Star Ferry between Kowloon and Hong Kong was crowded and noisy and marvelous. We took the Star Ferry a couple of times a day. Christy came to buy certain specific items. I bought pearl necklaces for Honey and me and some of the church ladies. I bought silk blouses for me and cotton shorts because it was hot and sticky.

We joined the group to tour the Night Market. A Chinese shopkeeper pointed out how long my pants were. The cuffs were getting wet. I clung to my purse with both hands as another "shopper" elbowed into me on the slick pavement. After he sidled away I bought the shorts the first gentleman was trying to sell. Christy approved. I passed my first challenge by pickpocket. I tightened the straps of the flat waist billfold under my jacket —where my passport was.

Next morning, with the group, we took a bus to the Stanley Market. I saw the teacher buy Jasmine so I bought some too. It smelled great. I turned to thank the teacher for this great idea but I couldn't find her. No one could. She was gone for several hours while we explored the Market. We marvelled at the Frangipani, flaming orange and breathtaking, at the top of the hill between our hotel and Victoria. Sea eagles cruised above the junks in the harbor. Steam buns were for sale on street corners. Heavy bicycles leaned against walls. Multitudes of temptations to buy were everywhere we looked.

Chapter 33

Our teacher finally rejoined us. She didn't bother to explain the long wait. At nightfall, our group took the ferry to Kowloon. The teacher and her family led us to a tiny restaurant above a shop. The narrow wooden stairs creaked in the dark. At the top of the stairs, a door was propped open for light and air. Our group was too large for the small crowded room. Stumbling among chairs and tables, her relatives, our host, made room for us. I discovered real Chinese food is entirely different from American Chinese food. During a vain search for somewhere to wash my hands, I got a good look at the dishwashing equipment. With a dirty grey rag, a petite young lady mopped plates and bowls in a tin basin of greasy water.

The following evening, we boarded a former ferry. Another relative of our teacher, a white uniformed waiter, welcomed us. Here many more people dined amid bright lights, balloons, and a band. Here again I was not keen on the sanitation. People in dinner dress dined and danced as we cruised the harbor. Squatting young ladies in dirty uniforms washed quantities of dishes in tin basins. The dishwater was neither hot nor clean. They sat back on their heels, now and then, to smoke a cigarette. I wasn't just worried about germs on dinner plates. Our list of things to bring to China did not include formal wear. For dress-up occasions I brought a sun dress from Hawaii. It was inappropriate, of course. Whenever I saw the teacher, she was obviously wishing she could lose me behind a paper palm tree. I expected one of her relatives to be someone capable of kidnapping me from the boat. Other relatives would rush me to a prison. There I would wash hundreds of porcelain plates in a basin of tepid water until I starved to death.

The next morning, we took a train to Quangzou through fields planted up to the railroad tracks. We passed soldiers in green uniforms, trimmed with small scarlet bands, working with picks and shovels on the railbed. Everyone stopped when they heard the train whistle. If the train was elevated at this point, they waited on a wooden platform built beside the tracks. We crossed into mainland China and carried our heavy packs into Customs. I was amazed when no one inspected our luggage. It was definitely June. We sat on ancient brown benches in individual pools of perspiration. We waited while passports were examined and finally returned. Once again no one could find our teacher—or her husband. Our group had the station to ourselves after a few minutes. Four hours went by. Other trains than ours came and went. We tried to look casual. Someone showed us her Swiss Army knife from a trip to Geneva. Someone else told us about the tea set she ordered to be shipped from Hong Kong. We discovered where everyone came from and what everyone did. Those who smoked did so, often. I remarked how heavy the bicycles looked in Hong Kong. Referring to the delivery bikes at the station, I noticed how American they looked. At last, our teacher and her family reappeared. The teacher said their video camera was a type unfamiliar to the Customs officials. They were allowed to keep it. We were put on a bus and driven to a school.

From the initial planning stage, we knew we were supposed to visit schools by formal prearrangement. The previous semester letters were exchanged between our teacher and several Chinese superintendents. Their school year was almost over and so was this day of our appointment. Some of us brought quantities of pencils (good wooden pencils with erasers). Some brought blackboard chalk and erasers, pens and crayons for the under supplied children we expected to meet. These were handed to the administrators in their office before we began our tour. Then we were ushered through an entirely Chinese compound with dragon roofs and red tiles and brick courtyards. We were encouraged to photograph the elementary and middle school students on their "free day." This was a private school where very small groups practiced violin or piano or did chemical experiments. In one classroom there was a computer with no one near it. I took a roll of pictures which never turned out. I forgot to remove the lens cap. Those dear smiling children were not captured on my film.

The next morning we went to a real Chinese market. En route, a child with a heavy wire basket, brimming with yellow baby chicks, tried to sell some to us. In the market we saw kittens lying in a basket, snakes in another basket, ducks in yet another reed basket. All were alive. The chopping block and cleaver were conveniently nearby. After the customer chose a kitten for lunch, it could be dispatched instantly. The customer brought his own plastic bag or reed basket to carry home the fresh meat. In the elevator to our hotel room, a lady passenger carried a small but lively snake in a plastic bag. We did not crowd her.

We went to the Swan Hotel to see the Jade Clipper ship. A bus took us to another school after the children went home. Here the superintendent proudly showed us the school compound. She directed our bus driver to a national monument. It was raining hard and my new umbrella did not work. She held her own umbrella over my head as we walked about the grounds. This was the site where Sun Yat Sen broke the yoke of the Emperor. This gentle person of my own size and age took my hand. She moved my fingers over the Chinese characters engraved on a gatepost marking her country's freedom. Yellow blossoms filled the trees nearby. "Huang Hua," she made me repeat several times until I got it right, "Yellow flowers." She was a real lady.

We flew to Kunming on a DC-10 and I thought about Claire Chennault and the Flying Tigers. One of David's friends worked for the Flying Tigers in the Eastern U.S.. We knew Kunming was where World War II war planes were delivered. I knew someone who flew over the Hump too many times. He now lived quietly in Pacific Grove, still trying to recover.

Three of us rented bicycles in Kunming and rode to the warehouse being used as a library. We were encouraged to pay a few fen to the lady who watched many bikes. We were not allowed to actually enter the "library." We rode completely around a gigantic cement statue of Mao Tse Tung. We never found any of the little red books we thought everyone in China knew by heart. We bought earrings frequently, turquoise butterflies in Kunming, scarves from the silk scarf factory we toured. We turned in our bikes. I asked where I could buy a lock and/ or a big silver bell to take home with me. I asked the question the day before we went to the western mountains. The guide asked how many I wanted so I ordered three locks and three bells. I received, our next and last evening there, three shiny silver bike bells and one lock with two keys. This was all I could get but I joyously paid more than they asked. I still use the lock and keys on my own bicycle.

I enjoyed the bus journey to a temple past the Chinese Sleeping Lady mountain. "She" looked less like an inert woman than the Anchorage version. I kept a log, sketching rice terraces in the south and swan-shaped lamps on posts. There were donkey carts in the far west where the Silk Road ran for generations. Our bus had a flat tire so we stopped beside the road, changed tires and left the flat to be repaired. On our way back we picked it up again, "good as new". I bought straw sandals from the wife of the tire repairman. Our group stood in front of the hay-filled barn. This sheltered both tire repair and sandal businesses—close to a gasoline pump.

The western mountains were wonderfully Chinese. We disembarked from the tour bus about half a day's ride from the hotel. The ancient bus climbed past many bleak farms, even past the hill where our guide pointed out a major catastrophe. This man-made ecological disaster was created when soldiers tried to drain a swamp for farming. The dry area protruded, like an immense sore thumb, from the natural greenery beyond it. We also came to a stop beside a living camel. My picture was taken astride the camel. Either the sun or the cameraman was in the wrong place for this picture also. Anyway, it was fun. So was the hike, up the mountain, led by Sunni women, real, living, dance-as-you-walk-and-sing, Sunni ladies. Three tribal guides in full costume led us about their Stone Mountain preserve chanting "Walk this way, Follow me, Watch your step." When the tour was over we could, and did, show our gratitude. From stalls strategically placed at the trail end, we bought things. There were belts, hats, wallets, even slippers, all intricately and colorfully embroidered. I bought vests for Honey and me.

Three of us rode bikes again in Chengdu and in the beautiful area surrounding the Bai Yun hotel. This compound included a lake with a boat. Weeping willows dipped into the green water. On a side street, we finally found hooded polka dot plastic raincoats first seen in Guangzou. Mine was blue. I got a green one for Honey. As our bus pulled away from the hotel I got watercolor brushes for David through the window. I hope I gave enough Chinese money to the enterprising salesman.

Another tour bus, with different guides, took us to Dahli Shan through forests of towering bamboo. I kept trying to see a panda but I never could. I did marvel at the faith of the highway designers who thoughtfully arranged spacing for concrete columns. These lay beside the road wherever a vehicle might slip in the rain. Hundreds of feet below lay a tangled ravine. These somnolent columns were too few and too far between to be an effective guard rail. As we chugged upward I did a lot of praying and I don't think I was the only one who did so. I heard we were scheduled to make an overnight climb to a mountain. We would not be climbing overnight, but climbing, then sleeping, then climbing with the light as long as it lasted. Accordingly, I carried extra clothing in the daypack on my back.

We did climb a mountain, all of us, a mountain with steps. From my point of view, Chinese mountain steps are not a full size nor quite a half size. I was forever trying to take two steps at a time or half my usual size step. It was not easy! Almost everyone else promptly hired a porter from the group near the entrance. I tried the steps until I couldn't see any of our group ahead of me. Then I, too, paid two strong Chinese men to carry me and my pack up the mountain. I hated myself for letting another human being carry me anywhere. This was how these people earned their living. When we finally toiled our way to the mountain top, we found a monorail to take us down the other side. They did the toiling. I tried to weigh less by thinking calm thoughts.

Then I discovered the overnight mountain climb was a macho male event. We leftovers were taking a boat to see a Buddha. This sounded like a great idea until we got off the boat at the foot of "the world's largest carved stone Buddha." We climbed up those hundreds of Chinese mountain steps in the carved stone face of Buddha. At the top our bus was waiting for us—just when I could not have climbed one more step. I heard the overnight climb wasn't really great and was appropriately grateful I missed it.

We took a train to Xian. I got the top bunk, Christy the bottom. Two others from our group shared the compartment. Their packs were getting as heavy as mine because their plans to ship things home miscarried after Hong Kong. One of the two who joined Christy and me read volumes of what Cal would have called "dime novels." As she finished reading a page she tore it from the binding and threw it away. All across China solitary pages of English print scattered to the winds. I hated her for it while the back country Chinese stared at us like newly unearthed Neanderthal bones. I thought I knew what any kind of English book might mean to someone who really wanted to learn English. At the train stops children tried to sell crickets in baskets. We saw no birds. The only visible animals were overloaded donkeys in the west, water buffaloes, and an occasional scrawny cow. There were no dogs or horses. I said, "The crickets in the baskets must be the only pets the children have."

Our teacher snorted, "Pets? Those are snacks. Crisp. Yum."

This was the college course in China for which I paid the price of a college credit.

In Xian we saw more temples. I bought a jacket with embroidered patches, frog, fish etc. on red cotton with a lining. I was ecstatic. I dreamed of this special kind of jacket for years. Now it was mine. Then, we took a bus through heavy rain on slick clay roads, to the excavated underground tombs of emperors. A few more miles by bus led to a low building about the size of two football stadiums. Under a corrugated metal roof were the clay soldiers, life-size and astonishing. We walked along a ramp, looked down and saw individual terra cotta people with different faces. Their different headgear or uniforms indicated specific ranks. Horses, also life-size, were, also, in military formation. I was glad our teacher's communication lines usually did not extend all the way down the social ladder to me. Christy already knew. It was her second trip. I felt like I felt the first time I saw the Northern Lights—really impressed. I bought a green Chinese soldier hat and a deck of cards to show Honey and David the clay soldiers.

We stayed overnight in what seemed something set apart like Camp David in Washington, D.C.. It was a heavy stone castle among other similar buildings, both peaceful and forbidding. It was the only place in the world (besides the American Museum of Natural History in New York or the

Smithsonian in D.C.) where I ever saw a Morpho Moth. Only this time it was not on a pin with an explanation and a scientific name. It was, they were, several huge, blue, gorgeous, moths. They flew freely around us as we waited for the porters. The porters were supposed to carry our, by now, enormous packs up a hill to our lodgings. I guess the porters saw the packs. After awhile we carried them ourselves. The moths were gone into the dusk and it was raining. Christy and I did our daily washing, scrubbed the road dust from ourselves, and went to bed. What sounded like distant explosions awakened us both. We threw on robes and ran to a balcony. There was our teacher with the guides and some of our "class." They were setting off firecrackers in a steady downpour, laughing hard, celebrating the Fourth of July.

We took another train to Beijing where we stayed, near the University, in the Friendship Hotel. Our teacher disappeared with more of her relatives. Christy showed me Tian Amen Square. Together we explored the Forbidden City. Then, she left me in order to make certain purchases. Grace, the girl who almost lost her retirement savings in the 1987 crash, rescued me. She and her friend, Louie, and I took a taxi to a huge modern American hotel. We split the fare three ways each day we remained in this city. I took Grace to Tian Amen Square and the Forbidden City. We looked for porcelain baby dolls in Lilioluang. We drank tea in a tea house and I bought the earthen tea set which would fit in my pack, a miniature. We went to the Zoo.

I love zoos. I loved the London Zoo where we watched elephants being bathed by attendants who chatted with them. I loved the Anchorage Zoo where a small brown bear huddled in a corner of a large bear area. The polar bears clambered up a concrete mountain from a real pool. Then I saw the Beijing Zoo. Grace and I almost wept. We tried to figure out whom to notify. It was a lot like seeing someone starting to have an accident in a car. It was like a fire blown larger by a sudden wind so it stops browning hot dogs and gets dangerous. First, we walked along the pleasant asphalt path to the Panda House. This was a real house with a step going up to it, wooden floors and ceilings. Above a platform was a high shelf containing a huge electric fan to cool the area. On the platform a totally loveable panda rested quietly. He was at ease beside a stack of fresh bamboo stems and a basin of fresh water from a dripping faucet.

Then, we walked a little farther and saw the concrete circle where the non-panda bears lived. It was like an inverted flat-bottomed ice cream cone topped by spiky metal "trees." These were similar to large bottlebrushes. Nothing but harm could come to whatever climbed the cone. A heavy cast iron fence capped the wall rising perpendicularly from a dry moat. In the moat-squeezed between the cone and its outer circle—were the bears. Those three brown bears looked moth eaten, wheezing and oozing from the eyes, sodden with their own excrement. There was no sign of food or water—no trees anywhere for shade. It looked like Hell. The temperature was almost 100 degrees Fahrenheit. We got out of there fast.

Louie needed more carrying space so we found a store with the new luggage on wheels. As he was extracting the money from his wallet to pay, a bell rang. Heavy metal doors slammed down from the top to counter level. We left because, obviously, the store was closed. Louie said, "The poor guys are hungry, so hungry they can't even wait to complete a business transaction." We got better luggage later at another store. One of the young people in our group brought scales for Grace and me. He heard us admire these portable weights and measures when we bought something at curbside or in the country. I chose the smaller scale for my kitchen, Grace the larger one for hers.

Our teacher, and her family, abandoned us the day before Grace and I caught our Fokker aircraft from Beijing to Shanghai. We just happened to meet our teacher as she left the hotel while we were buying stamps. She said something breezy like, "It's been nice to know you," trundled her luggage forward and departed. On the German plane condensation floated through the overhead bins. I remembered the miles of bamboo scaffolding in Beijing and wondered if the new buildings would last as long as the bamboo. I don't think any of us missed our teacher except, probably, her Chinese extended, very extended, family.

From the airport, we took a taxi to the Peace Hotel. As he paid the cabdriver, Louie tried to prove his rule. "Anyone can understand English. All you have to do is yell the same thing several times, patiently, until he gets what you mean." I rescued him, grateful I learned how to count up to ten in Mandarin Chinese. Moreover, hadn't I just travelled across China with a vocabulary of "Doo Xiao Chen?" and "Che, Che" (How much and Thank You)?

We did not have reservations at the Peace Hotel in Shanghai. It looked like Grace forgot to make them. I forgot the travel agent's warning she made no reservations at the Peace Hotel. I was so grateful to still be inside my own skin. Confirming our reservations never occurred to me. Suddenly, a clerk was assuring Grace there was no room available for any of us. No one cared how long we planned to share-one double, one single, bed in one reserved room. My knees turned to jelly. I could not afford to have anything go wrong. Neither could Grace, after spending too much for the porcelain baby doll for her coffee table. Nor could Louie, who pushed the new wheeled luggage crammed with bargains Grace and he, mostly Grace, were bringing home. In a flash it came to me, "Let's call the consul!" I asked the clerk, "Will you please help us contact the United States Consul? There must be some dreadful mistake." He did.

Political Science 101 came to my rescue. From the dim past I remembered. One of the functions of a United States Consul is helping American citizens in a foreign country. The hotel clerk called the consul. The consul called the manager. The manager assured me there were no rooms. I insisted on being put through to the consul. He assured me there were no rooms. I assured him we were stranded. We honestly expected to have reservations and we needed his help. The consul and the manager discussed this. The manager personally escorted us to a room with one single and one double bed. We dropped our luggage on the floor and sank onto the beds. We were in the Peace Hotel in Shanghai.

The Fun It Was To Be With You

Seasoned travellers all, we dug through our packs for whatever was needed to freshen up. A few minutes later we were in the restaurant. Each table held a set of white porcelain salt, pepper, and soy sauce dispensers. Grace wanted the tiny soy sauce pitcher with the blue rose. She asked the waiter who asked the person in charge of the dining room who asked the manager. For the second time in one day, the manager came to our rescue. It was impossible to break up the set. Grace bought the tiny pitcher and I bought the salt and pepper shakers. When we returned to our room two things were waiting. The huge thermos bottle of boiling hot water can be found in every hotel in China. Striding across the carpet was an enormous cockroach which Louie crunched underfoot.

When we ventured onto the street we found store windows featuring very small gas ranges and refrigerators. They were exactly like the ones at home but much smaller. On sidewalks shaded by huge leafy trees, men in loincloths, suffering from the heat, lay on cots. We walked along the Bund looking into the creature comforts of sampans. Often we glimpsed a lone child, harnessed and tethered so it couldn't fall over the side into the murky water. Now and then, a chicken would be tethered nearby. Laundry was strung on lines to dry. Pots hung on nails on a wall. More laundry hung from lines between windows as we ventured farther from the business district. One of our classmates appeared by prearrangement with Louie. He led us into a shop where I found the China doll Honey expected. I also bought clay animals and boat people for Honey plus a kite for David.

After dinner, we went for a walk along the Bund. In the teeming multitude, I was a little bit ahead of the others. A young man appeared at my elbow. "Change money" he pleaded. This custom was familiar. Everywhere people were eager to change money. My habitual "bu shiuan" brought his "Don't you speak English?" I stepped back, found Louie and said loudly, "I think someone is trying to pick me up." Louie is built like a linebacker even in the dark. The money changer quietly disappeared. Meanwhile, the clerk who misplaced our reservations returned from a day off. Our status with the hotel improved. Three Chinese pear apples were waiting in our room, compliments of the manager.

With the classmate who joined us yesterday, we took a cruise aboard a huge catamaran. We travelled to the mouth of the Yangtze River and back in three and one half hours. Part of the time we were involved in a traffic jam. A near miss occurred when the rules of the road were disobeyed. *MacTransporter-Istanbul* ran between a ship at anchor and a barge. Our catamaran came to a dead stop and remained still while the tanker cleared the barge. We saw a blue submarine and three blue destroyers. The river mouth was so wide we couldn't see either shore. We enjoyed creamsicles, cold sweet coffee, and several slices of watermelon. A steaming hot scented washcloth for our faces and hands refreshed us before and after the food.

Every morning we were in China we got a *China Daily* featuring international news in good English. Every morning a large thermos of boiling water waited outside our room. In the extreme heat, the shaded interior of our room in the Peace Hotel was comfortable. Still, I found myself going to the boiler room for more hot water for tea and packaged soups. It was a fascinating place with three sleepy attendants—one of whom filled the thermos from an ancient steaming boiler. Many boilers supplied water for the enormous hotel.

We went shopping for blouses in the lobby. Every evening we went to the night club off the lobby. The Jazz Band—a bass, trumpet, clarinet, saxophone, drum set and piano—performed American dance tunes. Elderly Chinese gentlemen in 1940 style suits played loud, slow, music, frequently emphasizing the wrong syllable, with wonderful results. Glen Miller, Tex Beneke, even Gene Krupa never enjoyed performing like they did. Grace and Louie danced and I drank two cans of cold Sprite. The band leader appreciated American dollar bills, which Louie frequently supplied, along with an occasional drink. At 11 P.M. the band played "Now is the Hour" and covered their instruments. We chatted in our sitting room before we retired.

From Beijing we took a taxi to the Great Wall of China, walked along its amazing width and photographed each other in various tourist poses. We climbed many steps to visualize thirty horsemen riding side by side on the bricks. We leaned over the wall on the Wall to look down. Louie took pictures of Grace and me when each of us rode the dromedary. This patient beast was stationed strategically in a bare spot in front of the parking lot.

Louie extracted an American cigarette, purchased cheaply in China, admiring the camel on the pack. I said, "It seems like every man in China smokes incessantly."

He nodded, "Yes. Wasn't this the second camel you ladies rode on this trip? One at Stone Forest? Another at the Great Wall?"

Grace and I agreed. I remembered aloud the oleanders and cacti between Chengdu and Emei Shan and the great variety of land forms we saw. In less than one month, our Chinese class went from desert, to mountain, to rice fields. We crossed corn fields edging up to the railroad tracks. The trains went through, not over, the loftiest terrain. Louie pointed out less energy is required to traverse a tunnel than to climb a mountain. Human energy was, in China, still the least expensive resource.

The heat was oppressive. We walked up and down Nanking Road, looked in shops, decided not to take any of six possible city tours. We breakfasted and lunched from our packs: soup packets, crackers etc. and quantities of good hot tea. The cold drinks (pop) were for evening when it was air conditioned in the bar with the band. After lunch, we hired a taxi to take us to the Tea House where Queen Elizabeth had tea on her visit. The Tea House stood on a zigzag bridge featuring large stone fish in a huge green-water pond. Many Koi struggled for oxygen near the intake. The garden was large and dry and elegantly Chinese. Many people fanned themselves or sagged on the benches. We saw the *Chinese Navy.* This full-rigged clipper ship was carved life size in stone at the Summer Palace. It was an Emperor's flagship frozen in a time before photography. What foreign power did he expect to be impressed by such a ship? How many man-hours created it? Another taxi took us back to the City Market where I bought another covered porcelain cup.

Back at the hotel we paid in full for four nights. We arranged for a wake-up call and a taxi to the airport in the morning. We shared dinner in the Chinese Dining Room: sweet and sour pork chops, mushrooms with asparagus, and chicken with bamboo shoots. We picked up our beautifully carved chops at the Friendship Store. I bought a suitcase on wheels, changing yuan into dollars "so we won't carry any Chinese money from the mainland." The taxi to the airport cost exactly half what it cost from the airport to the hotel. It was the same distance, same route, different driver. In the German airplane, a pregnant stewardess was violently ill. Most passengers munched stale peanuts or dozed. We went through customs without incident. Two hours after takeoff, we were in Hong Kong.

Grace and Louie dropped me off at the Peninsula Salisbury YMCA complex and headed for Thailand. I confirmed my reservations, met my classmate, and went with her to MacDonald's for lunch. We ordered Big Macs, French Fries, Apple Pie, and Sprite. We shopped at Sunni Rug Company and several shops. The ninety degree heat was relieved by a thin pants suit and sandals I bought to wear to dinner at the Malaya Restaurant. Here I ate my first Sate with peanut sauce plus Lamb Chops ala England on a bull-shaped black iron plate. It was a great meal with clean knives and forks and white napkins. Most people in the crowded restaurant were Indian or Chinese. I didn't even think of using the alcohol wipes we carried all through China to clean the chopsticks before meals.

We repacked before going to bed. There was no place for her Mah Jong set in my room mate's nearly bursting luggage. She started to leave it on the dresser. I volunteered to bring it home for her. I packed a fan from the pregnant stewardess, one of a few acquired in flight. It was one of many, since I bought fans and cups and bookmarks for souvenirs.

We had a leisurely breakfast before taking a taxi to the airport. As usual, we agreed on a price with the driver before we set out. The meter showed half the agreed price when we left the cab. Our driver insisted the original price included carrying our luggage the short distance he did. I lost many points with my classmate when someone adopted the luggage cart I was supposed to be watching. She brought her oriental rug as carryon luggage. I didn't even want to think about how heavy it was. I wore my conical hat from Beijing. How better to keep track of it?

At Narita we discovered the reservations made seventy two hours before were not valid. At the ticket counter, we started all over again. When we finally left Narita, after a three hour wait, we found ourselves in Business Class. Free SAS sox, eyeshade, shoe horn, magazine and movie, *Stakeout*, followed a five course dinner featuring smoked salmon and roast beef. After almost a month of packaged soup and various crackers for breakfasts and/or lunches this was pure luxury. I fell asleep listening to Beethoven's Sixth Symphony on the free headset.

At 11:45 A.M. we disposed of our orange juice glasses. We wiped our faces with the steaming white washcloths for a final time. The plane came to rest at Anchorage International Airport. From the window of the airplane I could see Honey and David waving on their bikes at the gate. After we cleared Customs, David told me Gorm Viking was waiting for Frode Viking (two 747s) at the SAS dock. Honey told me the date on my postcard from China was wrong. My dear little family wasted a full day, biking to and from the airport and waiting in vain. They biked home. I took a bus with my luggage from near the terminal to my home bus stop. The driver saw my Chinese attire and asked, "Did you have a good time in Hawaii?" It was good to be home!

For almost a month David watered the flowering plants, ran the sweeper, cooked and washed dishes. Honey did the laundry and cared about the pets. There was a mountain of clean dry clothing on my bed. Dishes not gotten around to yet covered the stove and drainboards. The plants never looked lovelier. The pets were healthy. We were glad to see each other. It didn't take long to fold laundry, change beds, unpack, and get in touch with the mail. They liked their souvenirs. I enjoyed giving bookmarks from Beijing to my co-workers. Everything was wonderful except for one thing—the ads.

Honey saw herself as getting too old to have her own family, her own home, even her own car. Working in a fast food restaurant was not what she wanted to do with her life. She believed having a boy friend would make her happier. I was away and not able to insist she do otherwise, any otherwise. Honey answered a singles ad in the newspaper.

When I came home, the telephone bill topped one hundred dollars, more than ten times what it usually was. I couldn't believe it so I inquired. Honey explained. It unfolded. Her answer to the ad was answered. A young man, currently in jail, chatted with her for hours from out of town—hence the large bill. At a halfway house Honey held hands with him. This was just the beginning. Within a few weeks, we innocents purchased a complete set of clothing for him. We bought him threes of sox and underwear, even sneakers. To top it off, Honey gave him my favorite guitar. He sold my spare guitar and came to our house. Honey introduced us. He took the clothing and told us he would be back in time for dinner. I rushed to the store, shopped, raced home to cook a suitable dinner. We waited, dusting and straightening. He never came back. Later, he told David, when they accidentally met, the guitar was always his and he didn't owe us anything. Meanwhile, Honey was fired for taking home catsup packets customers left on their tables. To her boss it was unseemly. To her it was basic conservation. Her world was pretty effectively crumbled. It took a while to rebuild.

We called the Fire Department because the dryer began to smoke. We raided savings and replaced the dryer. A couple of years later, the oven wouldn't turn off. Once more, the Fire Department rescued us. We replaced the stove. David's temporary employment with the Post Office paid for the stove. We three built shelves in the shed to ensure more, and better, storage space for books etc.. It was fun to build the shelves together. One Christmas Eve a young man came to our house for dinner and to play Trivial Pursuit. It turned out he was already living with a young lady. Honey was getting used to not having male companionship. She played banjo in the Community Dixieland Band with her usual skill and persistence. David and I were ticket takers again.

A young matron at work brought me a tiny stuffed llama from South America. I bought several scatter rugs from her sister and some earrings from her. There were potlucks at work. I brought unusual things like pickled beets, pickled eggs, homemade bread. When we had four potlucks in one month I wasn't happy. A co-worker snarled, "You mean you do the eggs in the same juice the beets were in?" I remembered the faces of the people who ate at Bean's Cafe where I took my annual rhubarb harvest. I made two decisions. This was the last time I would bring anything for the critic to analyze. Also, instead of bringing more rhubarb to work, I would take it all to Bean's Cafe. She moved, then became very ill. With spare paper from work, I made a poster to say "Get Well" in Chinese. This went with the other get well cards. Later, I heard she was dead.

For more than a year, the same generous and witty lady gave me rides to church. In a visit to her house, I learned something useful. If you make three changes in either the method or the ingredients, a recipe becomes yours. I always regarded a recipe as a map, not something to be followed slavishly. I used substitutions freely and found all kinds of unorthodox ways to use beans and hamburger. Therefore, despite the money we spent radically improving the appearance of the young man from the ads, we were solvent. We were even able to pay for a one-day train trip to Seward. This was our vacation the year after I went to China. The entire ride to Seward was beautiful. When we disembarked I found a store which had to be—could it be—owned by someone I knew? It was. Years ago, Lars and his family lived a couple of blocks from Ellen in Carmel. Lars and I used to ride my cousin George's tricycle when I visited Ellen. In the really spectacular tourist trap, I bought some earrings for Honey and me. I left a short message, "Tell Lars, Skinny's in town. I'm taking the cruise today."

An hour or so later, Honey was very sick amid the choppy waves of Kenai Fiord. Our tour boat guide pointed out puffins, cormorants, and otters while Honey upchucked over the side. The water became noticeably choppier when a cabin cruiser drew almost abreast of us. A tall man, holding a big sign breezed by. "Hi, Skinny. Welcome to Seward" was printed on the sign. Everyone on the boat looked at everyone else. I knew who it was even before the tour captain said, "Why that's Lars Thorvald! He owns the big store up there." When we finally got off the boat, after a tour shortened by foul weather, Lars was waiting on the pier. He gave me a tremendous hug. I introduced my children. I said something dumb about "Where can we have lunch?" I noted, "We have to catch the train back to Anchorage." I guess he

thought I wanted him to pay for our lunches. He suddenly explained he was supposed to be somewhere else. We didn't look like much in our old clothes and I definitely was no longer skinny. The moment was over. It was such a sublime moment. With my usual delayed gratitude—when someone complimented my Seward earrings—I ordered some by telephone. I mailed the check for them immediately. When they came I didn't sell them to the girl who liked them. I still have those two sets of earrings as a double souvenir.

When I first saw our church it was so perfect inside and out, I couldn't believe it. It was redwood and apple green inside and out, blending with nearby trees. There were large, lazy ceiling fans like I remembered from North Carolina and some New England churches. I loved it. For ten years, I loved teaching Sunday School. I loved encouraging the youngest children to draw and sing. When new people came and were welcomed, like I was welcomed, they took over various duties. I watched them water plants I watered last week without comment. I watched them substitute in Sunday School, without comment. I held on to what was left and kept going. When the church interior was painted ghastly white and the exterior matched a local apartment building, I quit. This meant we no longer rode the bike paths to and from church every summer Sunday. We did have more quality time together.

"You have old hands" a cherub beamed at me my last Sunday School morning.

"I have very useful hands," I explained.

Chapter 35

There were other church members with useful hands. My washing machine stopped working. I telephoned an appliance repair shop. Their serviceman charged $95 to look at the machine. The electric plug attached to the washer line was defective. He was not authorized to replace it. I paid the repairman and complained to an usher at church. This gentleman fixed the plug and, thereby, the washer. At the same time, he told me other ways to be energy efficient. Thanks to him, I replaced all our light bulbs. There was a noticeable difference in our bills. When we replaced our rugs, another church member helped move the piano. Another moved the gas range from our kitchen to the porch. My three summers of delivering newspapers on summer afternoons after work helped David. They made me late for several basic Russian classes. I biked an extra ten miles per day to deliver up to twenty papers. In each of three summers, I lost ten pounds and I loved it.

We replaced an arm chair and some well-worn curtains. Two consecutive years, I got our stock of posters, and David's smaller paintings, framed and installed on our walls. It was like living in an art gallery. From time to time we added another picture. Honey loved the band. She never felt she was wearing the right thing to a concert. She stayed after regular practice sessions to practice duets for a coming event. She really needed a new dress.

We went to the best local department store. From the catalog Honey selected a dress. As we placed our order the clerk insisted, "But it's a bridesmaid's dress! You can't just buy a bridesmaid's dress!" "May I speak to your boss, please?" I inquired as sweetly as I could. She backed down gracefully, "Well, I guess you can if you really want to." "I really want to," I said. It was a beautiful dress and Honey looked radiant in it. The duet brought compliments.

We went to see Kitty Dukakis at the Performing Arts Center and I actually shook her hand. In the audience was one of the Chinese 101 students, the one who came home with me. I reminded her I still kept her Mah Jong set. Two days later, she came to claim it. I gave her a children's story book from Beijing as well. When David's Flying Tiger friend came to visit, I asked him to bring me a Mah Jong set. He brought me exactly the same set I could not afford in Hong Kong. He brought aviation books for David, for which I am still grateful. There was a kind of post mortem at the college. Various complaints were lodged about the lack of communication between the teacher and students of CHIN 194. I heard about it later. I also heard our teacher decided not to teach there anymore.

We continued our association with Chinese in our own quiet way. Most of the birthday celebrations were "all you can eat" at a Cantonese restaurant. One year Honey bought a T-shirt for David. On it, she painted a Hot Dog because this is his favorite food. The concession where it was possible to paint one's own T-shirt went out of business. This made David's shirt really unique. We bought stock, just a single share, at first, and began enjoying our quarterly twenty-five cent dividends. Every year we went to the Air Base for Open House. When I was writing letters to the editor trying to halt reductions in bus service I mentioned the Air Base. I said the military wives could use bus transportation to work or shop in town. Then, the bus driver for the district began to make people wait outside the gates while a pickup was made. They could no longer remain on the bus if their pickup point came before Elmendorf or Fort Rich. This meant extra wear on buses and passengers. The Elmendorf bus schedule was dropped from the schedule book. Only the base hospital was listed for "security reasons". The two enormous bases, Air Force and Army, apparently lost their civilian bus service for a time. This did not help dissipate the carbon monoxide in the city.

Our neighbor told me she dated one of the Blue Angels. I was impressed. Every Elmendorf Open House, we stood for hours on the flight line. We watched the Blue Angels, the Snow Birds, the Thunderbirds, and the Air Force Band. We looked forward to finding out which one would come in a particular year We bought all kinds of souvenirs, hot dogs and pop. Honey loved the working dogs, David loved the airplanes. I loved the bike rides past Canada Geese and ducks and the garage sales. Open House was a summer event to which we all looked forward.

One August day I delivered eighteen newspapers. I picked up a Berlitz travel guidebook and our itinerary. I paid and thanked the travel agent and started my vacation. We watched the Blue Angels at the Air Base the next day. The day after, we took a taxi to the airport. Bus service to the airport no longer existed. Local cabdrivers were blamed. The local transit system was supposed to be federally subsidized. People wondered aloud how local cabdrivers could change a federal subsidy. Could five hundred people hold several thousand others at their mercy? No one knew. It certainly looked like they could.

We flew to Seattle to San Francisco to Honolulu to Auckland to Sydney. In Auckland, a steward walked down the aisle spraying the still seat-belted passengers like cattle. I was not the only one who was incensed. On the return trip I did not buy anything in Auckland. This was also because their prices were outrageous.

This trip to Australia was a special promotion David heard about. He longed to go to Africa like some of the church people. I could not imagine being able to afford a trip to Africa. When he told me the fare to Sydney was so little, relatively speaking, I decided to go. I did not want to disappoint him again. We would have to stay there a week. How? I talked to a church lady who suggested we write to people offering to work for shelter. We wrote and waited and, at last, we got a reply. Then we got another letter from the same person. There was an address and a telephone number and someone expecting us.

It was early evening when we landed in Sydney. A co-worker for the environment told Honey, "Whatever you do, don't miss the Taronga Park Zoo." So we went to the Taronga Park Zoo while the late afternoon turned to dusk. We rode a ferry to get there. We walked, among eucalyptus trees, past koalas, kangaroos, wombats and wonderful birds. At sunset, we rode a ferry back to the dock and walked to our hotel. It was great!

Now, came an educational experience. Our travel agent customarily booked one night in a hotel. We expected one room with one single bed, one double bed and a bath. We were given a key and directions. We took the lift to the top floor and found ourselves in a room which must have originated as an attic. There were low ceilings, no windows except one facing a chimney, bare floors and a tiny sink and toilet. When the cot arrived there was about a four inch gap between it and the double bed. Each bed leaned against a wall. We were exhausted. We slept in our travel clothes. Each of us thanked God it was for only one night. This must be a Japanese hotel. Only futons would work as beds in so little space. We checked out before breakfast, right after my telephone call. I called the neatest lady I will ever meet no matter how long I remain on this planet.

Without any preambles or platitudes, she gave us complete directions to her home. She was a lady after my own heart. She didn't ask how we were or how was the flight. She made sure we could find her. She reminded me of Ellen, who also assumed one was all right if one was talking. We breakfasted in the hotel coffee shop, a dreadful mistake. I thought nothing could be worse than climbing along beds to a bathroom where we couldn't even take a bath. The Lamb's Fry I innocently ordered was worse. It was greasy fried lamb kidneys too tough to cut with a knife. We went shopping for Kleenex, forgotten at home, in a downtown store. The store looked like a warehouse compared to San Francisco or Seattle or even Anchorage shops. I soon learned this store was not representative of Sydney. Then, we took the train to meet our hostess.

The first thing she did when she met us was give us a key to her house. I was absolutely thunderstruck. We came from nowhere she knew. We represented no one she ever met. A couple of days later we were watching her large beautiful television set. She said, "My uncle and aunt are in Alaska now. I hope they meet someone like you, someone who would be nice to them". I would have been her slave for life. She had two cats. We had two cats. We belonged to the same worldwide church. We could use the laundry and bath whenever we wished. She had her own bathroom. We shopped at Safeway on our way home from sightseeing trips. We dined with our hostess.

Our first day with our new friend she took us to lunch at a posh department store. We enjoyed great crepes. We usually ate Wee Bix or Rice Bubbles for breakfast. Lunch somewhere in Sydney, at a counter, was often Aussie pies. We ate hot dogs (frankforts) with potatoes, fresh vegetables and a salad for dinner. At a nearby Taiwanese store we bought shoes, jackets and a box of tropical fish erasers for my co-workers. We ate lots of frankforts to David's (and Honey's) delight.

We used City Rail to Town Hall and Circular Quay and strolled the Botanic Gardens. Six white herons with black bald heads lunched with us. We sat on a bench munching Aussie pies from a vendor near the Opera House. We took the Ferry to Manly our third day and walked along the beach crunching small shells. Hard salami and fruit bread were lunch at home. We walked around the Opera House. After church, a lady in a kilt drove us, in her Holden, to the Harbor Bridge. We walked across it to shop at the Rocks.

Another day our hostess took us on a tour of the Powerhouse Museum. She gave me a museum pin, David and Honey a key ring each. We watched the television set in the evenings. We admired the bougainvillea on her back porch and the rosemary growing above her kitchen sink. Then, our week was over and we were exchanging hugs and catching the Town Rail to the airport. At Christmas we sent calendars to each other, at other times we sent cards and pictures. She was, and is, a real lady.

For several years, David wanted to take "writing for children." Long before this, he entertained me with short verbal scenarios. At last there was room in the class for him. His first story began something like, "On our trip to Australia..." The hot shot in the class, a South American mechanic, snapped, "Not everybody can go to Australia". David did not reply. Laboriously, he put his second and third tries on the computer. He pushed the wrong buttons and lost them. There were papers to deliver on time. There were art assignments. He dropped out of the class. The mechanic became an elementary teacher. I pitied his students. After a semester or so, David told me more funny children's stories.

While I distributed the tropical fish erasers to my co-workers, a new employee introduced herself. I gave her an eraser. Some of her numerous relatives worked for a supermarket chain. Unsold vegetables and fruit or bread found their way to her house. She distributed them to her friends at work. When she insisted the food would rot if no one helped herself, I gratefully accepted some. What black looks I got when I accepted too many mushrooms someone else wanted! I won a permanent place on her black list by refusing to contribute to another money envelope. From a vacation in Hawaii, she brought real flower leis for everyone except me. For two days, each lady in the office wore a real Hawaiian lei. At Halloween I wore my two cloth and wire leis from Honolulu with a Chinese soldier's hat. I wished the flowers smelled as rich as the real ones Honey and I wore in Waikiki. The new employee came as a beautiful witch.

Already the "extra" food was being directed to higher echelons, to people who could hand out overtime. "What goes around comes around" she chanted several times a day. At Christmas I bought a sweatshirt, some fabric colors and a big box. On the shirt, almost touching each other, I printed the daily sayings of my new co-worker. On exchange day, I put the big box on her desk and waited. When she found and opened the box she exclaimed, "Wow! These are all my own words. This is what I say! Who did this?" She was delighted-so much so she wore the sweatshirt the entire day. I overheard many approving comments without lifting my eyes from my work or opening my big mouth.

I borrowed a series of Japanese videos from the library and watched them at home. One afternoon, I counted seventeen silver salmon in Campbell creek and a Kingfisher nearby. The muskrat in the ditch beside the bike path on C Street died mysteriously. One day he was paddling about the muddy water. The next day he was flat on his back with what looked like a BB hole in his throat. Beavers were felling the trees in the park by our bridge. The Coastal Trail was repaved twice while our bike path

continued to disintegrate. Frost heaves and roots broke through the asphalt. People voted down bike path (ski trail) repairs in our neighborhood. How was it the trail along the inlet was always so well kept?

The ravens fled from Fairbanks and Mt. Spurr erupted. For several days we wore surgical masks whenever we were outside. Our neighbor hosed the driveways religiously. She constructed a wooden walkway between her door and her car before she moved away. We went to the Governor's Picnic and delivered more rhubarb to Bean's cafe. For ten years I was not included in the double pay year-end activities at work. Finally, what I did was important enough so I was asked to work December 30. It wasn't as much fun as it was supposed to be. We supported the nature groups with purchases. Remembering Norman's, "All she buys is trinkets," I bought novelty earrings. I also bought household items, including a pineapple room deodorizer which worked.

Our moose trimmed the trees which grew beside our home. On one side an alder and a birch grew so close they almost shared a trunk. At first I cut them down to ground level. Then, I let them grow. They became ideal perches for birds, great spots to hang feeders and suet baskets. David blocked the hole where the mice came into the kitchen but now and then a tiny mouse would raid a feeder. Red Polls and Chipping Sparrows and Chickadees came to feed. Our indoor parakeet made the air busy with her chattering, especially when someone was using the telephone.

When it became possible to buy our own telephone we bought three, one for each of us. When we got a call from Grandma it was a conference call. Grandma sent us "Care" packages for Thanksgiving and Christmas, sausages and dried corn, relishes and candies. We sent annual commercial fruit cakes to her. At length, when the price of something local ceased to make sense it became possible to send for it. This blessed everyone, sooner or later. The local merchant eventually lowered his price to make it more competitive on the global market. Yes, we too watched television. I made my own lunches and lived on peanut butter sandwiches when we were poor. I took ham and cheese sandwiches to work when we were less poor. Honey and David ate thousands of mini pizzas and hamburgers. We learned to appreciate earthquakes and two foot snowfalls. We loved the wonderful long summer days when the Canada Geese took their families for a stroll to the library.

A Set of Trains/Late May

Chapter 36

We were selected to help with the Consumer Price Index. One year, a pleasant young lady visited us, at precise three month intervals, four times. In large ledgers, she entered our expenses for the preceding quarter. She noted what we paid for lodging, fuel, electricity, food, clothing, entertainment, and automobile expenses. This was before our lot rent jumped $20 and telephone use rose $2 (base price). The radio commentators assured us there was no inflation while all the prices crept steadily upward. She appeared to be honestly amazed we had no automobiles, no credit cards, no debts, and no overtime. We didn't frame our certificate because the pleasant young lady forgot to sign it. We missed the young lady but not the embarrassing questions about our lifestyle. She knew so much about us and we knew nothing about her. I hoped we were helpful.

There was a four foot snowfall followed too closely by six more feet of snow. Our heater stopped. The expert who repaired, and restarted it, first suggested we have the snow removed from the roof. Our problem was a snow-choked rooftop vent. I put down the telephone and called for volunteers. Honey and David put on their heavy weather gear and shovelled vigorously. From the dining room, I heard a loud thump. I opened the porch door. There was Honey. She literally dropped in through the porch roof. She was unhurt but it was spring before the porch roof was mended. Meanwhile, everyone in the park borrowed ladders. David spent his Christmas money for our own aluminum ladder. Now and then our favorite neighbor borrowed it.

Fur Rondy came again. We rode the dog sleds behind a masked husky, lunched at Blondie's, and bought books at Cyrano's. At Iditarod time we tracked the race on a map and wore our Iditarod headbands. The Roto Rooter man came again but this time he made two trips. His arrangement was, for a set price, he would clean out any drain. What I initially thought was excessive turned out to be a real bargain. After hours of his hard work, we could use our kitchen sink in the accustomed manner. The questions for the Consumer Price Index made us seem so far behind "civilization." Then I recalled my father's water supply—a creek, frozen solid about six months every year. I felt "spoiled rotten modern."

April 2, 1993 I paid our travel agent a little more than $4,000. This was for airfare and Euro-rail tickets for three adults. There was a month's vacation: two weeks to clean the house, and two weeks to travel. The last half of April I spent training another new worker. There were several clouds on the horizon at work. A lady who was there when I arrived began to bring me small Tupperware bowls of soup. She invariably explained her husband didn't like soup and she didn't want to throw it away. I accepted the soup because she insisted it would be discarded if I didn't. A lady in another department sold hand -decorated aprons. I bought one for the soup donor. Then, the lady for whom I decorated the sweatshirt began to insist I contribute to the envelopes for four company weddings and the needy. At one time or another, four members of her family held well-paying jobs with the organization. Three of us were paying for unsubsidized college courses. I didn't explain this. I just didn't put any money in the envelopes. The young and beautiful new employee learned how to do my job. My month of earned off-time began, leaving those three ladies together.

We house cleaned thoroughly and took the sweaters to the dry cleaners. The porch roof was replaced. We got the yard in shape and left utility payments with a reliable person at work. We watered the plants and said good-bye to the neighbor who would care for our house. We took a taxi to the airport. Honey and David carried luggage packs like the one I bought for China. Each carried a flashlight because we expected to stay in hostels.

We carried a list of hostels, a guide book, and traveller's checks. David carried the new camcorder proudly, at first. We went to O'Hare and Dulles and, finally, Paris.

Bedraggled from the long journey, we claimed our luggage and headed for a bus into the city. As we passed a ticket counter, someone in full airline uniform asked me, "Is this your first trip to Paris?" He looked exactly like an airline pilot in the movies. He was scrumptious, delectable, all right!! I mumbled, "Yes." So much for a semester of trying to learn French!! He hugged me lightly, tenderly, and gave me an enormous kiss on my cheek. I shall remember it forever. "Welcome to Paris!", he said. Because I was too shocked to say anything he added, "I just wanted you to be welcomed properly!" Then, he turned back to the counter. Honey and David and I tottered under our packs toward the line of buses.

We went into the city, found the bus stop nearest the Louvre and disembarked. Next we learned it was too late to be able to see much in the Louvre. We decided to get something to eat in an outdoor cafe. It was not yet tourist season. There were literally dozens of empty plastic chairs. We were allowed to purchase baguettes. We were not allowed to sit down while we ate them. I learned this when I sank into a chair. Two waiters zeroed in on our table, each loudly insisting "No." In a small shop, I bought vanilla perfume because a girl in my French class recommended it. Then, as dusk was falling, I said, "Where should we go first?"

David said, "Let's go to Barcelona."

We took a bus to the Euro-rail station. A Spanish General, in full dress uniform, waited for something beside a slowly starting train. I asked him if this was the train to Barcelona. He insisted we could not ride his train, pointing to a sign, "POURBOU." Running to catch the train nearest the sign, we asked another passenger if it was going to Spain. It was. We used our Euro-rail pass to get a good night's sleep in a compartment.

Barcelona was glorious. Even the way to Barcelona was glorious. Our train rambled along the Mediterranean. It was mid-May, not yet full tourist season. We could buy baguettes with tomatoes and genoa salami and cheese at a railroad station. We could reboard the train, and eat them as we travelled. We could see moonlight on the Mediterranean. There were red tiled roofs and sailboats and yachts under a radiant sun. A conductor came along to check our passports. At Pourbou we changed trains and our passports were checked again. In Barcelona, we got off the train and walked a block in the warm spring sun. We checked into a brand new hotel, the Barcelona Sants. We spent two nights in an upper floor room we could exit (or enter) without going through the lobby. The manager welcomed us like we were friends. He took us to the large room with sitting room and bath. He even explained the rear exit stairway which was close to a bus system. He was very nice.

"In the excitement the conductor rang up the right amount of fare," the Foreign Cars bookkeeper in Philadelphia used to say. Now I knew how fare on the bus he rode to work was handled. We entered a modern bus in Barcelona. An attendant extracted bits of numbered paper from a machine and handed us each one "ticket." In English, he said, "Keep it till you get off." At our chosen bus stop, we walked to the rear of the second section. Another attendant accepted our tickets and coins which he deposited in a coin box. I thought his knowledge of basic math must be incredible. How would he handle rush hour crowds? It looked like an opportunity for either petty larceny or classic confusion. The Olympics preceded us, which was why the new hotel was there. It was also why there weren't many people around a year later. David wanted to see where the Olympic marathon was run. We took a bus to a high hill where he pointed out the exact spot Olympic racers passed on TV. I saw a bus going the other way and we ran to catch it. In my rush to cross the street, David missed the snapshot he wanted. We looked for an adaptor for the camcorder. I kept asking people, in my California high school Spanish, for directions. One lady actually took us to a metro station. She walked half a block with us before heading back toward her original destination. We looked for a hostel. When we finally found one, it was exclusively male. We found a camcorder adaptor, at last. Then we found a wonderful restaurant with a beautifully dressed lady manager. I gave her all my remaining Spanish coins for lunch for three. When what David ordered turned out to be raw fish she took back my portion. I tasted it before I knew what it was. She brought me a pasta. David found the meal just great. We agreed lunch was perfect and the atmosphere old world elegant. I hoped we didn't diminish their profits much.

A fountain, on one of the lovely shaded avenues, was a cast bronze little girl with a frog from whose mouth water spouted. David snapped pictures of the fountain and a bike shop where Honey purchased a bicycle pump and a lock. We never found a hostel where all three of us could stay. We loved Barcelona. David wanted to stay longer. I reminded everyone we already spent three days so we reboarded the train the next morning.

It was warm and rainy in Nice. There was a public shower in the train station. We walked from there to buy a Flan. I noticed a canopied shop featuring umbrellas in beautiful pastel colors. I bought one for each of us. We went back to the flan shop and dropped some of our luggage on a nearby picnic table. We bought another three pieces of flan. While I was paying for it, David tried to open his new umbrella. Someone adopted the carryon briefcase which came with his pack. It contained the video he made in Barcelona, postcards, and film. It did not contain passports or traveller's checks or money. These were in the flat wallet belted onto my waist. We didn't see who took the carryon. No one did. Whoever did it was a pro—in and out quickly. We looked, found no one near and finished our flan.

Our showers at the station were rushed because the proprietors were in a hurry to close the facility. Then we walked, probably for miles, to the Nice police station to report the carryon theft. Alone with a pleasant pudgy policeman, we filled out three copies of a complaint and kept one. We walked back, through lovely tree-shaded neighborhoods, in the light rain to the Euro-rail. I deliberately skipped going to Marseilles because I was afraid the city might be unsafe. Now I could have kicked myself!

We went to Rome, arriving in the morning. Back in Anchorage, Honey promised to buy a scarf for someone. Just outside the Rome Euro-rail station was a kiosk where scarves attached to the frame waved in the wind. We bought one for Honey, one for her friend, one for me. Then, we took a bus to the Vatican to see the Sistine Chapel. We lost our way and found ourselves in a small apothecary. An aging gentlemen gently shoved us away like trespassing birds or squirrels. I remembered cockatiels and parrots in Bondi Junction when we got off the train after a day in Sydney. The people there were indulgent with the big colorful birds. The people here were indulgent with the big colorful tourists.

We went to St. Peter's Square. A black-robed priest recognized and greeted David. They were members of the same high school graduating class. They chatted briefly. He was showing his visiting mother the famous landmarks. He told us where we could safely store our packs. We marvelled at how immense the square itself was and how overwhelming the buildings.

The Sistine Chapel was being restored. We got to see most of it. We shuffled along very slowly in a tightly compacted mass of tourists disgorged from countless buses parked nearby. We bought ROME T-shirts from a sidewalk vendor on our way back to our bus. We drove past the Coliseum, getting to see it from two sides. We marvelled again at how huge, how cavernous, it was. We stayed in a hotel, did our laundry in a laundromat, and ate pizza at a tiny niche in the wall. The owner, Patrizia, gave us her business card and asked us to send her a post card from Alaska. We did so when we returned home. The address was so short I thought it might not reach her. We never knew.

We went to Florence for two days of looking at bronze doors which were copies of real ones being repaired. We climbed many small steps to a balcony overlooking the city. We stood overlooking red tile roofs and orange-brown brick churches, towers, and homes. We strolled the not very crowded streets. We climbed one tower which tapered to nothing at the top. We lodged above a restaurant in a room with a red bathroom whose floor leaked after a shower. I thought the manager came from the United States. He understood us perfectly and brought us bottles of water from his own refrigerator. At any time of day he willingly sold us sandwiches built like hoagies. David got a pair of Italian army shorts from an Italian haberdasher. A life size plastic horse pranced in front of his niche in the wall. Honey and

I got scarves and rings from other shops. We ate spaghetti and decided my homemade sauce has more flavor. I make my sauce from scratch with basil and oregano, tomatoes and hamburger, onions, salt, and garlic. David wanted to stay in Florence to look at more statues.

We went to Venice. Our lodging was, again, upstairs in a small hotel. We rode on a motor launch. We walked across curved stone bridges and enjoyed more flan and gnocchi and more pasta. We bought T-shirts. As we strolled across a delightful shaded park, an elderly lady waved her umbrella and shouted, "No." Her intent was to prohibit entry to a private neighborhood. We waited on one of the benches till she went about her business. A walk along the park perimeter revealed a boring backyard. We retraced our steps to the livelier, more entertaining, tourist area. David wanted to stay in Venice to explore some more.

Back on the train we rode through Milan at night. I kept waking up and going back to sleep and we were still in Milan. The train changed cars, gathered speed, slowed down, and changed more cars. We seemed to be in an endless freightyard. I didn't even think of trying to get off to explore the area. Two conductors checked our passports on two separate occasions this night. Once we heard shouts and running.

We went to Lausanne for Honey's birthday. The train ride through the Alps was just wonderful. We saw ranks of towering mountains. Here and there, cattle grazed in pleasant valleys. We saw tree plantations, not forests or woods, but plantations. Trees stood in rows like tufts of a gigantic carpet. They were all the same height and width, in squares or rectangles, isolated from fields or villages. We didn't see any wild animals or birds.

The entry of a Lausanne bank was a clear shatterproof glass cubicle, almost the size of a small hotel elevator. Here an individual waited for another customer to complete a transaction in the bank lobby. Waiting there, I wondered if the box was designed to protect me from some dangerous tellers or them from me. I only wanted to change a traveller's check to local currency. Across from the bank was a bridge and near the bridge was a delightful vegetable market. There we bought fresh fruits and vegetables to take back to our hotel. This hotel was next to the station. For relatively little money we enjoyed a great breakfast with choices of fruits and rolls and juices. The beds were perfect. Everything was clean and cheery. We bought pant suits for Honey and me, a Swiss army knife, and some books. We got more books at the museum on a square. Here gentlemen played chess with wooden pieces the size of a kindergarten child. They pushed the chessmen about painted spaces on the brick square. It was so much fun to walk the crooked streets. Cars toiled up impossible grades. Motorists rode their brakes down incredible slopes. Pedestrians ascended or descended stairs or evaded traffic on the stair-like roads. A visual feast of flowers, trees, glimpses of mountains and the lake below, appeared between the stately old buildings. We were there for another two days. Honey's cake was a creation from a chocolatier whose shop also sold chocolate frogs. We ate the frogs the same afternoon we shared her birthday cake in our room. None of us wanted to leave Lausanne. In Geneva, a young man stood holding the reins of a horse. Both man and horse were life-sized bronze castings. Due to overcast skies, Lake Geneva itself was rarely blue.

We photographed swans before taking a boat ride. The guide pointed out the houses of illustrious poets and famous people. I bought professional toenail clippers from a drugstore. Really good clippers were less expensive than they would be at home, if I could find them at home. The clerk gave

Honey and me miniature bottles of perfume. We strolled the parks and hiked to the Botanical Gardens which were wonderful. I bought a hat there.

We also walked the great distance from our centrally located hotel to the United Nations Headquarters. On our way, after much walking, I led us to an official looking building. A guard, with a gun on his hip, pointed out we were not allowed to go any farther. This was GATT headquarters and not a tourist attraction. We backed away from the grim grey fortress. At last, we found the UN, where we listened to a discussion of the world's refugee problem. We learned every day at least ten thousand people leave home without wanting to do so. We acquired free literature and bought souvenirs and walked back through the late afternoon. At a park restaurant, we enjoyed the best omelettes we ever ate. Several times we passed the house where Woodrow Wilson worked to establish the League of Nations. The wooden structure was rotting away on a main street with a great view of Lake Geneva. A billboard about the building and our World War I President was fading in the sun. Then it was time to return to Paris.

Chapter 37

The Geneva railroad station was different from other Euro-rail stations. Waiting patiently in line, I found myself paying for an express train trip to Paris. It wasn't really expensive and it did save time. On arrival, we took a bus to the Paris Opera. We discovered a tiny hotel at an angle from this marvelous structure. The hotel elevator was about the size of the Lausanne bank cubicle. Wearing my overloaded pack, I couldn't close the door. We walked up two flights of narrow winding stairs to our viewless room. The hotelkeepers ran the restaurant downstairs, looked totally Parisian, and didn't speak English. We were in the middle of everything, a short walk from the Louvre, two blocks from a major department store. Here we bought bottled water.

We went to the Louvre. After buying our tickets, we were informed bottled water could not be carried away from the I M Pei entry area. David volunteered to hold our freshly purchased water bottle while Honey and I explored. We mounted the escalator, walked a bit, and began to climb stairs. I looked up. There at the top of the stairs was the Winged Victory of Samothrace in a fantastic golden light. "David has to see this!", I exclaimed. Honey agreed to wait there while I went back for David. He was deep in conversation with an attractive English speaking French guide. We drank the water, left the bottle in a garbage can and went up to see Winged Victory. The light was still fantastic but David would have preferred to keep chatting with the guide. A couple of hours later Honey and I used a rest room. There was a tourist with two large bottles of water. They protruded from the top of her shopping bag, not even concealed. "Who does she know?" I wondered, in American, licking my dry lips.

We spent most of the day at the Louvre. For dinner we found another sidewalk cafe, this one owned or, at least, operated by a young Englishman. He cleared a table for us, named today's special and brought it to us in good time. We were delighted to find a Paris cafe where it was possible to both buy something and to eat it. In the morning we found another cafe where the English proprietess brought me the worst coffee I ever tasted. She went back to hide behind her newspaper without wasting any unnecessary words or time on us. Honey and David liked both the food and her Springer Spaniel.

Paris itself was all we expected. We walked for miles along the Seine to buy books at the Museum of Man. We were almost run over beside the Arc de Triomphe. We got Eiffel tower earrings at the Eiffel tower. We admired the latest Sports cars in automobile showroom windows. We bought more baguettes and carried them to our hotel where we ate them with more bottled water. Preserves from an English store and fresh lettuce and tomatoes from the food section of a department store augmented our meals. The landlady watched us carry food past her restaurant and smiled.

We bought perfume for Honey and me at Lafayette. I asked for Quelque Fleurs which I remembered from high school. It was too expensive for me then but it smelled so good. The clerk asked an older clerk if she was familiar with such a scent. The older lady remembered it, but it was a Houbigant creation. To her sorrow, and mine, "Houbigant no existe." The first clerk found my perfume, Regina. She kept it for me while Honey made her selection. We took the sales slips to the cashier whom we paid before we went back to claim our merchandise. I recalled the procedure from Chinese Friendship Stores; choose, get sales slip, take sales slip to cashier, pay, and return for purchased item. I was astounded. The French are supposed to be trend setters for America. The Chinese are supposed to be backward. Both used a system no way superior to an old-fashioned American store.

We went to Monaco. Passing a tourist near our hotel, we exchanged smiles. She said, "Have you been to Monaco yet?" She gave us directions to the appropriate stations, said, "You'll love it," and kept walking. We followed the directions and found ourselves amid a quaint cluster of steep hills. What looked like flats from a stage set were set up in several directions.

These were arranged to make it impossible for us to see any of the automobile race. We could hear cars screeching and whining somewhere off to stage left. We were allowed to buy a pin honoring a specific racing car from a garage which also sold souvenirs. When we tried to descend the hill past those huge canvas obstructions, policemen wouldn't let us pass. Somewhere out of sight was Jacques Costeau's Marine Museum. We were forced to turn back to the station without having seen it. The huge billboards of a cigarette company were everywhere. I was so grateful I no longer smoked. I was even grateful I did not know anyone who did smoke.

Throughout our European vacation, I kept aside money to pay the airport departure tax. We reached the airport two hours before departure time. I looked for someone who could tell me more about the tax. No one could. Ticket agents assured me, "Your travel agent gets paid for taking care of such things." Since my travel agent was the one who reminded me to save for the departure tax, I didn't believe this. When we finally reached Anchorage, there was enough cash to pay for our taxi home—plus, exactly the departure tax.

David's partial plates came too late in his life to be very helpful. Honey's glasses didn't attract men but they did help her see better. Two acquaintances from where I got my traveller's checks planned to go to Europe on vacation. Someone slipped several thousand dollars from an envelope for which they were responsible and their jobs ceased to exist.

I was still mourning their loss when David's boss decided to stop handling the newspaper. For fourteen years David gave his all to this job. He scheduled art classes around deliveries and walked miles five days every week in all weathers. In winter, his bus fare frequently cost more than his monthly check. In summer, his bike tires were replaced frequently as he crossed and recrossed the city. He replaced a bicycle every four years. The friendly people at the Bike Shop always commented, "Well, whoever stole that particular bicycle didn't get much. It was just about worn down to the frame." Three times we faithfully filled out a police report with data pertinent to the disappearance of another bicycle. Three times no one officially found the bike. When the paper folded David could finally schedule classes unattainable before. Deprived of my summer deliveries I no longer lost ten pounds each year from riding my bike.

Patiently, persistently, Honey tried to find her niche in life. She tried to be what she always wanted to be—a music arranger. Because she had no access to a piano, she failed her first attempt. When we did get a piano she was taking archaeology classes. Chemistry, biology, food service, dancing, all the basic requirements, one by one, required or elective, she took.

One day, in desperation, she asked, "What am I going to do?"

I asked, "How many credits do you have which belong together—like a major?" She added her credits and came up with anthropology. So I said,

"O.K. get a degree in anthropology. Then, decide what's next. You probably should have a degree. When I went to college I followed one piece of paper, one list of subjects, for four years, till I graduated. Afterward, when I could, I took the classes which interested me. Try it!" After consulting a counselor, she followed my advice.

When we first came to Alaska we left behind two people, a house and a cantankerous parrot. We also left a dearly beloved, mixed beagle as well as a Siberian blue cat. When their father sent his annual birthday cards he relayed important news. For example, we knew Norman took the cat to the pound because Norman hated him. Charlie, the dog, froze to death because Norman wouldn't let him inside the house. It did not matter how much snow filled his dog house or how frozen his water dish was. Sam, the parrot, starved to death. The house was paid for and David's brother was kicked out. I received a small check from Norman's lawyer. It was enclosed in a letter of praise for not having interfered with the divorce. When I told Honey and David I was divorced David said, "What took you so long?" Honey said, "It's about time." I felt like a truck was lifted from my shoulders. Or was it the nine used cars Norman bought on the installment plan while we were married?

Ten years later, in May, just before prices went up for tourist season, my son Bruce visited us. He, whom I last glimpsed on his way to a prestigious college, sent us a letter typed on his computer. He wanted to know if we would welcome him to our home since he was on his way to Alaska. When he telephoned from a local motel I insisted he come to be with us. Instead, he slept at the motel for the week he spent touring what we regarded as our country. He went to Homer and Seward and Fairbanks. Without advance notice, I could not take off from work. Bruce spent lots of time with Honey and David. He took me along on a Saturday trip to my father's old home. He took many pictures with his rented camcorder and smiled a lot. After he left, I learned he owned a bigger and better mobile home than we did. He invited Honey to share it. I did not hit the ceiling. Then, Honey told me Bruce flunked out of college because of my divorce. Then, I hit the ceiling. This was the family success, the A student, honor roll, the big man on campus who dated a cheerleader. This was the self-sufficient independent who drove two of his own used cars and sold shoes at an outlet for pin money. Now, he was running some company's computer and blaming me for his troubles. This smiling face was my middle child, Bruce.

There was a time in November, just after tourist season, when tourist rates were again lowered. Norman sent a post card announcing his forthcoming arrival. As usual, Bruce went before. Norman followed. Of course, I invited him to dinner at our humble abode. He came wearing penny loafers, levis, shirt unbuttoned at the neck under a cashmere cardigan. For years, I tried to get him to even try on loafers or levis. He would wear nothing in public but a suit and tie and wingtip shoes like his grandfather wore. Once, when colored shirts were in style, I bought him a pink shirt. He never touched it. Now here he was—only the disapproving frown and disgusted grimace on his face were unchanged. Oh, yes, there was one other thing. When I handed him the platter from which to serve himself, he snapped, just like he always did, "What's this?" I told him it was halibut, a local fish. "I know what halibut is," he responded. I did not cringe.

After Bruce left Alaska, Honey described their lunch for me, chiefly the offer to come and share his abode. I was impressed. Now, both David and Honey were busy during the week. Weekends, I made sure there was never a moment when either was alone with Norman. Norman went to Seward, Homer and Fairbanks, alone in a rented car. I remembered my shaking knees when I told Norman we were not going back to the East Coast. I also remembered his instant reply, "That's fine. I already cut off the insurance so if any of you gets hurt it's not my problem. You stay there. Only send Honey home. You and David stay there." I hung up then. Now, I tried to be cordial and polite. He didn't even try for polite. Actually, this was a blessing. Honey and David were not impressed, not even by the penny loafers. Several years passed. Bruce married and had a baby which we bombarded with toys for her birthday, Christmas, and Easter. Norman retired early with a sizeable pension. He still sent $50 each Christmas and another fifty each birthday to Honey and to David.

Honey relied on the bus, or her bike, for transportation. There were frequently inconsistent work schedules and very few full semesters she could afford. She was too shy to push to the front of the class and demand attention. She was patient, persistent, and devoted to her wind instruments, flute, piccolo, and clarinet. The French horn was always too heavy to carry. Now and then, someone would give her a ride home from a class for a semester. Now and then, someone from my language class would give me a ride home for a semester. These were our friends for a time and we treasured their kindness.

Honey earned her degree in December. She planned to participate in the Graduation Ceremony in May, in the same auditorium where she got her Associates Degree. Once in awhile, she mentioned what fun it was to be on the Swim Team. How neat she thought it was to be in the Marching Band in her Pennsylvania high school. I wouldn't say anything. I would just hurt inside because I wished she would love Anchorage like I did. I cared enough to see what was wrong with the city and try to help it grow. Concern was my motive when I wrote letters to the editors while the bus system started coming apart. I knew there was a good chance if Honey ever returned to Pennsylvania she might never come back.

It didn't help matters particularly when a passerby stopped to chat. One summer day after work I was waiting for David to bring my share of the papers. He said, "I'll bet you're from the East, New Jersey or Pennsylvania."

I said, "How could you tell?, He said, "Easy. If you're not a native or an oilman you're probably from the East or Middle Atlantic." Then, he told me his sister tricked him into going back to Pennsylvania to visit his ailing father. She promised to pay round-trip fare. When he got there, his father wasn't ill and there was no return-trip ticket. So he hitchhiked from Philadelphia back to Anchorage in 110 days. "Here I stay," he added. "Me too," I said.

Honey needed a graduation present. For her there never was a Prom, never a real date, never even someone male to take her to the movies. Those things never happened before her Junior year when she came to Anchorage and they never happened in Anchorage. Bruce tried to get her to go back when she was less prepared than she was now. For the place in her heart, where the Swim Team and the Marching Band used to be, she needed something. It was arranged for Bruce to come to get her and bring her back. She would be in Erie over the Christmas holidays. This was the loneliest Christmas David and I ever spent. I expected never to see Honey again.

Bruce came to our house by taxi, bringing a sweatshirt for David, a nightshirt for me, and nothing for Honey. He explained his round-trip ticket was from their long ago remarried father. He nibbled at the dinner we shared and then they were gone. I said, "Call me every night, and, have fun." The house was emptier immediately.

Honey did call every night—sometimes twice. She described the days she spent using Christmas money from Norman to buy bicycle equipment for all three of us. She bought bird feeders for our bird tree, earrings for herself and me. Then, late one night, she telephoned from Seattle. Bruce did not bother to bring her back. In fact, on the way to Seattle from Anchorage, Bruce surprised Honey. He said he was not going to entertain her over the Christmas holidays. He had his own family and she was old enough to find her own amusements. Honey was shocked. Norman and his wife invited her to her former home to go through things to bring back with her. They took her out to dinner once. A mutual friend from high school also took her, with Bruce and his wife, out to dinner once. The rest of the time she rode a bus to shop or revisit a site from her childhood. Honey was more alone than in Anchorage, where, at least, she had David and me and the band.

In Seattle, she missed her plane and slept on a bench. Thanks to a perceptive stewardess who made sure she was on the right plane, she returned to Anchorage. She came home in a taxi from our airport. Then, we celebrated Christmas! From her luggage, Honey unloaded the bongos I bought long before. She brought pictures and souvenirs David and she collected when they were children. There was an early plastic horse from her former bedroom. She said, "The little porcelain Pug Dog I bought for you, Mom, is still in the living room. I couldn't take it because it's part of their home." That's my girl who said that.

We planned a week in Grand Cayman this summer. Bruce telephoned several times after his visit. He insisted Grandma's health was deteriorating at an alarming rate. He wanted to be sure she got to see us again. He suggested we meet in Chicago. When he learned where we were vacationing, he said he and his family would bring Grandma to Chicago. They would meet us on our way home from Cayman. We had a glorious time in a great hotel. Every night we parked the rental bikes just outside our room near the pool. We biked to Georgetown almost every day, loading the bicycle baskets with souvenirs and food to eat in our room. At a restaurant, we ate the native dish

recommended by the cab driver who met us at the airport. There were three sprawling stories in our hotel with a pool, gazebo, dive shop, and barbecue. We kept the driver's card for the return trip to the airport.

We went to the Museum to learn about the seven ships sunk on a reef. This happened exactly three hundred years before—when treasure galleons plied these waves. We printed our own coins in another shop. We swam and sunned and ate at a different fast food restaurant every day. We did our laundry where lizards sunned on a wall and bougainvillea and oleanders splashed color. We swam in the Caribbean and took two Captain Marvin boat tours. I held a sting ray on the first, smaller, boat, and swam beside a turtle on our second cruise. A father and son from Honduras introduced us to conch salad. We saw puffer fish and a barracuda. Both Carnival and Princess cruise ships floated on azure seas nearby. We were politely asked not to use a private beach before we found the public beach for more swimming. We dined in a Bootlegger's Cove—all you can eat—of several ways to serve conch. We dined in a rooftop restaurant beside two huge parrots amid white tablecloth and napkin elegance. We turned brown and sunny and happy. We chatted with the dear little maid who took care of our room and approved our purchases. We watched TV while coating each other with sun tan lotion. We even got a rebate on our room after we returned our bikes. At the rental agency we paid less than expected because the bikes were in great shape. We bought key chains from the bike rental agent. He said, "Cayman is O.K. but if you want a real vacation go to Jamaica. That's where I came from."

We went to O'Hare Airport. As we left the plane and entered the waiting area, we met Bruce, his wife and daughter, Grandma and Lisa. Grandma was definitely not deteriorating.

Spring Break

Chapter 38

On stopovers, during our various vacations, we made two trips to the Boeing factory. We explored Pike Street Market and the Seattle area three times. We loved the city. This time we walked, rode one bus, walked more, and rode another bus. We found ourselves surrounded by dry lawns exactly like those I remembered from Los Angeles. Honey wanted to meet the publisher of a bicycling magazine. We did. His living room was more sparsely furnished than ours. His entire approach to bicycling was as a means to visit Africa. We bought a T-shirt for Honey and some fruit at a nearby Farmer's Market. It looked like we were the only people we knew who really used bicycles. We used bikes like cars and trucks, like the Chinese used their bikes. In summer, our bicycle cart carried more groceries than would conveniently fit in a modern car. Our bicycling adventures happened every day all summer. We watched Canada Geese from mating to migration for the price of an occasional new tube or tire. As usual, David loved the sights and sounds of the 747s under construction. Honey and I loved to shop. This time we brought Seattle brochures back to our travel agent.

Later this summer David found a beautiful blue bike, with a damaged front wheel, in a dumpster. He manipulated it free from other debris, repaired and tried to ride it. It was too small for him, too big for me, and too good to throw away. We sold it when we replaced Honey's old bike. Honey was disappointed because there were no men in her life.

As we biked home from church, she threw her bike down on the unforgiving asphalt. "Why can't you move to a neighborhood where some men are?" she demanded. Down went the bike on the asphalt. "Why did we come to Alaska where there aren't any men?" she agonized. Down slammed the bike. It was old and worn. We bought a mountain bike for Honey. Breezing down the C Street hill near Campbell Creek, one day after work, I fell in love. A prematurely grey gentleman was sauntering along on his bike. I passed him. Then he passed me. Then we slowed down and he said, "I'm Gary. Who are you?" I murmured my name and "Isn't it a great day?"

"Sure is," he agreed. "You live around here?" I thought this was a bit sudden so I pedaled faster. He said, "You know you drive altogether too fast. Slow down."

I braked slightly, descending the curves of the hill. When I came to the bridge and looked back he was nowhere to be seen. I lost him without even trying, the first and last man who wanted to know who I was! What a catastrophe! I knew how Honey felt.

A couple of weeks later, near the Arena, I bent from my bike to pick up an aluminum can. Another grey haired gentleman was walking with his dog nearby. He asked, "Do you collect cans?" I said, "Yes," a bit defensively. My family was the only one who did as far as I knew, from a bicycle, that is. He whistled. A stunning black Labrador Retriever appeared. The man took one of the cans from my pack and held it near the dog's nose. He whistled again. The black Lab went to look for, found, and retrieved a similar can. Then, another one. Each time he patted and praised the dog and gave me the can. It was fun for all of us. As I peddled rapidly to work, I thought, "Who needs Africa?"

Honey went to the school to prepare for graduation. She came home in disgust. She needed more credits. So her graduation was delayed a year. I bought an electric wok and plastic-coated pancake turner so she could heat something for a classroom party. I stayed out of our kitchen for hours. Honey ground, sliced, grated, pulverized and deep-fried various foods to make several kinds of Indian delicacies. At the appropriate time, on my bike, I carried the wok and utensils. Meanwhile, on her bike, she carried the carefully wrapped foods. Without fanfare, but with permission, she set up her presentation. She even brought computer printed recipes from the subcontinent of India for each member of the class. Honey was the only one in class who followed the instructor's suggestions for the last day's party. One student brought popcorn balls. Another student brought potato chips and another a plastic jar of commercial potato salad. I waited unobtrusively in the hall. Finally, she let me know it was time to carry the culinary equipment home. No one ate any of her careful concoctions. Neither of us said a word. I heated her Indian delicacies in our microwave for dinner. They were simply great! At Christmas, Honey and David came as my guests to the sign language semester end banquet. We loved it. For a time all of us finger spelled.

Walking homeward from the bus stop after work, I was mentally fingerspelling. A lightweight camper driver hurried past me, stopped, made a complete circle and backed into a dead end street. I thought the driver must be on drugs so I diagonally crossed the icy street to avoid him. Then, I looked up—right into the myopic eyes of an enormous moose. He was plodding straight toward me. I swerved and strode rapidly to the side of the camper farthest from the moose. While the animal moved purposefully down the street toward the bus stop, I edged behind and to the driver's side of the vehicle. The driver opened his window. I asked, "What would you do if the moose saw me?"

"I planned to keep my truck between him and you," he said. I thanked him and he drove away. The moose encounter made an entertaining subject for a sign language video. We became friends with our dentist, his secretary, and especially the hygienist. Honey invited her to the graduation when it finally occurred. Meanwhile, she refused to clean my teeth again unless a blood blister was removed from just inside my lip. I did not smile for years because of the blister but I dared not do anything about it. Since we had our teeth cleaned every six months or so, the blister had to go. The dentist talked to a friend of his who scheduled an appointment. One day, after work, I took a bus to his office. The oral surgeon and his nurse removed the blood blister. It was kind of awesome to have two people working inside my mouth at the same time. David accompanied me on the bus home and I was glad he was there. I paid by check, as usual. Some time later, the oral surgeon notified me the company insurance would not pay the entire balance of the bill. Apparently a biopsy to determine whether the blister was cancerous was performed. The law required the biopsy and the law required me to pay for it. I did so, reluctantly.

The snow came in sheets on fields and mounds on roadsides. David met me after work one day to help carry food home on the bus. I followed David up a mountain formed when snow plows cleared the highway. No one had cut or worn the last step. Apparently, one was supposed to jump to the ground. There being no alternative, I jumped. At the most, it was three feet. My landing was less than successful. I put down an arm to break the fall and felt a snap. Suddenly, I knew how our dachshund felt when she broke her leg. I got to my feet and followed David to the grocery store.

We did our necessary food shopping. At the checkout counter, I asked the clerk where the nearest emergency center might be. He suggested one. We called a taxi and loaded the food into the trunk. David dropped me off at the emergency center, taxied home, and unloaded the groceries. He paid the driver and walked back to join me. I was still waiting for someone to do something besides write down my name, address, work phone, etc.. When it became clear I was not alone, X-rays were taken and studied. My arm was put in a sling and I was given some pills. I paid for all of this, of course. Then, David and I walked home.

It was Easter vacation for the school district. Most of the orthopedic surgeons were at conventions or on vacations. The emergency center people spent a lot of time trying to locate one. I always felt they earned their money. So did the rest of the experts who converted a fractured wrist into a working wrist. Honey and David went with me, on the bus, twice to surgery at the hospital. Both times I climbed on a gurney. Tubes were attached to the normal arm and I was anesthetized. A structure remarkably like the Golden Gate Bridge was attached to my arm. Several weeks later, the steel wiring was dismantled. We took a taxi home the first time. We took the bus several times to the surgeon's office. We made several more bus trips to physical therapy. I learned how awesomely dirty the unbandaged part of my hand could become despite frequent washings with diluted peroxide. I learned how to doze, not sleep, with a miniature Golden Gate on my arm. I got my first and only flowers from my co-workers, a Safeway bouquet. There were forms to fill out at the company office. There were days of practicing Kanji and sign language. I emerged with two stress balls, one quarter pound of putty, and four ace bandages. I got a D in sign language and a B in Japanese 301. Honey and David were superlative the entire time. They accompanied me wherever, whenever, I went. They swabbed the edges of the holes where the Golden Gate was attached. They folded laundry, washed dishes, did all kinds of chores. The physical therapist advised me to ride a bicycle to increase the strength of my wrist. She said bicycle hand brakes would be more effective than a set of hand grips. Twice I rode my bike alone to the therapist. By then, I was riding my bike to work.

This semester, one of the wisest young women I ever met volunteered to provide transportation home from Japanese 301. My having to leave early enough to catch the last bus from the college disrupted the group. After Spring Break, she came to get me before class. In the most ingenious manner she maneuvered lessons for her children around collecting me. She went to Tokyo for a short trip and brought me back some elegantly wrapped scarves. She also brought books back to class. They were so attractive I asked her to get some for me. She offered to save me freight charges. A friend, who was coming to visit her in the summer, could carry my books along. I tried to tell her this was going too far. I remembered my luggage usually bulged—without other people's gear. I could not bother her friends with my merchandise. I wasn't clever enough to say this properly. To my surprise, suddenly we were no longer friends.

I ordered the books from one of my favorite stores in Seattle, Uwajimaya's. They arrived soon after the semester ended. The same dear lady took me to the class party at our teacher's home. I sat there with the Golden Gate Bridge on my arm. Something I ate for lunch disagreed with me. It was all I could do to stay in my chair and try to concentrate on what was happening. Finally, we departed. The next morning our teacher telephoned to see how I was. I was embarrassed to the point of tears. I knew the bus schedule would not change between semesters. I could not expect anyone to replace my dear ride giver. With a heavy heart, I said, "Sayonara" to my favorite teacher in all the world, to my classmates, and to the university.

Then, it was time for Honey to get her degree in Anthropology. Honey bicycled to the arena, changed to her cap and gown, and carried her outerwear in her pack. David and I came later by bus. As we entered the building, our hygienist greeted us. In the crowd of graduation candidates, Honey's pack was noticeable. David saw it and ran back down two flights of stairs. He brought her coat, gloves, purse etc. to me. We were too far away to hear well or, even, see some parts of the ceremony. David videotaped it. Even this wasn't much of an improvement. When Honey found us outside I sent her back for refreshments. Then David and I returned to the auditorium also. People we knew, from when Honey tried to become a chef, served sheet cake and punch. Honey rode her bike home while David and I took the bus. We remembered the young black woman's major speech was the main event of the day.

At a pregraduation reception one of Honey's professors said he might be able to help her find an Anthropology job. Honey went to see him. Two of her teachers said, "Come to see me about a job." Nothing came of it. No one needed an Anthropology degree. There was a newspaper ad from the organization which still employed me. Honey went to their employment office only to hear the usual, "Don't call us, we'll call you." Once, disgusted with my job, I tried to work for a local newspaper—when there were two. I even knew the editor, slightly, having been invited to her house for a meeting. She, too, said brightly, "Don't call us. We'll call you." Very patiently, Honey reconstructed her clarinet with slender cotton strings.

I didn't know she literally rebuilt her clarinet until two days before the Spring concert. Then, I came upon her practicing and asked about the thin strings between the keys. "You can't take that on the stage," I insisted. I took it, in my bicycle saddle bag, to the Music Store. The horn repairman kept it until the next afternoon when I biked back for it. The repairman insisted he was afraid to touch Honey's handiwork. "She did a wonderful job! It sounds exactly like it should! I couldn't have done so well with cotton string, or anything else, for that matter," he said. Very carefully, I replaced the clarinet in my saddle bag. Riding slowly around the bumps on the bike path, I brought it home to Honey. At night she played it, very well, in the Spring Concert. Amid the band members on the stage, under the lights, who was to notice the tiny threads holding everything together? I was angry with myself for not seeing the problem sooner. I was so proud of Honey for finding a solution. We returned to the music store to buy her a new clarinet-a red one. It was especially created for a marching band. We loved it!

There'll Be Some Changes

Chapter 39

After I went back to work things were different. The people who were doing my job changed the job itself. It was inevitable, of course. Four years earlier, my boss predicted "Within five years automation will take over." As usual, I tried to make as few waves as possible. One by one, integral parts of my day were shifted to someone else or removed altogether. I learned other things, of course. I still had a month of vacation and neither the date nor the destination changed.

We flew to Seattle, took the bus into the city, dined at Pike Street Market and went to our hotel. The next morning there was a harried hour at the dock while we waited for someone to find our reserved tickets. We cruised to Victoria, buying T-shirts and pins on the catamaran. The hotel in Victoria was magnificent. Due to another mix up, we were assigned to the Penthouse. We ordered pizza from room service and sat in semi darkness at a table looking out over the city. I flexed my left hand and remembered the therapist said not to miss Butchart Gardens. It was a beautiful evening.

We went to the famous Butchart Gardens on a tour bus. They met all our expectations. When we toured the White House years before, I was amazed how small the rooms actually were. Now, I was amazed how large the Butchart Gardens were. These were proportions which could only be learned by being there. We stopped to sit on a bench and admire a waterfall in the near distance. Some Japanese tourists were on a nearby bench. I remembered the Japanese lady from Nagasaki. The airport chat with her before I went to China was such a joy. Tentatively, I began a conversation with a lady of about my size and age. She promptly stood up, shook her head and snapped something I could not understand. She departed, in a huff, with her group. In the summer I read Joy Kogawa's *Obasan* and understood, or thought I understood. The Canadian government's World War II detention policy was even worse than California's. There was time enough to retrace our steps to many of the famous special gardens. The therapist was right. This was no ordinary tourist attraction.

Back in Victoria, we went to the Butterfly Museum and to look for an ATM. I brought a list of Canadian automatic teller machine locations. Of the many banks on the list, we could find only one which would accept my ATM card. It was The Hong Kong Bank. We tried, without success, to find someone who rented bikes. We walked about the city, admiring, enjoying. The next morning we went to the Museum to see Empires Beyond the Great Wall, a wonderful Chinese exhibition on tour. There was just time to check out and carry our luggage to the bus before it left for Vancouver. We passed huge tented areas where the BC tomatoes available in Anchorage, at a reasonable price, were cultivated. There were many modern farms and dairies.

In Vancouver, we checked into our hotel. We hiked several miles of city streets looking for a famous tea importer. The attractive tins of loose tea fit nicely in our packs. Then, we found a bike rental company. David and I rode a bicycle built for two while Honey rode a girl's mountain bike completely around Stanley Park. We got lost on the way back to the bike rental agency. Arriving just before it closed, we claimed our deposit. We found a little shop where we ate big sandwiches for dinner.

From Vancouver we took the Canadian Pacific train. For a few minutes there appeared to be another mix-up. Our travel agent told us an overnight case, of some kind, would be available at the enormous railroad station. As our tickets were checked, I inquired about this. An attendant gave me a quizzical look, disappeared and reappeared with three lightweight carryons. This was fortunate because our toothbrushes, change of clothes etc. were in our backpacks. They were encased in a single embarrassing layer of plastic. The carryons were attractive and practical. Prominent railroad officials welcomed the large tour group aboard with speeches and fanfare. This was a trip created for tourists and I was thrilled to be included. The train climbed and cruised and descended past vast expanses of trees. There were miles of clearcuts in the not so far distance and small pulp mills with mounds of saw dust. A few eroded hillsides were streaked with muddy rocks. There were tiny rushing streams. We saw a grizzly bear and some mountain sheep. More glorious green trees reached for the sky. Railroad cars on a siding waited for sawdust at another pulp mill. We felt the gushing joy of big mountains in the spring and the deep sadness of the clearcuts. The food was good. Sandra, the lady attendant, answered David's many questions like answering questions was her reason for being. At Kamloops we left our huge backpacks on our seats. We carried the overnight cases to the school bus which took us to a lodge. There we stayed overnight while our train was readied for the next day's journey.

After a great breakfast in the lodge, we reboarded the school bus back to our train. The video of our journey and Aussie type hats, ordered the day before, were waiting for us. We headed deeper into the mountains. Along the way we watched the approach to a tunnel which made a complete circle. Meanwhile, it rose nine hundred feet through a mountain pass. What an engineering feat! And then we were in Banff. One of the people I knew in grammar school honeymooned in Banff. Like the White House, like Butchart Gardens, Banff was not what it looked like in books. The famous hotel was not a jewel in the wilderness. It was surrounded by city streets and traffic lights.

We remembered Euro-rail travel in Switzerland where the mountains seemed higher but much more tame. The ski resort at Banff was surprising. A bus took us from the train to a famous local ski lodge where we dropped our packs in our room. We walked uptown a few blocks to find dinner in a diner packed with tourists. It was too late to check out the gift shops. We chose a side street to avoid a trio of elk. There was a Safeway store. We bought white nylon carry home bags—not the heavy cotton ones available in Anchorage, but neat foldable nylon. Expecting to find them later in the U.S., I only bought one for each of us. They never did appear in Anchorage despite my verbal and written suggestions to two store managers. So much for conservation! We went to bed early. The town was retreating into bedrooms light by light.

The next morning we waited thirty minutes for the tour bus to pick us up. Fifteen minutes after that, someone named Monte appeared. He swung our packs into luggage spaces accessible from the exterior before he gave us the city tour. At the Gondola, he told us when to report back to the bus. We hurried into a long line which climbed many steps to the observation deck. From there, a great valley spread before us. I thought we were doing well. All around me were people from our bus. We left the line once to buy two magnets as souvenirs of Banff. Then, we got right back into line. The snakelike, people packed, line—elbow to elbow, hip to thigh, thigh to hip, reached a narrow shelf. We loved the view from the gondola but when we reached the ground—there was no bus. Two other people from our group were standing in the empty space where we left it. After a short wait, in case the bus was being refueled, we telephoned the bus company. Someone there suggested we take a taxi to the station. The mother and daughter, who also missed the bus, split the taxi fare with us. To an older, disapproving station agent I explained we were left at the Gondola. He called a young lady who reimbursed the taxi fare. In a company van, she gave us the guided city tour. All we missed was the famous hotel in mid-city, the one which used to be surrounded by wilderness.

We saw several small herds of elk, ski trails, movie set scenery and many local buildings. Our guide answered David's questions like she enjoyed doing so. I think she did. We learned and observed. It was much more fun than it would have been with Monte. When she took us back to the station, we waited for Monte again. Monte was not glad to see us. He impatiently explained he had a schedule. We found the mother and daughter and reimbursed their half of the taxi fare. Grimly, Monte drove us to Calgary and left us at the airport. Calgary was another surprise. From a distance, appeared a treeless golden wheat plain, miles of wheat. Suddenly, there rose a city as cramped as Venice. It looked like the buildings were wall to wall condominiums, no single family homes. It was a triumph of city planning. Here agriculture was not displaced by suburbia. It was refreshing to see. In the airport we found real root beer which we enjoyed at comfortable tables. The gift shop sold leather earrings I first bought in Niagara Falls when Honey was an infant. I bought as many as I could. We flew back to Seattle and home the same day. I gave our neighbor a nylon Safeway bag for keeping our home together.

When I studied Japanese, I occasionally bought supplies from a tall, friendly Japanese lady at her store, Sakura. One day there was a garage sale sign on the shop door. When I went inside her husband told me she was in Japan. He was going there after the business was sold. Everything in the store was available for purchase. I bought more covered bowls and soup spoons. Picking up a large frying pan I inquired "Ikura desu ka?" He said I could have it for nothing. It was his wife's favorite skillet. He could think of no price for something she used every day to make such good meals. Sadly, I carried my purchases from the store. I missed those amiable people.

I sent our Australian friend a snapshot of the group in our office which stayed together for the most years. It was a good group of which either my boss or I was the eldest. Then, people started peeling off. Two went back to college. Two retired. Others got better jobs for more money. Our group's secretary went to work for one of the executives. She was a lady for whom I still have boundless respect. She was an expert secretary, a lady of practical knowledge and sweet disposition. She also used the plunger when the plumbing on our floor required attention. This unpleasant chore was performed with the same impersonal expertise as a computer project. We heard from her now and then. One day our boss also left us. When she announced she, too, accepted a promotion we cheered. Suddenly, I said, "You realize, of course, you are leaving me in the lions' den." It was one of the many times I asked myself, "Where in the world did that come from? Did I really say that?" I really said that. The boss just stared. Dead silence followed. I picked up some papers to hide my face. The boss said, "Oh, it's nothing like that." It was.

For many years, I sat in a corner of our office, quietly keeping track of specific company matters. In the telephone book, my name was the only one under three small but, I thought, relatively important functions. I tried to keep the company from being sued by making sure there were as few mistakes as possible. A lady in one of the other departments regularly sent me small pieces of candy via interoffice mail. Sometimes she sent thank you notes which I treasured. The boss was always my court of last resort. She was thoroughly familiar with every job in the department. I counted on her support when it was necessary to point out a major error to someone in another department.

Our new boss was her second in command for a relatively short time. She never considered me a valuable company asset. The girl who gave away leftover food, decorated for parties and started the birthday lists was obviously more talented. I could understand this. Year end arrived and the state monies were to be disbursed. No one accumulated the pertinent data on which one of my annual duties depended. I was unable to attract the attention of my very busy new boss. Taking my job in my hands, I telephoned my former boss to ask if the function still existed. It did. The new boss was not pleased. I did not go through the proper channels. The office was being automated and put on a military basis at the same time. The former department secretary came back to work for her, our, former boss. They were in another office higher in the chain of command. My new boss got a second in command who was strictly professional and computer literate. Even her haircut was military. I was, to put it bluntly, extra baggage. The state monies were taken care of in a timely manner. I breathed a short sigh of relief as I completed the year end procedures pertaining to my job.

Each member of our crew took a series of classes from a local computer group. I asked the girl who was trying to do part of our former secretary's work if we could go together. After all, a written notice listed her name beside mine. Then I learned her husband was coming to get her and she expected to drive him back to work. It was too late to make other arrangements. How could I know hers was a one car family? A lady, who joined our group a year after I did, was evidently commandeered to take me to the next class. For years she made wisecracks like "woof" whenever I passed her desk. She mellowed when it turned out we were equally computer illiterate. By the time she decided to retire we were almost on speaking terms.

Another year, another month's vacation, and this one was as absorbing as any other. We hired a contract laborer to build a workroom for Honey's papier mache. When we lived in our second tiny apartment, Honey constructed an elephant. She also made a Flicker and various vases from newspapers and glue and some chemicals. Then she went farther into music and college. Now with time of her own, she returned to papier mache—at first in our laundry area. Then, I would find large trays with various pieces under construction getting dry on my bedspread. So I signed a contract with an earnest, honest, capable young man. It was for building the workroom plus a series of bookshelves, repairs, and general shoring up of our abode. It became a thorough housecleaning, painting, and replacing of obsolete items. It was a month of eighteen hour days with heaps and piles of things to be sorted, cleaned or discarded. The massive group effort successfully ended the weekend after I went back to work. The trailer and the shed were each levelled. Doors were rehung. One room became an office. The files were repainted, the windows repaired. The BB shot in the living room window became a memory. I washed all the curtains, the rugs, most of the clothes. The real triumph was the workroom. Our neighbor insisted it could not be 8X12 without infringing on her area. It became 7X20 which fit against one side like it was designed to be hiding (behind a tree) from the streetside.

My sewing machine broke. After I made the workroom curtains by hand, my favorite neighbor fixed the machine. Then she moved out so her son and his wife could take her place. We became friends of the contractor and his family. David gave one of the contractor's daughters rides on his shoulders while I scoured the workroom windows. Our yard looked like a junk yard for a month. Permission, and understanding, came from the management who initially approved the project. When it was all over the contractor put down his white paintbrush. He said, “That ought to hold you for another five years.” He promptly moved his family back to the northeastern United States.

I bicycled to Penney’s and bought two blue denim comforters at half price. I bungeed them to the sides of my saddlebags and conveyed them home. It was bike riding Chinese style and it worked. One of the two plastic bags, carrying comforters, split as I brought it onto the remodeled porch. It was the last word in efficiency—the final touch on our new-old home. My vacation exhaustion dissipated at work where, for a while, people seemed glad to see me.

We Did A Good Job

Chapter 40

David saw a TV commercial featuring a do it yourself haircutting machine. It seemed foolproof so we sent for it. When it came we learned our vacuum cleaner was not strong enough to support the haircut machine. For another $100 we replaced the vacuum cleaner. Murmuring not very nice things about TV commercials, I encouraged David to trim my hair. It worked! It was fun! The grill we bought because we watched it work on

TV was even better. However, this summer our part of the country was rife with forest fires. It was illegal to burn anything outside. Honey needed newspapers to make papier mache and I refused to subscribe to the local newspaper. My news came from TV and radio. For the bottom of the birdcage we used the college paper for which we paid scandalous fees. Other papers came free, regularly, as advertisements and junk mail.

We habitually dined out on every birthday and at Fur Rondy. This year, Honey calculated the day she spent half her life in Anchorage. She invited David and me to her Half-A-Life party—Thai dinners. We biked, enjoyed the meal and bought rings for her and me to celebrate. Next weekend we biked the Kincaid trail where Honey skated while I looked for mushrooms. In the spring, Honey bought a kite which we took turns flying. This spring, we heard, Grandma flew a kite for the first time. It was fun!

When we first came to Anchorage, our friends learned David could draw. They suggested he have a one man show. At the time, and under the circumstances, this seemed impossible. Then we were invited to a show in someone's home. It was very well done. Now, a friend of David's asked him to let her show one of his prints in a group show. While she was going through his portfolios, Honey's prize winning pieces from the Fair were displayed in our workroom. David and his friend asked Honey if she would make something for the show. She did. No one bought the print David submitted. Honey's handiwork came back. There were favorable comments but no cash. The lady who took care of our house, on our vacation, was impressed by Honey's entry. A life size Boston Terrier stands looking through the living room window like a guard dog. It looks aggressive—just too well trained to bark. Tentative dates were set for David's own one room, fifteen print show. Honey worked on projects for the next State Fair and practiced for the Spring Concert.

For more than two years, a new person at work tried to meet increasingly rigorous standards. Meanwhile her home life fell apart. Another worker with sickly children surrendered and quit. She did not. Her excuses came in, sore throat, headache, periodic pain, too late or not appearing at all. Then she was fired. Replacements appeared. Another worker snapped at people. Her target burst into tears and ran to the boss. She continued this practice, with apparent impunity, because she was really a skilled worker. Her fingers were both fast and accurate on the computer keyboard. These were background events. My own struggle to survive kept me on the edge of my new ergonomic chair.

The entire procedure required six months. Now I realize I was the only one in the building who did not know this. One of the company's favorite employees was being feted at her departure. Meanwhile, in an isolated room of the same building, my new boss interviewed me for an evaluation. This was an unexpected event My first boss and I always talked informally, in her office or at my desk, about my work. Now, I sat opposite my new boss. Without preamble, she said, "You are the rudest person I've ever met. You are inattentive, inept, insolent, an instigator." Was this a spelling list? I stopped listening and looked at the clock on the wall. When the sound of her voice stopped a few minutes later, I said, "I tried to." She snapped, "I have never even seen such a rude person." Three times I tried to speak. Three times she talked right over me. I just sat there dully for forty-five minutes. Then, I really looked at the clock, sprang to my feet and said, "I have to go now. I missed my bus." I ran from the room. Hot tears streaked my glasses, made it difficult to see the way out of the building. For the first time ever I forgot to turn in my badge.

Then the ordeal began. First, I was required to move from my corner to the center of the room. Then, my desk was replaced with a table. Then, my telephone number was deactivated so it ceased to exist. Then, my files were removed to a most inconvenient area. All of this was just part of the changes in the system. Months before, we were advised both verbally and in writing, there would be some changes. I was the only one from whom all these changes were required. My changed job required learning three new computer systems and several new procedures. I did so while two people who could have taught me left the state forever. My new boss informed me, "You've been here long enough to know how to do these other people's jobs." I was ordered to ask no questions of anyone other than herself. When I did collect enough courage to interrupt her, I was told, I should know that.

I would have two chances to learn something. The job would be taken away. Three weeks later, I would be held fully responsible for that job. Quite sure I was losing my mind, I began to lose sleep and to skip every break. What used to be my responsibility, my work piled up insurmountably. I was learning. I knew I was learning. But there was no one to actually teach me. The girl for whom I decorated a shirt one Christmas became my boss's right hand man. Then, another girl who was there when I arrived, years before, was transferred to our area. She was there almost a week before both my boss and her right hand man were "legally absent." I found myself teaching the new girl how to do my new job. We worked at breakneck speed because we alone had to pay certain bills that Friday. The item count at week's end was higher than ever when we did it together. Normally, three of us performed this function. The absent one did it for the entire preceding year. I was jubilant. All weekend I felt good.

When both boss and right hand man reappeared, a relatively quiet week followed. The right hand man even spent less time on the telephone trying to find another job. I took this as an indication she felt more secure. A casual observer would have noticed nothing unusual. Tuesday morning I locked my bike near the entrance bike rack. Absentminded, I ran my tongue across my teeth. My upper plate was still in a glass in the bathroom. From my desk, I telephoned David. Within forty-five minutes the guard telephoned me to say my son was outside. I met David and took the small ZipLoc bag from his hand. En route back to my desk, I returned my upper plate to its normal day time position. There was a second evaluation. Again in writing, I was informed my work was inadequate. Several people from other departments, whose work affected mine, came and went from the company. I kept trying. A third evaluation came. As I returned to my desk, the girl who worked alone with me the successful week said, "You know when you and I were doing this job together, we really did a good job. I want you to remember that."

It was vacation time. This year I expected to be sort of watching David's prints at the gallery. Why, I don't know. His friend came to our house twice, went through his work, and made suggestions. After the remodelling, she and he worked together on advertising, matting, and framing. Finally, they set up the room where the lithographs would be shown. I held one of the announcements in my hand and admired it. Then I put my name on the vacation list, telephoned our dear travel agent, and gave her the dates. Between the end of David's show and Honey's spring concert we could travel. I wrote a letter to the editor of our surviving newspaper about the Canada Geese. These creatures were in line for extermination because their nesting grounds were preempted by a cluster of immense hotels. "While the hotels ran each other out of business, what would happen to the subsistence hunters along the Pacific Flyway who relied on their annual migration for food?" I wondered in print.

David looked fantastic in his very old corduroy jacket, matching tan cords, and Chuck Taylor high top sneakers. I found him at the gallery, after biking there from work. I tried to help set up the potato chips and dips. Everything was already most efficiently taken care of. David introduced me to four of his art teachers as they wandered in gradually on opening night. Several other people introduced themselves. Honey arrived and we checked out the pictures together like we were art critics. I was impressed. This was the first time I saw many of those prints. "Sydney's Aquarium," showing the children looking through the glass tank at swimming sharks, impressed me the most. Another of bicycles and another of trains—close ups and in the distance—in the same space, blew my socks off. I went with Honey to see other people's work in other parts of two buildings. It was well done—all of it. When we returned someone's critique impressed me. "I keep having to come back here because every time I do I find something new in a picture." We helped gather up the leftover food and bicycled home through the golden evening light. No one bought any of David's work. Next morning, we were on our way to Jamaica, West Indies.

At the airport, there was plenty of time to wait between checking in and boarding. We browsed the gift shops. I found a paper back book about Aikido, a way of conflict resolution. Between Anchorage and Seattle, Dallas and Miami, I either slept or read the book. I enjoyed the airline food or watched a movie or slept some more. We registered in the Montego Bay airport. An attendant named a cab driver he said would take us to our hotel. Out at the cab line, the driver I asked for wondered where we were going. When I gave the name of our hotel, he refused to take us. Another, more adult, driver spoke up. He took us to the hotel—explaining the young drivers didn't want to take the short runs. At the really spectacular hotel, we had to leave the completed registration forms from the airport. "Remember to get these back when you leave," said the clerk. We paid our bill in advance and collected our keys. Our room was four large rooms. There was a fully equipped kitchen, living room with day bed and couch, full bath, and double bedroom. There were also two closets and a wide balcony with table and chairs where we dried our bathing suits.

We left our luggage in this air conditioned apartment and descended winding stairs to street level. We walked a couple of blocks to Burger King where we found Whoppers and colas and cheerful attendants. Fortified with familiar food, we walked farther. A young cab driver overtook us. He agreed to take us to his grocery store and to wait while we shopped. I hesitated till he insisted there would be no charge for his wait. Since the cab was innocent of a meter, I gratefully agreed he should wait. It was not the tourist season and our faces were painfully white. Inside the store, ours were the only white faces. The former warehouse did not accept traveller's checks. So we went to a nearby bank, then back for Jamaica Blue Mountain Coffee, some cereal, and fruit. We also got wooden turtles from a Grandmother in a nearby crafts center. She saw us coming, seized our arms, and shepherded us from stall to stall past various wood carvings. She was totally friendly so I was barely able to stay within my daily budget.

Back at the hotel we found the dining room and the pool. From the desk we got huge towels. We swam before dinner despite a light thunder shower. That felt good in the warm air! After dinner we ate fruit. We surveyed the balcony's drying towels and swim suits, and the few people lingering on the street. We went to bed. There was no radio, no microwave, and no television. The electric stove and refrigerator worked well and everything was clean and quiet.

In the morning we looked for, and found, bus tokens. I chatted with the clerk in the grocery store. I needed enough tokens for three people to make three round trips. With an air of disbelief, she counted them out. We three crossed the street to a bus stop sign where we stood waiting. A passerby went to join the line of waiting cabs at the rear of our hotel. Soon he, and three of the drivers, crossed the street to join us. Words tumbling over each other, they informed us: 1) this was a bus route which wasn't used for a long time. Someone forgot to take the sign down; 2) the bus wouldn't come for three hours and wasn't it hot out here? Too hot to stand and wait; 3) the bus would be too crowded for three more passengers; 4) there really was no bus. Four more passersby came to add their voices and their reasons why we should not take the bus. Abruptly, I swung on my heel and walked down

the other side of the street. Two cab drivers followed us. I led my family into a souvenir shop where we bought a box of dominoes and a deck of cards. When the street was clear and our purchases paid for, we returned to the grocery store. We bought food and returned all but three of the bus tokens. We kept those as souvenirs. The clerk could not explain why the bus did not come while we were waiting. She still thought it came, every half hour on the half hour. She would not look at me as she spoke.

At the foot of the winding stairs leading to our apartment, a lady set up a fruit stand. We bought bananas and pineapple, took them upstairs, and ate them. We looked at travel brochures from the hotel desk. After lunch we arranged, at the desk, for a cab to take us to Dun's River Falls. Then we went back across the street to the beach for some sun and cool breezes. We got started on our tans. We went from the beach to the pool to dinner at a spaghetti restaurant. We played dominoes while rain splashed on our balcony and we sat snug inside.

Our cabdriver was waiting at the desk after breakfast. He took the winding front entrance route through parched country. An occasional scrawny cow was tethered to a concrete block. The pasture invariably looked seared and sparse. There were few trees, few tumble-down houses with barefoot children, few yachts visible on the azure sea. At the Falls our driver explained he would meet us after we climbed the Falls. When I tried to buy three tickets, the clerk insisted I walk down the wooden steps. He wanted me to see the way I would have to go to get back up. So we descended wooden stairs to the bottom of a low hill. We climbed the same stairs back to the top. Then, we bought our tickets and went down again to meet Hubert, our guide.

Rainbows on Rhubarb

Chapter 41

Hubert worked with a video cameraman who taped our journey upward. Through a continuous, natural, pleasantly warm shower, we climbed huge blocks of white stone. We occasionally slid on the slimier rocks. Sometimes Hubert backtracked to find an easier route. The actual climb didn't even take an hour but it was exciting, sometimes scary, always wet. I wouldn't have missed it for anything. Hubert led the way. I clung to his hand while Honey clung to my other hand. David found his own route, preceding us to the top, amid hanging hibiscus and bougainvillea. We previewed parts of our video in a sort of souvenir village. A throng of salespeople were leading us to their kiosks. We finally paid for and carried our armsful of carvings to our cab. A last salesman walking before us played a bamboo fiddle. I bought one as we came abreast of our driver, Dudley. He took us to a dining room where lunchtime reggae music was normally available. We heard the last few strains of something while we munched.

Honey wanted earrings so we found a shop nearby. I didn't have enough local small change to pay the entire bill. Graciously, the clerk waved her hand to indicate three cents didn't matter. Outside, a young man entertained David by telling him some Jamaican history. We emerged from the shop into the strong daylight. The young man told David there would be a charge for "being a friend and telling so much." I leafed through my paper money, found a small bill and gave it to David. He gave it to his friend who shoved it back and spat on the ground. "That's like five cents in Jamaica," he said. I took the money and marched back into the shop. "Here," I said to the gentle clerk, "I found the extra money." I pressed it into her hand. She gave me the most beautiful smile.

On our way back to Montego Bay, Dudley stopped at a very old church. We walked through it with an ancient lady who showed us her favorite relics. In the graveyard were thin stone markers. I reminded Honey of the New England churchyard where we found Lidiane. "What a lovely name, I thought." On her granite gravestone were these words, "Ever she sought the best, ever she found it." Dudley of the radiant smile waited in the taxi. In the morning we rode the glass bottom submarine and loved it, too. An attendant swam outside the glass walls in scuba gear. He lifted mollusks and pointed out several kinds of fish and corals. For two hours, we lived in a blue undersea world with shrimp and sea cucumbers and Sergeant Majors. In the afternoon we took another cab to buy reggae tapes and CDs. Our guide showed us a small brick box, about the size of a man. This was where slaves were kept while being shown to prospective buyers. He knew his music much better than we did, of course. He helped us make our selections with evident pleasure.

Another day, Stanley drove us, in his Cadillac taxi, to the Great Houses. In the cool interior, there was an ancient timeclock, formerly used by slaves. David tried for a snapshot. It was too dark in the corner for him to capture the ornate instrument on film. Stanley stopped the cab so David could take pictures of a cricket match. He explained parts of the game and patiently answered David's unexpectedly knowledgeable questions. A real scissor-tailed Hummingbird was resting under a trellis at Rose Hall. This tiny glorious bird was in the right place to keep cool. It was the wrong place to be photographed. A new neighbor was watching our house. When I asked her if she collected anything, she said, "Hummingbirds."

On arrival, I started looking for hummingbirds. The first day I bought a small tree of carved birds. Now that I knew there really was a Jamaican hummingbird I looked for, and found, some to take home. They were refrigerator magnets. Then we found postcards featuring Jamaica's national bird.

Honey needed something to give her ride-providers to show them she valued their steady, friendly support. We found drums, carved and painted and covered with taut skins at the ends. They were small enough to carry, big enough to sound good. For herself, she chose a carved giraffe. David waited for his carved red snapper to reach the burnished look. The guide at Rose Hall pointed out a tremendous tree with really red wood. We believed the red wooden carvings were from the same kind of tree. Imagine our surprise when David chose a carving. The carver brought forth a can of oxblood shoe polish and a rag. He calmly applied these to the carving and waited, we all waited, for the polish to dry. The carvings we bought were beautiful—all of them, in several colors of wood. Honey bought a fan and I was given one while I bought shorts and a wicker jewel basket. We bought several T-shirts and some books.

We set out on short hikes, before the days became too warm—to buy food or souvenirs or both. We dined or lunched in different restaurants each day. We swam in the pool and lazed in the sun. We played dominoes in the evening and listened, once, to a live band on the roof. We finally tried breakfast in an outdoor cafe, fleeing inside to get cooler. The night before our return to the real world, I paid our bill. In the morning I collected our registration documents from a new clerk. He took our key and said, "Your bill is only $90." I said, "No, it isn't. We are paid in full. Here is my receipt." He swallowed and wished us a safe journey home. Dudley took us to the airport. He seemed sad. He said, "Come back. Come back again to see us."

In Miami, there was a long wait with time to browse so we bought salt and pepper shakers. In Dallas-Fort Worth there was too little time between planes. An alert lady, driving a cart, asked where we were going. She sped us to our gate just in time to board and take off. In Seattle, a plane from New Jersey was late. The pilot announced we would have to fly at thirty two thousand feet to make up time. We were still an hour late on arrival. We didn't mind because at the Seattle airport we found a really superb restaurant.

There we were, rumpled and travel worn and hungry. There was plenty of time because of the other (late) plane. Several cafeterias were closed. We rounded a corner and beheld a plush dining area. I hesitated. I knew how we looked under our heavy packs. An attractive cashier asked us if she could help somehow. I asked her if we could possibly have a hamburger there. She found a closet to store our packs and David's walking stick. She led us to a table in the back of the, not very crowded, room and brought us menus. We got three superlative dinners with desserts for a reasonable price. I signed off my last traveller's check and we departed in good spirits. I blessed the lady for being able to look beyond our dirty faces.

After our trips to Australia and Europe, and after my trip to China, it took time to recuperate. Priorities were sleep, unpack, sort out, launder, straighten the house, sleep, shop and cook, organize everything, and sleep. This time we were well rested when we came home. I brought ideas from the Aikido book and a sense of hope from many dear Jamaicans. They owned so much less property than we did. There was, instead, a sense of confidence and trust. I thought it was, probably, because they weren't waiting to be downsized. That already happened. They were survivors. Maybe we could survive too.

I remembered the time I was taking a midtown class. I tried to study on a bench at the new mall. A guard walked up to me to explain a municipal ordinance. He pointed out the benches were exclusively for sitting on. One could legally sit there no more than ten consecutive minutes. The local mini libraries were closed. It was not tourist season. My alternative was to take a bus home from work, turn around, and take a bus to the class. There were no tourists. It was the empty time—nothing but empty benches. I thought, if I really wanted to, I could go and study on the bench in a shoe store. There, I would be unlikely to be disturbed! In Jamaica, and wherever else we travelled, a bench was a place where people sat and talked or rested. Not all of those people on benches were tourists. I wondered how long it would be before this concept reached the last frontier. One day the telephone rang. I answered it. "Is this the last frontier?" a voice queried. "It's Alaska," I replied. "I think I have the wrong number," said the voice as she hung up.

Honey's concert was always a triumph from my point of view. I loved to see her on the stage with her red clarinet. David and I sold tickets to the concert-goers and collected tickets from the ushers. I bought Tupperware from another band supporter. Our care package from Grandma came one Wednesday morning by parcel delivery van. Pen in hand, ready to sign for it, I heard "$98 please. The package was from Grandma's home town. Its contents were supposed to be what must have been really glamorous shoes. I refused to accept delivery. In the evening, we telephoned Grandma to report the loss. The next day another delivery man, from the same company, came to collect money. Again, I explained none of us ordered shoes. I said the package contained perishable food. I suggested he X-Ray the package to see what was in it. Again, the van left. On the third day, a supervisor appeared. I remained adamant. I would not pay for Grandma's present to us.

We biked to Eagle River on Saturday. In the box on the back of my bike,

I carried food and water. In my saddle bags, I carried extra clothing in case it got wet or cold. There was a repair kit for the bikes. Between noon and 8 P.M. we covered forty two miles to and from the Subway Cafe in Eagle River. We thought of going to the nature center. Those extra ten miles would have doubled our journey. As we descended the Eagle River hill, I knew I could not retrace my steps upward. There must be a better way back to Anchorage. We shopped at Safeway and lunched at Subway. David led us from the town by an alternate exit. I could not believe there was enough intestinal fortitude in my whole being to bike so far in one day. When we finally reached home the care package from Lebanon was on our porch. We called Grandma to report its safe arrival. It appeared, a clerk in Pennsylvania made a mistake. Forever afterward, when one of those delivery vans passed, one of us would say, "There goes D'Nunzio's shoes." The family returned to the USPS for package deliveries.

The next weekend, we bicycled to Bird Creek. Several times, David threatened to go alone. I remembered how few places there were to get help so, for some time, I discouraged him. He made a solo trip to and from South Bivouac and didn't tell us about it until afterward. Now having covered, at least, forty miles without mishap, I was game for a longer trip. Again it was noon before we actually started and I carried more gear, just in case. We rode at a fairly steady pace to Potter's Marsh. This was familiar territory. There were remarkably few birds and no red kings this time. We stopped at the restored mine where I bought silver mosquito earrings for Honey and me. They seemed to be the size of those hordes we slapped at Denali, on our field trip, years before. We bought blueberry muffins at the bakery in Bird. David changed his rear tire at the waterfall between the mine and McHugh Creek. It started to rain. We changed into raincoats and pants near Potter Marsh. We travelled at least fifty miles that day.

The really wonderful weather of this particular summer made it necessary to water the rhubarb. Usually, there was enough rain at the right times and in the correct quantities. Usually, we only watered the begonias, fuchsias, and geraniums etc. on the porch. This year we set up sprinklers. They set up rainbows on the border of our lawn. This year we found a large green frog beside our house. This year we harvested seven peas and three beans from seeds planted along edges. Normally, it would not be too dry for them to grow. Our real harvest, of course, was the rhubarb. With the bicycles, we delivered thirty eight pounds of fresh rhubarb to Bean's Cafe. They pulverize and boil it into pancake syrup for local citizens who are less fortunate than we. I gave away several bunches and froze some for us.

The third week we biked to South Bivouac. We saw red kings in Upper Campbell Creek, seven huge red-orange salmon, the biggest red kings I ever saw. They must have slipped by the fishermen lining the C Street Bridge while it was dark. I felt a great sense of relief because some of them made it so far. This year, they were the only red kings I saw. I saw beaver sign, too, well above C Street where the dam they built a year before was broken. For 15 years, I counted up to 10 kings per short bike ride near C Street Bridge. Now, this was changed. For 15 years, I counted 64 Canada Geese all summer, from eggs to migrants. When I delivered papers, and covered more ground, it was 120 per season. This year, I counted 19 at the most. On the last day, the count was 18 plus a carcass left by a speeding car.

On the radio, someone pointed out Canada Geese were not native to Anchorage. A businessman lured them from the Palmer Flats, where they really belong. He brought them to Anchorage, because he liked their calling. Another person pointed out they did not supply food for native subsistence hunters. They merely migrated to Washington state. In the vast distance along the way, there were no hunters. The nature organizations I supported, for almost 20 years, agreed with a local committee. It was unanimous. The geese were messy and should be removed. Listening to the various geese detractors, I remembered one wonderful morning. The department secretary and the girl who said, "We did a good job," stopped traffic. One stood in the middle of the street in front of the company office. The other shooed a family of ducks across the street—all the way, safely, while traffic piled up. This was a great memory!

We biked all the way to where a sign read "North Bivouac" and pointed one way. Another sign read "South Bivouac" and pointed the other way. We rode familiar bike paths to Muldoon. On less familiar city roads, we reached those signs. Then we travelled an extremely long bike path which must be a ski trail when there is snow. It rained. We put on our raingear. The hills were steep and my ancient Schwinn heavy. David formed the habit of walking his bike down, slipping and sliding up, then walking my bike down. He fought the bike's weight while I walked along the grassy edges. I moved slowly enough not to slip more than a few times. We came out near Hilltop, and sat on each of the last benches for several moments each. I marvelled on our ride to Eagle River there was a great bike path. There, too, all the benches were in the last mile or so before the trail rejoined the road. I brought home a round white rock which we christened "the roc's egg" from the original Arabian Nights.

Christmas Trees

Chapter 42

Walk a mile in another's shoes before you pass judgment on his words or actions, is an Aikido principle. I tried, even when I was using five different passwords for the two new computers our department acquired. I tried, even when those passwords would not open programs. I tried, when ACCESS DENIED flashed on the screens no matter what I did. I tried to keep cool when my boss made me choose a new password, sometimes twice a day. There was no opportunity to write it down. She raced through further verbal instructions, usually for something I would not need to know for ten days. I tried to remember everything even as she changed her mind, swinging like a pendulum. She said, "We'll do this from now on." Five minutes later, she said, "We don't use this method, never have." I tried to be patient and considerate when I could see a staff meeting was going on. No one told me there was going to be a meeting. They were laughing. I was working. When my boss said, "Don't bother the staff," what did this make me-cold spinach? Chopped liver?

One totally beautiful morning, the clock radio awakened me. The cats marched in parade before me to the kitchen. Their worry bag of cedar chips was tugged from the drawer of cat things to the floor. I biked down the street to work. I remembered the gentleman who used to smile and wave while he came toward me walking to his job. Every day for several winters, we waved at each other. One morning, he stopped to chat. He told me he was going back to the States. He told me he was going to tell his grandchildren about the day the moose followed me to work. He said we kept the same pace for several blocks. I remembered having felt strange and looked around. I saw the huge antlered moose behind me, turned back and kept walking. What else was I to do?

The day was relatively normal. I consulted my tiny sticky list of passwords and, for a change, they worked! There was another staff meeting of which I was, again, not notified. The same girl still looked for a better job, and visited her friends, by telephone. This no longer bothered me. A friend walked by my desk, asked, "How you doing?" I replied, "Hanging on." She nodded, "By the skin of our teeth." Five minutes before quitting time, my phone rang. "Come into my office," said the office manager. I did.

She pointed to a chair, handed me a paper and pen, and said, "You'll have to sign this." I didn't quite believe it, even then. "I'm terminated?" I asked. "As of right now. You got all the warnings. You signed everything but this. You'll get your last check in the mail next week." I signed the termination notice. My boss walked me to the street exit. "Have a good life," I said. "Uh, huh," she murmured, her thoughts elsewhere. On my way home, I shopped for milk and bread at Safeway. I packed them in my saddlebags and on my bike rack. I counted the Canada Geese, the eighteen survivors. For six previous months, I described the increasingly degrading environment at work to Honey and David. They were not surprised when I told them I was no longer employed.

We went to the Social Security people. They were superb. After a required waiting period, I would be receiving monthly payments from taxes already paid. We went to the state employment agency and searched their computers. We found interesting jobs, for none of which any of us could qualify. We went job hunting systematically through the course of a month. The places where I really wanted to work, I haunted twice a week. Every job application said, in print, "we reserve the right to fire you at any time without notice." I thought this was an odd way to attract an employee. When someone finally gave me an interview, he said I was overqualified.

There was time to watch movies set aside while I wrote procedures for my recent boss to call "garbage." There was time to read a whole book or an entire magazine. There was time to really take care of the yard and the porch. There was time to get ready for fall, then winter, time to really listen to the radio. We were listening to KENI one day when the announcer intoned, "A gunfight in a trailer court resulted in injury to one man and additional shots in four trailers and a car."

"One bullet per trailer, very efficient shooting," quipped David.

Having time to really listen makes a difference. Someone on Channel 2 informed us, "the plane struck a hill containing 250 people." There was even time to check out the bird feeders. I watched a camp robber go by and a blackbacked woodpecker catch a snack.

The first weekend of my unemployment we biked to Kincaid and on the Coastal Trail. We stopped at the Saturday Market for a huge zucchini and some free Capucchino. The weather turned sour with days of slashing cold rain. I was grateful not to have to go through such a storm system by bike or bus to work. Piles of unread magazines lay where I had to see them in our dining room. We got some more bookcases and organized the two dozen books from the library sale. We planted bulbs for the spring, mowed the lawn, mowed our neighbor's lawn because he suffered a heart attack. He got a notice from the management just like ours, the first and only one we got this year. "Mow, trim … etc.," it said. He brought us a meal, salmon and rice in a great sauce.

The snow came two weeks early. It was heavier than usual and it did not melt immediately like it was supposed to. It did not precede a couple of more weeks of sunshine, as it did in prior years. We took the bus to the Hygienist and chatted with the dentist. My glasses made green marks on my cheeks where the metal frames were worn. I got plastic frames like Honey's on my new glasses. I read all the magazines. Our neighbor's wife moved out. Another neighbor brought a chainsaw. In four minutes he cut down four trees in his yard, trees which took long years to grow. He dug up one and I asked for it, set it in our yard behind the shed, and hoped our moose would enjoy it in the winter.

Our neighbor who planted our rhubarb when he was a child was unemployed for months. His telephone was disconnected. He came to use our telephone several times. The day he presented me with our first touch-tone phone I overheard him pleading with the finance company. He begged them to take back his truck because there was no way he could meet the payments. His electricity was turned off. The gas was turned off. His water pipes froze. The winter became savage, strong winds, heavy snows, a record snowfall for the month of November. The truck was not in the driveway for a while, then, it was. Then, his mom came back and straightened out the house. I was extremely grateful to see her, to think the young man was going to make it.

She came to us for warm water to clean things up. She came to bring me her house key and tell me a Realtor was coming to see the house. She came later with a box of salad dressing, etc.. She asked me to pack what was still unpacked in the house. She said, "take whatever you want." When I used the key to get in, envelopes from the management and utility companies hung from the door. Ice coated the floors wherever there was linoleum. I found a lamp without a shade and took it home. It was perfect for my bedside table. I packed all the boxes left from our last major grocery shopping. Still there were untouched closets, whole rooms strewn with books and papers and clothes. There was ammunition and a holster but no gun. I would find a boot in one room and its mate under something in another room. It was a nightmare day. I was nowhere near done when I ran out of boxes. I called my friend to thank her for the pressure cooker I found. She mailed the pressure gauge back to me. Meanwhile, her son was having another heart attack, then living with friends, then coming back. I would take late rent notices from her door and read their contents to her over the telephone.

David forgot his combination when his bike was parked at school. This time, someone adopted his bike. He needed to clear the area where his art projects were. We went grocery shopping again with sleds. We got a good deal on two replacement TVs. The antenna required readjustment because an earthquake squeezed it between the work-room and the house. David used one of the sleds to bring his equipment from the school art facilities. He pulled it into the side yard where two feet of snow promptly covered it.

Our rhubarb planter's truck was again parked in his driveway. He came to use the telephone. Overhead cargo planes droned all summer. Business boomed, especially airborne business. Now the same air was still and very quiet. The young man tried to get himself admitted to a treatment center. He was quietly freezing alone in the cold dark next door. I kept his mother informed and tried to give him meals, which he usually refused. When the truck was gone again, I took back more boxes for more packing. Two empty liquor bottles stood upright in a wastebasket. A newspaper clipping attached to a shelf proclaimed, "Alcohol will dissolve anything. This universal solvent works on paint, marriages, children, parents, homes." His mom came back with reinforcements, family members, who moved things out. She asked me to look around the house to see if there was anything I wanted. The Realtor was coming. I chose three books Honey might like. Her son found someone who helped him.

We received invitations to eat Thai food with a nature group. I told someone I was reading Jane Holtz-Kay's *Asphalt Nation*. A former co-worker told Honey she would call her "and we'll go to lunch sometime." Why do people say this? Honey waited expectantly. No one called. We also received invitations to participate in a rally to protest logging roads being built in the Tongass. We heard fifteen million dollars were

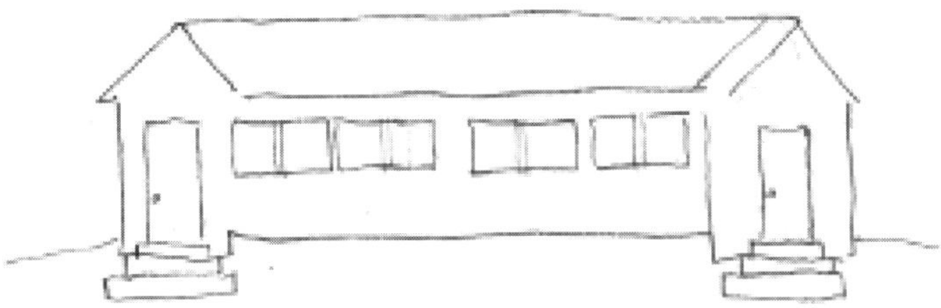

federally provided to build these logging roads. A total of more than ten times any single timber subsidy in the nation went to this area alone. The mere presence of these roads caused great harm to wolves and goshawks. Logging roads created land slides, polluted streams, and decimated fish. In the long run, they destroyed jobs by destroying their bases. We marched for two hours in the early autumn chill carrying signs and waving at motorists. Many drivers honked their support. That evening I tuned in the TV news. There were the rally leaders, handcuffed, being shoved into a car. One of them was an elderly lady from the Tongass. They were jailed for trespassing on federal property. I wrote a protest to the Governor, requesting an apology for the lady. The next morning we carried copies to both local nature groups and the newspaper. Nothing happened. Nothing at all. When I tried to call one of those who was jailed, his telephone was disconnected. Later, we learned more from our magazines. For example, "The Tongass timber industry is the most federally subsidized of any in the Western world. In the Tongass region there are only 32 inches of annual snowfall, but the Tongass rainforest was aptly named. Its average annual rainfall is 162 inches or 13 1/2 feet. However, more roads were built on this particular earthquake and landslide prone area than were built anywhere else. They stripped its vegetation and reduced it to a really dangerous place." No wonder those who protested went to jail. We voted for the people who sold us out because there were no alternative candidates. So much for showing the way to the third world! So much for Western Civilization!

Some of the things I ordered for Christmas remained on back order. We heard so much about downsizing for so long. I decided the shippers were probably trying to do too much with too few employees. We filed our usual report with the police when David's fourth bike was adopted. I was assured we would be notified when it was found. It wasn't. A policeman found David reading the tracks in the snow two miles from the site where it was stolen. He listened to David's complaint and drove away. David was heart sick. For Christmas he got another bike. Honey and I got videos and all of us got telephone calls from Grandma and Bruce. As usual, I sent commercial fruitcakes and magazine subscriptions to our relatives.

The first Christmas we spent in our trailer we owned two fake trees. I bought one the first year in Anchorage, a very small one for the apartment. Then we were given a very large one. After we replaced the couch, and moved the furniture to make room for books, there was no place for a tree. I hung our felt ornaments on a grill between the piano and the dining room table. Each year I sent two felt ornaments to our friend in Australia and hung two on the grill work. This year we just exchanged calendars and I loved mine from down under more than ever. I was idly thinking about having a Christmas tree. Our chainsaw neighbors strung lights on the remaining fir in front of their house.

I read and returned to the library, for resale, nine of James Michener's later books. The smell of beans in the slow cooker refreshed my nose.

We ate our turkey and stuffing and all the usual good stuff. I heard a thump on the porch roof. I walked from the electrically lit dining room to look through the living room window. A Red Squirrel was dashing from branch to branch on what I thought of as our bird tree. The intertwined alder and birch was moose trimmed several times each winter. The birds used plastic milk jugs by choice. The plastic feeders tended to clog and become unuseable when most needed. The squirrel was chasing five blackcapped chickadees from the feeders. He was almost flying, knocking the snow from the thicker branches as he tried to divert a redpoll from a meal. It didn't work. The birds came back to the milk jugs. He scurried to the ground so I could see his three snow tunnels. The birds gathered seed from where it fell on the snow. David pointed out another set of tunnels to the neighbor's house.

David said, "Cal had a squirrel named Squiffy. Let's call this guy, Squiffy Two."

"And let's call this our Christmas Tree," I suggested. He nodded. Honey agreed.